T0301305

The State, Regulation and the Economy

The State, Regulation and the Economy

An Historical Perspective

Edited by

Lars Magnusson

Professor of Economic History, Chair, Department of Economic History, Uppsala University and National Institute of Working Life, Sweden

and

Jan Ottosson

Associate Professor, Department of Economic History, Uppsala University and National Institute of Working Life, Sweden

Edward Elgar

Cheltenham, UK • Northampton, MA, USA

© Lars Magnusson, Jan Ottosson 2001

All rights reserved. No part of this publication may be reproduced, stored in a retrieval system or transmitted in any form or by any means, electronic, mechanical, photocopying, recording, or otherwise without the prior permission of the publisher.

Published by
Edward Elgar Publishing Limited
Glensanda House
Montpellier Parade
Cheltenham
Glos GL50 1UA
UK

Edward Elgar Publishing, Inc.
136 West Street
Suite 202
Northampton
Massachusetts 01060
USA

A catalogue record for this book is available from the British Library

Library of Congress Cataloguing in Publication Data
The state, regulation and the economy : an historical perspective / edited by Lars Magnusson, Jan Ottosson.
        p. cm.
    Includes bibliographical references and index.
        1. Trade regulation—History—Congresses. 2. Trade regulation—United States—History—Congresses. 3. Trade regulation—Case studies—History—Congresses. I. Magnusson, Lars, 1952– II. Ottosson, Jan, 1958–

    HD3612 .S73 2002
    338.9'009—dc21

                                                                                            2001040113

ISBN 1 84064 128 2
Printed and bound in Great Britain by MPG Books Ltd, Bodmin, Cornwall

Contents

Figures

Tables

Contributors

Lena Andersson-Skog, Associate Professor, Department of Economic History, Umeå University, Umeå, SE-90187, Sweden.

Frank Dobbin, Professor, Department of Sociology, Princeton University, Princeton, New Jersey, 08544, USA.

Timothy Dowd, Assistant Professor, Department of Sociology, Emory University, Atlanta, Georgia, 30322, USA.

Colleen A. Dunlavy, Professor, Department of History, University of Wisconsin-Madison, Wisconsin, USA.

Carl Jeding, Phd, Department of Economic History, Uppsala University, SE-751 20 Uppsala, Sweden.

Ronald N. Johnson, Professor, Department of Agricultural Economics and Economics, Montana State University, Bozeman, Montana, 597 17 USA.

Gary D. Libecap, Professor, Department of Economics, University of Arizona, Tuscon, Arizona, 85721, and National Bureau of Economic Research (NBER), Cambridge, Massachusetts, 02138, USA.

Lars Magnusson, Professor, Department of Economic History, Uppsala University, SE-751 20 Uppsala, Sweden.

Jan Ottosson, Associate Professor, Department of Economic History, Uppsala University, SE-751 20 Uppsala, Sweden.

Thomas Pettersson, Phd, Department of Economic History, Umeå University, Umeå SE-90187, Sweden.

Sven Steinmo, Associate Professor, Department of Political Science, University of Colorado, Boulder, Colorado, 80309-0333, USA.

Acknowledgements

This collection of essays is the result of a workshop held in Stockholm, in June 1999. The editors would like to thank all participants. The Swedish Transport and Communication Board (KFB) were generous sponsors, and we are most grateful for their dedicated interest and financial support. We want especially to thank Magnus Carlsson for organizing the workshop. Ann-Britt Hellmark helped us to correct the language. For stimulating discussions, practical help and constructive suggestions we would like to thank all members of the research project 'Transport and Communication in Perspective': Carl Jeding, Magnus Carlsson, Rikard Skårfors, Eva Liljegren, Lena Andersson-Skog, Thomas Pettersson and Olle Krantz.

Lars Magnusson and Jan Ottosson
Department of Economic History
Uppsala University, Sweden

1. Private actors, policy regulation and the role of history: an introduction

Lars Magnusson and Jan Ottosson

There are two facts of history that seems undeniably true. First, that regulatory regimes appear everywhere where market economies exist and where there is a competition for limited resources (free choice). Second, that over time there is stability as well as change in such regulatory regimes. However, the rationale of public regulation of markets, as well as the mechanisms that cause such stability and change in regulatory regimes are not well understood. Hence, we argue here that economic theory, whether of a positive or a normative stance, is not convincing in explaining the stability and change of regulation over time.

There are mainly three theoretical traditions in economics that discuss regulation and the role of the state in economic activity. First, in 'normative' economic policy studies – neo-classical welfare economics – the aim of governance is mainly to correct for market failures. According to this view, stemming back to Alfred Marshall, market imperfections, which lead to welfare losses, could be countervailed by an omnipotent state, which serves the common good. Moreover, once these 'perfect government measures' were found it was often supposed that they would be implemented without problems. There are at least two arguments, however, which can be raised against this Panglossian view of the world. First, it can be doubted that the state really is a servant of the common good. This question is not only of philosophical interest, or a mere sophistry, but has a number of important implications. Hence if we doubt the benevolent character of the state we cannot be sure that it only and always intervenes when there are market imperfections and market failures. Should we not instead expect that 'market failure' might also be the excuse and veil of state intervention in cases when no such failures are due? Without doubt, the historical record of the last couple of centuries provides ample evidence of such instances where the state introduces regulative orders mainly, it seems, for its own (selfish) purposes. To some extent public choice 'capture theories' from Chicago (formulated by George Stigler, Sam Peltzman and others) which argue that market failure (monopoly and so on) provides an opportunity for monopoly profit and gives rise to a market for regulation, can be questioned for the same reason: is it not just as likely that self-interested actors would try to enforce regulation in order to create monopolies or other market 'failures' (Baldwin and Cave 1999, p. 22 for references)?

Second, as, for example, Dixit (1996) has demonstrated, it is certainly necessary to differentiate between the *aim* and the *outcome* of policy action. Between these two entities there is a process of implementation which may result in less-efficient solutions and less social welfare than might have been perceived *ex ante*. In other words, there may be a process of unintentional outcomes at hand. Certainly, such a process of implementation may even lead to *lower* welfare and *less* efficiency than some other policy action, when we include the role of implementation in our picture. (Pressman 1999; Dixit 1996, p. 9).

Moreover, the traditional argument of market failures and the *raison d'être* of public ownership and nationalization, gives little guidance in explaining, for example, *why* publicly owned enterprises, or a certain set of regulatory standards, is preferred to other regulatory regimes. Increasing returns to scale and positive externalities might produce two different policy options – regulations or public ownership. Hence, market failure does not explain why, for example, the first has been favored in the US, while the second option has been chosen in many European countries (Domberger and Piggot 1994, p. 34). In the case of nationalized industries, the market failure argument does not help to explain entirely why differences in the mix of public and private ownership structures appear in sectors of the economy showing similar signs of market failure. For example, in the British case some network industries were nationalized, while other industries facing even worse economic or organizational problems experienced a diminishing state-dominated ownership structure (Millward and Singleton 1995).

The second, and quite different attempt to explain regulation and state intervention is provided by positive theory and public choice economics. Hence, public choice theory regards the state as being a nexus of individuals who are self-interested, rational maximizers. Here, rent-seeking behavior on the part of various interest groups is seen as crucial in the making of regulatory orders. Moreover, the contest for power between different interest groups is seen as pivotal in the process where a specific policy action is selected. Further, as argued by Olson and others, a large and homogeneous interest group will have a greater capacity to influence politics in the desired way (Olson 1965; Kanazawa and Noll 1994, p. 23).

A major problem with the positive view is that interest groups are viewed as rational actors with stable preferences. An important underlying hypothesis is that the actors within interest groups are aware of and understand their self-interest (Krueger 1996, p. 173). For very good reasons sociologists and political scientists have, however, raised considerable objections to these assumptions. They argue that the making and subsequent change of interest group preferences are of vital interest in an attempt to understand the rise of regulations in various countries (Wilson 1980; Knoke et al. 1996). One example of this critique is the important work by Krueger (1996). In her study of American Sugar, she points out that shifting actions of state intervention contains elements from the two mentioned theories regarding the functions of the state. However, simultaneously she shows that neither of these approaches actually explains *why* and *how* the state intervened in the case of American Sugar. More important than the state was the role of interest groups; on several occasions the actions of these interest groups contradicted theoretical predictions of group action based on the public choice perspective. For example, groups with opposing interests worked together, sharing similar viewpoints. Krueger also points out the importance of studying policy changes over time. She incorporates a dynamic element into the analysis of state intervention, while recognizing that, once initiated, policy programs seem to take on a life of their own.

In recent years a third theoretical position regarding the role of the state has become widely discussed. This approach is influenced by the transaction cost theory and is mostly known as the 'New Institutional Economics' (NIE). According to this approach, bounded rational actors try to cope with an uncertain and complex political world, where transaction costs are an important element of real world economies. In an important contribution drawing upon Williamson's (1996) model, Dixit (1996) has developed a set of analytical tools that can be used to discuss 'political transaction costs'. Dixit applies the familiar 'transactions cost' notions of uncertainty, complexity, information impactedness, opportunism, and asset specificity, within the field of political decision making in a dynamic context. By applying these notions also in the field of policy, Dixit shows that given such restraints, the analysis of policy measures necessarily needs to include the difference between policy aims and policy outcomes. The reason for this difference is constituted by the incompleteness of contracts. A central theme is the complexity of the political contract, exemplified by the constitution. These contracts are less complete than economic contracts, due to high transaction costs in the political environment. The consequence of such incomplete contracts is seen as more problematic in the political field, compared with economic transactions. The reason for this is the long-term character of constitutional arrangements. The incompleteness of political contracts also gives 'large variations in the way a given rule operates'. In other words, 'an incomplete constitution can be manipulated by the participants to serve their own aims' (Dixit, pp. 20–21). Due to the differences between the economic and political fields of decision making, it is more costly to enforce policy reforms, since monitoring and incentive contracts are more complicated to use in the political arena. The case with state agencies implementing various policy decisions further illustrates the complexity of the principal–agent problem. Since there are a multiplicity of agency relationships in public administration, this complicates the moral hazard problem. The crucial point of this aspect concerns the chosen path of implementation. Implementation in this sense can be seen as a rather wide range of policy measures. One of the most important aspects of implementation is the making and function of multipurpose, multi-principal state agencies. In contrast to principal–agent relationships in the economic world, it is not always clear which of the parties in the political world are agents and which are principals. Instead, government agencies are often responsible to several principals, sometimes with diverging interests, leading to a higher degree of incomplete contracts and unclear lines of authority (Wilson 1989, ch. 17; Dixit 1996, p. 56). These agencies are seen as crucial regarding both the timing and the content of political reforms.

Since such agencies implement policies in different ways, the outcome is not always predictable. Moreover, as political reforms will be implemented through state agencies, earlier lock-in events will affect the outcome of such policy measures in ways not always anticipated by the actors themselves. This is close to the view of Krueger (1996), who argues that regulatory systems after a while seem to live their own life. This discussion shows the importance of taking into account the transaction costs in the political system, characterized by a higher degree of uncertainty, different rules of selection (voting systems and so on), and unclear principal–agent relationships. It also highlights the role of government agencies and allows a more sophisticated discussion of the actual function of interest groups.

Linked to such a discussion is a fourth possible alternative in discussing the make-up and shift of different regulatory regimes. Hence, we argue that it is of utmost importance to treat regulations as historical phenomena, which occur over time. Such an understanding is particularly pertinent when we are interested in why regulative orders seem to have stability over time but also why they are changed and transformed. Hence, regulation and policy action must be analysed in terms of lock-ins which might shape path-dependent patterns. This may lead to (suboptimal) institutional settings enduring for long periods of time. In a broad sense this notion of path dependency challenges the neo-classical paradigm through its recognition of the importance of institutions and the role of history (North 1990; David 1985, 1994; Setterfield 1993). Thus, increasing returns, network externalities, and learning effects all reinforce the path chosen in the past. It is of course important to acknowledge the two major conditions that, for example, North (1990), emphasizes. To apply the notion of path dependence within the analysis of institutions, both increasing returns and imperfect markets must exist. Most certainly, in this context interest theories – capture theories or others – might help us understand why regulative regimes are defended sometimes for a very long time and seem to give rise to path dependence. Consequently, when there is a shift of power between various interest groups themselves and/or between interest groups and the state – probably mainly due to external forces propelled by economic change and development – this means that 'old' forms of regulation may fall and new ones appear.[1]

* * *

The aim of this collection of studies is to discuss various aspects of the rise of regulation as well as its change with special reference to one policy field: the infrastructure and network industries. There are few such areas in the economy where the pendulum has swung so fast regarding the view upon regulations and the actual role of the state during the two last decades. Not so long ago, market failure arguments, mainly based upon natural monopoly reasoning, were used to defend a large degree of state involvement in the infrastructure sector in terms of state ownership, subsidies granted as well as direct control and regulation. The fast-changing attitudes and policy actions regarding regulations and the position of the state might be better understood when applying a somewhat longer time horizon.

The infrastructure sector also provides a challenging empirical field to examine further regarding the role of interest groups, their constitution and evolution. Since there are large investments at stake in projects with extremely long time horizons regarding planning as well as duration, the long-term interaction between the state and interest groups is of particular interest in this respect.

We believe that the studies presented in this volume demonstrate the fruitfulness of understanding regulation as a process over time. Moreover, we suggest that they show that the form and content of state interventionism in the economy – although not necessarily its explicitly formulated *raison d' être* – is strongly influenced by historical and path-dependent factors. We also suggest that the welfare-maximizing and public choice models of state economic intervention only partly explain the complex patterns of interaction between the state and the market. This becomes explicitly obvious when we understand the political process as a process of implementation in which various rules, routines, and the actors' mental models in a complex environment shape path-dependent behavior by actors. Hence, neither the normative version of political economy, which takes for granted that the political process of state intervention is a simple response to market failures (and thus leading to increased social welfare), nor the positive version, which always sees open or veiled 'interests' as the backbone of political action, is very realistic or useful. Instead, we put forward a historical approach to state interventionism, which illuminates the important role of specific historical events in forming regulatory processes. The results from the contributions in this volume suggest that the interaction between institutions and dynamic market forces is central in understanding factors underpinning economic growth. Therefore, concluding that the role of the state and the interaction between polity, regulation and the economy is complex and dependent upon historical specific events, might be a good starting-point in which to explore further the reasons behind state involvement in the economy.

* * *

The book is divided into two parts. Part I contains general aspects of the question of how regulations and institutions are decided upon. In Part II, we use Sweden as a role model of a regulated economy.

In Chapter 2, Ronald N. Johnson and Gary D. Libecap investigate the reasons behind the development of the ethanol program in the United States. Johnson and Libecap suggest one important factor behind the apparent success of the corn farmers to the continuity of the transfer programs. This is due to the structure of the political contract, and the incentive politicians have to cover the real costs and benefits of long-term transfer programs, as well as the strength of the interest groups. Without accurate information, voters will not be able to make decisions regarding politicians' support of such programs. Johnson and Libecap's clearly argued chapter makes important contributions to the general discussion of the role of the state and the interest groups by pointing out the relation between the incentives for politicians and interest groups.

Chapter 3 deals with the development of the American railroads and the various steps of regulation that emerged during the first railroad decades of the nineteenth century in the United States. Colleen Dunlavy uses a model that incorporates the dynamic stages from local, to state, to federal level in the US regulatory regime, using the example of rate regulation of railroads in the United States. In Dunlavy's view, the state-level government and the railroad companies are acting against each other in a repeated game, where the local government always loses. One central aspect concerns the interrelation between regulators on the state level and the private actors, finding a number of strategies for escaping such state regulations by moving to other states. Dunlavy raises the question of the limits of regulations in a globalized economy in recent times. Her chapter concludes from the insights raised from the nineteenth-century railroad tycoons' aggressive strategies towards state regulation and the corresponding shift today from state level towards international regulatory orders that 'the prospects are exceedingly dim'.

In Chapter 4, Timothy Dowd and Frank Dobbin also use the case of the American railroads to demonstrate the relation between implementation and decisions regarding the regulation of the American railroads. They argue forcefully against the neo-liberal notion that a low level of state intervention accompanied the development of advanced market economies. They suggest that the interplay between public policy and private interests is a powerful force behind economic activity. In particular, the introduction of new policy regimes created similar responses among the railroaders. After a while, the shift in policy was adopted as a 'natural' economic law. The second part of the chapter studies the importance of shifting policy regimes in the acquisition and founding of railway firms. Contrary to common belief, the US policy was far from *laissez-faire*. Also, the initial effects of the antitrust policy towards the railroads actually led to the consolidation of the railroad companies. This might be looked upon as a nice example of unintentional consequences of regulatory activities. Also, this case highligths another set of mental strategies among railroaders in adopting to policy regimes. Thus, the study shows that institutional settings are important in determining firm behavior, but not always in the way politicians and other actors assume.

Sven Steinmo's 'Taxation, redistribution and regulation: fiscal policy in a changing world economy?' (Chapter 5) points out some important implications of the role of the state in an internationalized economy. With a background in historical institutionalism, Steinmo argues that the recent policy changes – and responses – in the taxation policy area has been influenced a great deal by the development of more flexible markets, and a fast-changing globalized economy. Steinmo examines actual changes in tax policy in a comparative setting, as well as discusses the recent development in a historical setting. Both the redistributive functions and the regulatory instruments are, according to Steinmo, abandoned. The reasons why this has happened come close to a central question of this volume, that is, the driving forces behind shifting policies regarding various policy regimes. Steinmo points out the dramatic changes in the world economy during the last years, but is careful also to point out that different governments might still be able to respond in various ways. Here, changing relative prices, new technologies and so on are seen as important driving forces behind the changing policy.

In Chapter 6, Lars Magnusson discusses how the notion of path dependence can be used to understand regulations. In this sense, he here returns to the discussion we presented earlier in this introduction. By studying the present discussion on path dependence, he shows the fruitfulness in applying -- which is the central theme of the chapters in this volume – a historical approach to regulation.

In Part II, the Swedish economy, with special emphasis on various parts of the transport and communication sector, is used as an example of some important aspects regarding the formation, transformation and change of institutional settings. Chapter 7 presents a brief introduction.

In Chapter 8, Lena Andersson-Skog examines how regional interest groups are formed in a specific political environment, and the longevity of the struggle over infrastructure investments in a new railroad located in northern Sweden. In particular, she points out that new regional formations may be decisive when formulating a new strategy for interest groups. Also, the crucial role of the state, the parliament, and the actual parliamentary setting opens up for logrolling among politicians and the political parties. In such circumstances, interest groups comprising local and regional public officials as well as private investors might be important in shaping 'a defining moment'. Also in this chapter, the historical and dynamic perspective of the role of interest groups points out not only the winners, but also the losers – in this case, the voters and taxpayers in a political system characterized by high transaction costs in certain political sectors, such as the infrastructure sector.

In Chapter 9, Jan Ottosson suggests that the making of a new technology also fosters the search for regulations. He argues that neither simple positive nor normative theories are directly applicable to answer the questions why some European states adopted their initial positions or changed their attitudes towards state ownership, subsidies, and regulations of the first civil aviation companies. He emphasizes the importance of bringing in a dynamic element in the analysis of regulatory change, and of incorporating the notion of learning processes in political markets. In the case of early civil aviation, existing governance models from the railways and the shipping industry influenced the first choice of governance regimes. The model of state-subsidized private lines and collectively owned infrastructure was chosen in some European countries while others were more influenced by the continental railway governance regime, with a single state-owned company.

In Chapter 10, Carl Jeding argues that, in line with Vogel, deregulation may actually increase the number of regulations. Using the example of the deregulation of the Swedish national telecommunications market, he shows that the number of regulations has actually increased. The creation of a new watchdog agency in Sweden is also examined. Contrary to common belief, the introduction of more competitive rules for the telecommunications market was followed by a changing set of regulations, but no decrease in regulatory activity. In Dixit's and Williamson's terms, this case might further be interpreted as one of a multi-principal agency, with multifunctions. The effect of an incomplete political contract, where the state is still an owner of the old monopolist company, will probably be an increase in the gulf between political intentions and implementations.

Finally, in Chapter 11, Thomas Pettersson interprets the forces behind the longevity of a subsidy in the context of Swedish economic transport aid. The notion of path dependence in a Northian sense is used in order to understand the mechanisms behind the decisions to keep on allowing resources to flow to this kind of subsidy, despite the fact that all other relevant economic factors were changing. One important factor behind this development was clearly ideological, expressed by the political compensation for long distances. Also, various levels of institutions are discussed where changing conditions on one level might be leveled out by stationary conditions on other levels in a complex system of formal and informal institutions.

NOTE

1. The relation between regulations, the role of the state and changes in economic activity is perhaps best illustrated by the recent discussion of the 'defining moment' in US economic policy during the New Deal (see Bordo et al. 1998).

PART I

General Aspects of Regulation and Institution
Decision Making

2. Information distortion by politicians and constituent groups in promoting regulatory transfers: the case of ethanol

Ronald N. Johnson and Gary D. Libecap

INTRODUCTION[1]

In his seminal article, George Stigler argued that there is a market for regulation whereby constituent groups bargain with self-interested politicians for beneficial policies (Stigler 1971, pp. 3–21). Politicians use the power of the state to assist organized constituents through a variety of methods: direct subsidies, the provision of control over entry, regulations on substitutes and complements, and policies that increase rivals' costs. One of Stigler's primary objectives was to debunk the view that government regulation reflects the public interest. The preambles of major enabling legislation promote such notions by describing how programs improve safety, provide national defense, or protect the environment.[2] Despite these claims, Stigler's assessment was that government regulations are often merely masked efforts to transfer wealth via the political process. His argument has become a prominent part of the rent-seeking literature.[3]

More recently, however, these rent-seeking arguments, which imply that government regulations and transfer programs reduce aggregate wealth while benefitting certain constituencies, have been criticized as ignoring the incentives of politicians in representative democracies to promote wealth-maximizing outcomes.[4] Using an analogy with competitive markets, critics argue that entry by entrepreneurial politicians and competition between them and incumbents generates sufficient information about the benefits and costs of regulation and government transfer programs to allow voters to reward efficient behavior.[5] Market-like pressures provided by competing politicians discipline government policies and institutions, and those that survive over time are presumed to be reasonably efficient, given the transaction costs of changing them. In this chapter, we concur with Stigler's skepticism of the public interest objectives of regulation. Further, we question the claims of a close analogy between competitive markets and the political process in a representative democracy.[6]

The focus of our analysis is on the extent and basis of voter information about regulation and transfers and the role of political competition in providing it. Our contention is that obtaining accurate information about the costs and benefits of regulation is more difficult than suggested by those who argue that competition will adequately discipline politicians. Investigators, as well as general voters, must often rely on the government for provision of information about underlying program parameters and functional relationships. We argue that politicians have incentives to limit and distort the information that is released by the government to voters and that competition for elective office alone is unlikely to be an effective remedy. Our approach builds on Gordon Tullock's insight that politicians engage in information obfuscation because direct transfers 'would be just too raw. The voters would not buy it'.[7]

The analysis we offer distinguishes between competition among politicians for political office and competition between powerful competing interests groups as a means of policing the flow of information.[8] We argue that although competition among politicians may not generate sufficient information to allow voters to assess the welfare effects of regulation, competition among interest groups might. That is, if a regulation seriously disadvantages another cohesive group, then it will be in the latter's interest to organize to counter the policy. It is this process, competition among concentrated interests and the spillover incentives of aligned politicians, that is most apt to release information to general voters. Even then, however, voters will be faced with assessing the relative claims of competing parties, and if the issues are complex, voters may not have sufficient unbiassed information to make informed judgments. Information distortion is difficult for voters to counter, and as such, assists politicians in providing transfers via regulation to important constituencies.

In politics, there are incentives to provide focussed benefits to influential constituents and to spread the costs among all taxpayers. As we argue, obfuscation or the opportunistic distortion of information about the benefits and costs of regulation by sponsoring politicians makes transfers to influential interest groups more likely. Although government programs are usually aimed at specific constituents, typically there are important external effects whereby costs and some benefits are spread to other voters. Politicians have an incentive to take advantage of these externalities by overstating benefits and understating costs. The emphasis on the external benefits of programs decreases opposition from general voters for what otherwise might seem to be blatant special-interest legislation. As such, information obfuscation can enhance the re-election prospects for politicians.

Information obfuscation by politicians raises the costs of program evaluation by general voters. The incentives to distort information and the opportunities provided by the political process to do so, explains the commonly viewed phenomenon whereby politicians wrap narrow, special-interest legislation with broad external benefits.[9] We argue that linking narrow transfers to broad externalities is more than mere window dressing. Despite Stigler's challenge, there remains the sense that regulations can, and sometimes do, promote the general welfare. But, we argue that it is difficult for the general public to know when the public interest, rather than a narrow private interest, is being served. This difficulty in assessing the actual beneficiaries is recognized by politicians and that is why they publicize special interest transfers such as solving a natural monopoly or externality/public good problem. Such practices are an integral part of the political process whereby politicians provide transfers to key constituents, while distorting information on the broad benefits and costs involved.

The institutional structure of the political system allows politicians to engage in information obfuscation with few negative electoral consequences. This condition challenges the analogy between competitive markets and the political process in a representative democracy. Whereas in competitive markets, firm shareholders capture the benefits and costs of adhering to or cheating on product quality, in politics property rights to program benefits and costs are much less well defined. Given the property rights structure in the political arena, the resort to information obfuscation by politicians as a means of advancing special-interest programs appears to be widespread, and competition among politicians alone will likely have little impact in reducing the use of information distortion. Where competition exists among two or more powerful interests groups, information distortions are more apt to be revealed. But that form of competition is far from ubiquitous, and even where it occurs, voters may not be able to disentangle successfully the claims made by the competing interests. The resulting uncertainty may facilitate the provision of special-interest benefits.

We develop our arguments in the following section and then illustrate them with reference to the ethanol program, a long-standing subsidy and regulatory program that benefits corn farmers, but is advertised as having significant benefits to the environment, rural development, and national security.[10] The documented efforts to disguise the actual costs and benefits of the program are important for gaining a broader understanding of the functioning and costs of government transfers in the economy. In the final section, we consider how our analysis contributes to recent discussions on the usefulness of labeling transfer programs as 'efficient' or 'inefficient' once information costs, which are the basis for transaction costs, are included.

THE COMPETITIVE MARKET ANALOGY AND INFORMATION DISTORTION

The notion that there is competition among politicians and political institutions and that their actions can be analysed by applying the same tools used to explain the behavior of individuals and firms is widely accepted, certainly by the two authors of this chapter. We question, however, how far the underlying paradigm of competition and resulting optimization can be applied to the political arena.

According to the market analogy, competitive entry and exit among office holders and seekers is a necessary condition for directing political outcomes towards aggregate wealth maximization. It generates the desire among politicians to invest enormous funds in campaigning, in learning constituent demands, and in mobilizing resources to satisfy those demands. Politicians who fail to be responsive to influential constituents will not be re-elected. Further following the market analogy, competition among politicians can also mitigate the problems commonly associated with rationally ignorant voters.[11] Since most models of government failure are premised on voter ignorance, this is an important point. Although voters may not be fully informed, competition in the political arena is argued to release information about program benefits and costs. Entrepreneurial politicians are rewarded for assessing program effectiveness and for finding new funding sources or ways of reducing taxpayer burdens. Fraudulent claims and behavior by some politicians will be revealed by other politicians because they will be rewarded by voters for doing so. The process of information generation and revelation provides voters with sufficient insights that they will not be swayed by mere rhetoric.

The problem with the analogy between a representative democracy and a competitive market is that the property rights structures are so different. For example, while there are similarities in the relationships between stockholders and firm managers and between a constituency and its elected officials, there are important differences in the recourse general voters have with elected officials compared with that available to consumers in dealing with firms. Consider the incentives and penalties a firm manager faces when contemplating whether to lie to customers about product quality. If the deception goes undiscovered, at least for a substantial period of time, the stockholders will likely support management. The competitive process of new firm and product entry, however, generates needed information for evaluating firm quality claims. Discovery of quality deception can be extremely costly for the manager because stockholders will turn on management if asset prices plummet. Firm reputational costs seem to be substantial compared to civil penalties (Karpoff and Lott 1993, pp. 757–802). Accordingly, there are market forces for assuring contractual performance between a firm and its customers.[12] Moreover, the US legal system allows consumers to sue for damages, including punitive damages, and agencies like the Federal Trade Commission monitor fraud and false advertising. At the very least, consumers can cease buying the product. Accordingly, consumers have recourse and thus, discovery of deception posses a threat to both managers and stockholders in private markets.

Now consider the incentives faced by an elected official to deceive voters outside of his or her district about special-interest program costs and benefits. In contrast to consumers, the general populace who often pay the bulk of program costs have little direct recourse against deception. If they do not reside in the politician's district, they cannot vote directly against him or her, nor is it clear that they would be in any position to inflict much harm against the constituents in the politician's district. In a federal system such action would require a considerable degree of collective behavior on the part of general voters. Unlike consumers who can discontinue purchasing a commodity, the comparable option for general voters is a high-cost one: leaving the country.[13] Thus, under a federal system in a representative democracy a politician may be largely immune from any penalty so long as the deception benefitted the local constituency.[14]

The standard market analogy also glosses over the structure of district-based representation and the weak property rights that exist over tax revenues and program costs and benefits in the political arena. Competitive market outcomes result in wealth maximization when property rights are well defined and enforced. When they are not, competition among agents results in rent dissipation. The classic example is the open-access fishery where entry by fishermen is free.[15] Once there, they compete to harvest prior to other fishermen, resulting in the dissipation of the rental value of the fishery. The weak property rights conditions that result in the wastes associated with open-access fisheries seem more like those that exist in politics than the fully defined rights that underlie standard competitive models.

Consider tax revenues. These are not a pure open-access resource with complete rent dissipation since there is only a limited number of politicians in a representative democracy to compete for them. Even so, no individual politician has a clear property right to tax revenues. Politicians and their programs compete for budgets in order to satisfy constituent demands. As in the fishery, the rule of capture defines property rights to the budget at any point in time, and funds migrate, like fish, to the most effective competitor. Politicians who are particularly skillful in securing taxpayer largess for their districts become locally notorious and typically, are rewarded with repeated re-election by grateful constituents.[16] Majority voting rules for funds allocation requires logrolling and other exchanges among politicians. These trades result in program benefits being concentrated on certain constituencies while the costs are dispersed to general taxpayers and voters. Hence, the underlying property rights structure in politics equates neither constituent program benefits with relevant tax costs, nor constituent benefits with overall social costs that would account for externalities. As in markets, the failure to equate private benefits and costs with social benefits and costs leads to non-optimal resource allocation.

In politics, the lack of a well-defined residual claimant fosters information distortion. It is, of course, in the interest of the sponsoring politician to make sure that key constituents recognize how much they are served by his or her actions. In contrast, however, those bearing the program costs will typically be less informed, and it is in the interest of sponsoring politicians to keep it that way. Elected officials have substantial control over the flow of information that could expose deception. We argue that if narrow-interest programs can be portrayed as providing positive externalities across jurisdictions, it may not be in the interest of other politicians to reveal the information distortion by one of their colleagues.

Because of the nature of many government-provided goods and services, there are generally externalities and information problems. These information problems create uncertainty for voters in the assessment of program benefits and costs.[17] As voters' agents, politicians are expected to provide public goods and information about their benefits and costs. But, politicians seeking re-election also have incentives to provide transfers to key constituents and to shift the costs to others. By distorting information about the true social value or cost of those transfers, such as by linking them to public goods, politicians can provide more private benefits to the targetted constituency. Through exaggerating the social benefits or minimizing the social costs of transfers, politicians can increase demand for a particular program or regulation, or reduce opposition to it. Rather than resolving the information uncertainties facing general voters, politicians take advantage of the situation and further distort and manipulate information flows in order to provide more transfers to favored constituents.

Consider the case of a single political jurisdiction wherein all the benefits and costs of a program accrue to the voters within that jurisdiction. Assume two groups of voters. The first group is composed of the direct beneficiaries of the regulation. These may, for example, be agricultural producers benefitting from a regulation that restricts output and rises prices. The second group is composed of consumers harmed by the higher prices, but who may experience a positive environmental spillover effect from a reduction in output. Now consider an incumbent politician who attempts to maximize expected votes in the next election.[18] The incumbent faces an opposing candidate and will be judged, in part, on the positions taken on various bills. While voters decide to vote for or against the politician on the basis of an array of issues, the focus here is on a single issue, the extent of the output restriction. The probability that members of the farm community vote for the incumbent is positively related to their net income, which in turn depends on the degree to which output is restricted. The probability that the consumer group votes for the incumbent depends on the trade-off between higher output prices and a cleaner environment. The politician is also confronted with a trade-off between the support of the farm and consumer groups.[19] To maximize votes under these circumstances, however, the politician may turn to information distortion and obfuscation.

The politician can exploit the situation through the control and manipulation of information. Assume that the farm group carries out their transactions in the marketplace, and knows with certainty what their net gains are. On the other hand, consumers may find it difficult to measure the environmental effects of the input restriction.[20] If the incumbent can control the information the consumer group has about environmental benefits, as well as the degree to which the restriction impacts price, opposition can be reduced. But, there is likely to be a cost if the incumbent is discovered lying to consumers, his or her own constituents.

Although it would seem that the political challenger would have an incentive to expose the incumbent, there are complications. By exposing the incumbent, the challenger gains support from the consumer group, but suffers the displeasure of the farmers because future restrictions will be less stringent or not adopted. Whether this is sufficient to deter the challenger depends on the reactions of the two groups of voters, but it should be clear that competition among politicians can differ substantially from competition for control of a firm. Compared to a political jurisdiction, stockholders in a firm are likely to have very narrow and similar objectives.[21] While management may attempt to fool the stockholders, there is really only one group the challenger need address, not two as in the scenario offered here. Thus, the incentives for the challenger to expose an incumbent's obfuscation seem greater in contests over the control of a firm compared to contests in the political arena.

We emphasize that it is the diversity of interests that provides the underlying incentives for the type of obfuscation addressed in this chapter. If instead of two distinct groups, we assume there is only a single group, composed of both the producer and consumer groups, the challenger would have a clear incentive to expose the incumbent. This appears to be the condition that those who rely on the role of competition in the political marketplace have in mind, but it fails to capture much that goes on in representative democracy.

Consider, instead, a system that more closely resembles representative democracy. Let there be two districts, one that contains all the members of the farm producer group while the other district contains the consumers. By engaging in information obfuscation, the incumbent in the farm producer district can attempt to influence voter perceptions in the district containing the consumer group. The goal would be to shift perceptions so that the consumer group believe they are experiencing greater spillover benefits. While the incentive for the incumbent in the producer district to engage in obfuscation is clear, the reaction of the incumbent in the other district is not as apparent. The politician representing the consumer group might actually want the obfuscation to take place, or simply be ambivalent about it, because by raising the perception of benefits from this particular regulation it will make a vote in favor of the regulation, made as part of logroll trade, easier to justify to the voters. Logrolling is an integral part of the working of a representative democracy, but it requires that elected officials impose costs on their own general constituents in exchange for specialized or targetted benefits to specific constituents (Weingast et al. 1981, pp. 642–64). That is, in negotiations politicians trade off support for narrowly-based programs that impose costs on other, typically broader, constituents. Since obfuscation reduces the perceived cost by convincing the voters in the paying districts that they are actually benefitting from the transfer, it facilitates logrolling.

Much will depend on the incentives of the challenger in the consumer district to expose the distortion. A political challenger in that district might choose to expose the information distortion as a means of attracting voter support, but if the challenger is to benefit from the exposé, the incumbent must be made culpable. That may not be easy. First, it is the incumbent in the producer group's district who will take the lead in distorting the information flow, while the incumbent in the consumer district can simply act passively. Second, as soon as it is recognized that a challenger is about to expose the distortion, the incumbent could pre-empt the challenge with his or her own attack on obfuscation, thus reducing the rewards to the challenger. Importantly, the incumbents in both districts can have an incentive to block information flows that would reveal the obfuscation. Together they will attempt to control the flow of information and win re-election.

Furthermore, if the benefits of a program remain concentrated, while the number of electoral districts expands, costs will become dispersed. While both obfuscation and discovery require effort, the rewards to the latter will decline as program costs become dispersed. Thus, elected representatives may have only a very limited incentive to expose the obfuscation of fellow representatives because the rewards of doing so are likely to be small and they too benefit from engaging in that same practice.

Politicians, then, are motivated to act collectively and adopt policies that reduce access to information. Indeed, if a politician stridently exposes obfuscation by politicians in other districts sufficiently to attract widespread voter attention and negative reaction, the logrolling trades among many politicians who depend on it may be disrupted. While politicians may gain broad voter approval across many districts, as whistle blowers they may not be invited to engage in logrolling trades of their own. Hence, they may not be able to deliver to specialized constituents within their own district, jeopardizing their re-election. Accordingly, the returns to obfuscation for politicians suggests that they will attempt to control the flow of information that may weaken or bolster their claims. In particular, the use of information from neutral, scientific agencies can be very important in adding credibility to political rhetoric. Hence, if agency reports, which are often vague, can be interpreted and presented as consistent with the political rhetoric, politicians will do so. Clear reports that are inconsistent with the rhetoric will be suppressed through a variety of means.[22]

The arguments presented thus far should not be taken to imply that elected officials have no incentive to expose information obfuscation by their colleagues. There are situations where the incentives could be very large, but these are likely to be cases where certain well-organized interest groups are adversely affected by a distributive program and know that they have been harmed. Indeed, we should expect that when competition among relatively powerful interest groups occurs, there should be a substantial amount of conflicting information generated and studies inaugurated aimed at offsetting or discrediting the information advanced by the opposing group. This process may provide useful information to general voters, if they can evaluate the competing claims. But in the absence of those circumstances, there will be little in the way of systematic cross-examination of political claims about transfer program benefits. The ethanol story illustrates both of these scenarios.

OBFUSCATION OF INFORMATION IN THE POLITICAL ARENA: THE ETHANOL SUBSIDY

In this section we describe how the ethanol subsidy was linked by sponsoring politicians to a variety of externalities that were positively viewed by general voters – energy independence, environmental benefits, and rural economic development. Importantly, the ethanol subsidy was also tied to an alleged reduction in government support payments to farmers. Since 95 percent of ethanol is made from corn, ethanol production became a convenient alternative source of demand for corn stocks to reverse the fall in domestic corn prices that began after 1980. These externalities were used to increase general voter approval of the ethanol subsidy. Such linkages allowed farm-state politicians to provide greater benefits to a powerful constituency, the corn growers. Because ethanol's actual contributions to energy independence, clean air, and rural economic development were tenuous, politicians had to control the flow of information to the public so that supportive information was released and negative information was suppressed. As a result of these efforts, voters received a distorted assessment of ethanol's broad contributions to the economy that went largely unchallenged until the late 1980s. No competing interest group was seriously harmed. While the major oil companies may have viewed the subsidization of ethanol as a potential threat, there was no plan to promote ethanol to the extent practiced in Brazil and the energy crisis was viewed broadly as a serious problem. A criticism of the ethanol subsidy by oil companies would have appeared as self-serving as those firms were also developing their own alternative fuels, such as methanol, with government encouragement.[23] Methanol, made from natural gas, was less costly to produce than was ethanol, and it captured a larger share of the alternative fuels market.

In the late 1980s, however, competition among interest groups began to develop, with more information about the nature of the ethanol subsidy being generated for voters. Stricter air quality standards and requirements for the use of reformulated gasoline (RFG) under the Clean Air Act Amendments, proposed in 1987 and adopted in 1990, opened new markets for oxygenate additives.[24] Corn-state politicians sought to mandate a share of this new market for ethanol at the expense of MTBE (methyl tertiary butyl ether), a natural gas derivative. Legislation and administrative rulings on behalf of ethanol were introduced. These efforts led to the mobilization of the natural gas and chemical industries to protect MTBE. Congressional hearings and other public testimony contained the claims and counter claims of the proponents of ethanol and MTBE, and through this process the external benefits of ethanol were challenged systematically for the first time. As a consequence, ethanol supporters were unable to secure preferential treatment in the new developing market for oxygenated fuels. Even so, given the scientific nature of the claims and counter claims made by ethanol and MTBE proponents and the absence of neutral bodies to assess the arguments, it is not obvious that this conflict among interest groups has released useful information to voters for weighing the social benefits and costs of the ethanol subsidy.

Externalities and the Ethanol Subsidy

The Arab oil embargo of 1973 and the related oil price shocks made the United States' growing dependence on foreign oil supplies a political issue, and politicians searched for ways to promote domestic, renewable energy sources.[25] Although the cost of producing ethanol in 1980 was nearly twice that of gasoline, forecasts of high future gasoline prices (as high as $4.00 per gallon) by 1990–91, issued by the US National Alcohol Fuels Commission, made ethanol seem like a reasonable alternative.[26] The 19 congressional members of the commission were predominately from agricultural states, most likely to benefit from greater ethanol production.[27] They repeatedly stressed externalities as justification for an ethanol subsidy.[28] Foremost on their list were: (a) energy independence; (b) environmental benefits linked to the Clean Air Act of 1970 and its mandate for cleaner burning fuels; and (c) rural economic development and reduced farm program costs, achieved through lower domestic corn stocks and higher corn prices as corn was diverted to ethanol production. These concerns were heightened by President Jimmy Carter's embargo of grain sales to the Soviet Union in 1980.

Although those external benefits were described in 1980, 18 years later, in 1998, political proponents of the ethanol subsidy have continued to tout the same benefits. The claims made by Representative Richard Gephardt of

Missouri in May 1998 are typical: 'ethanol is good for our environment, our nation's energy security, and for American farmers'.[29]

The feasibility of ethanol as an alternative fuel in 1980 was strengthened by expected technological advances that would further close the gap between (rising) crude oil prices and (falling) ethanol prices. Further, the potential for correcting externalities in energy security, air quality, and agriculture meant that government intervention in the market was appropriate. If the externalities were substantial, a subsidy for ethanol could have broad economic benefits beyond directed transfers to corn growers, and hence, the subsidy could merit support among general voters. Farm-state politicians continually re-emphasized these external effects throughout the 1980s, and for the most part were successful in obtaining favorable legislation, because no other constituency had the incentive to evaluate their claims critically.

The Energy Tax Act of 1978 authorized the first federal excise tax exemptions for biomass derived fuels, chiefly gasohol, a mixture of 90 percent gasoline and 10 percent ethanol. The Crude Oil Windfall Profits Tax Act of 1980 extended the tax exemption through 1992 and added income tax credits for blenders of ethanol and gasoline. The Energy Security Act of 1980 set a goal for alcohol fuels production equal to 10 percent of motor fuel consumption by 1990 and provided over a billion dollars in loan guarantees for ethanol plants.[30] The ethanol subsidy has amounted to more than $7.1 billion between 1979 and 1995, and is projected to equal an additional $3.3 billion between 1996 and 2000.[31] The largest component of the subsidy is exemptions from the federal excise taxes that have ranged from $0.50 to $0.60 per gallon of ethanol or $0.05 to $0.06 per gallon of gasoline blended with 10 percent ethanol. Currently, the tax exemption equals $0.54 per gallon of ethanol. In addition, at least 20 states provide exemptions to state motor fuel excise taxes for ethanol, providing an added subsidy of $0.20 to $0.30 per gallon of ethanol.[32]

Comments stressing the benefits of ethanol beyond the pecuniary gains to corn farmers were especially important to corn growers because they helped camouflage larger direct transfer payments to that group. As such, externality assertions are part of information obfuscation in the political arena. But politicians have gone beyond mere rhetoric. They have also taken actions designed to control or distort potentially damaging counter information and to circumvent administrative processes that might reveal such information.

The Ethanol Subsidy to Corn Growers: Masking the Transfer

To illustrate the nature of the ethanol subsidy to corn producers, we consider how feed grain programs operated prior to the Federal Agricultural Improvement and Reform (FAIR) Act of 1996.[33] These programs used a number of policy instruments, including target prices and deficiency payments, an acreage reserve program, and nonrecourse loans.[34] When market prices were below the target or support price, farmers who met the eligibility criteria (usually participation in whatever supply control program existed) received payments equal to the difference between the target price and the higher of the average market price or the nonrecourse loan rate. The total payment received by each farmer was a function of the difference in those prices, multiplied by the number of eligible acres times the normal yield for each participating farm, and most corn producers participated.

Throughout the 1950s and 1960s the target price typically exceeded the market price. In the early 1970s, increases in foreign demand drove corn prices above target levels. As shown in Table 2.1, however, this situation was relatively short-lived. By 1982, target prices were once again exceeding market prices and large deficiency payments were a mainstay of the farm program.[35]

Table 2.1   Corn prices, target prices, and deficiency payments

Year	US corn prices ($/bu)	Target price ($/bu)	Deficiency payments ($ millions)
1975	2.54	1.38	0
1976	2.15	1.57	0
1977	2.02	2.00	0
1978	2.25	2.10	88
1979	2.48	2.20	0
1980	3.12	2.35	0
1981	2.47	2.40	0
1982	2.55	2.70	291
1983	3.21	2.86	0
1984	2.63	3.03	1653
1985	2.23	3.03	2480
1986	1.50	3.03	6195
1987	1.94	3.03	5910
1988	2.54	2.93	2163
1989	2.36	2.84	3504
1990	2.28	2.75	3014
1991	2.37	2.75	2080
1992	2.07	2.75	3625
1993	2.50	2.75	1502
1994	2.26	2.75	3199
1995	3.24	2.75	0096

Sources: Lin et al. (1995, pp. 51, 52); USDA, *Agricultural Statistics 1997*, Tables 1–37 and 1–44; and USDA, Farm Service Administration, Economic Policy and Analysis, Seed Grains and Oil Grains Group.

Figure 2.1 helps to illustrate the ethanol subsidy. Panel A outlines the pre-subsidy situation with the curve D_0 representing the aggregate demand function for corn in the United States. The domestic supply curve for corn without government intervention is denoted as S_0. With implementation of the government's price support program, accompanied by an acreage reduction requirement, the supply function shifts to the left. The target price is denoted as P_T and intersection with the restricted supply function, S_1, determines output under the program, Q_1. Note that the restricted supply function is a function of P_T, with the market price, P_{M0}, determined *ex post*. As drawn, Q_1 is the same output that would prevail in the absence of government intervention.[36] The per unit deficiency payment is the difference between the target price and the market-clearing price, P_{M0}. Assuming that all producers are eligible, the federal government's total outlays for deficiency payments is area $P_{M0}baP_T$. Even though output is the same as in the non-intervention case, this program results in an increase in the cost of production, generating a deadweight loss equal to area eba. It is assumed, of course, that the gain to producers under the program, area $KeaP_T$, is larger than would have prevailed in the absence of intervention, area KbP_{M0}. In the long run, these gains are typically capitalized into the value of farm land.[37]

Now consider the introduction of a subsidy on ethanol and how it affects the demand for and supply of corn. Although the actual shape of the new demand curve will depend on how the subsidy is implemented and conditions in the industry, the primary effect, as shown in panel B, is an increase in the demand for corn to D_1. The market price increases to P_{M1}, but, given our assumptions, the output of corn is the same. Unless the demand for ethanol is sufficiently high so that the market price exceeds the target price, there is likely to be little effect on output.[38] Between 1950 and 1985, for example, the average market price for corn was greater than the target price in only 13 of those 36 years.

But, if the ethanol subsidy had at most a minor impact on the output of corn, then that would seem to suggest that corn producers did not directly gain from the ethanol subsidy. There was, however, a clear political benefit to corn producers from the ethanol subsidy. It *masked* the costs of the federal farm program by reducing deficiency payments. With the ethanol subsidy, deficiency payments could be reduced from $P_{M0}baP_T$ to $P_{M1}caP_T$. Continuing the subsidy for ethanol was important if agricultural program costs were to be kept in check.

The political importance of concealing deficiency payments is indicated by the data in Table 2.1. Deficiency payments ballooned in the 1980s, rising from $88 million in 1978 to $25.8 billion in 1986, and became one of the largest components of agricultural commodity program costs.[39] At the same time, the federal budget deficit was increasing and a source of considerable political and financial concern.[40] In 1985, the Congressional Budget Office (CBO) estimated

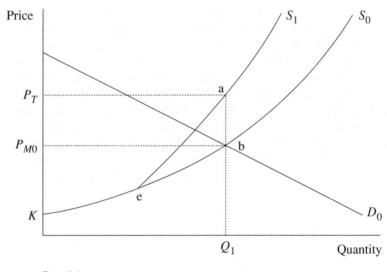

Panel A

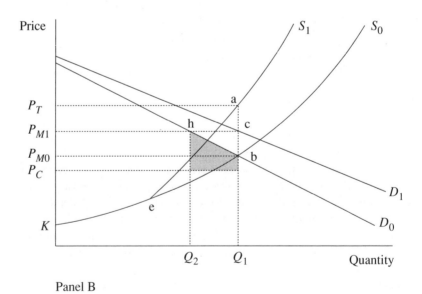

Panel B

Figure 2.1   The market for corn

that elimination of deficiency payments would save taxpayers $28 900 million over five years.[41]

As farm deficiency payments grew, a 1984 General Accounting Office (GAO) report suggested that the cost of ethanol subsidies might be offset by the reduced costs of agricultural price support programs.[42] Given the analysis in Figure 2.1, it should be clear that such an outcome is possible. The GAO report, however, was not conclusive, and the trade-off between ethanol subsidies and agricultural program costs remained unanswered. Moreover, even if that trade-off proved positive it would not have amounted to a full cost–benefit analysis.

Most studies of ethanol acknowledged that without a subsidy for the fuel, there would be little or no production of ethanol.[43] Even at the subsidized price, there are a number of competing alternative fuels, and ethanol is confronted by a somewhat lower priced and easier-to-use substitute in the oxygenate market, MTBE. These other products set a limit on the price that can be charged for ethanol. Despite the subsidy, ethanol has managed to obtain only a small fraction of the alternative fuels market, and barely a third of the larger oxygenate market in the 1990s.[44]

Accordingly, as shown in Figure 2.1, panel B, after the subsidy has been deducted, the per unit value of corn in producing ethanol, P_C, must be less per bushel than the market price P_{M0}, implying that corn is being used inefficiently. If there are no rents earned by ethanol producers and there are no other significant price effects for any other commodities, the partial equilibrium analysis shown in panel B reveals that the subsidy to ethanol results in a deadweight loss equal to the shaded area, a combination of lost surplus by other buyers as the price is driven up to P_{M1}, and the inefficient use of corn.[45]

Of course, there may be rents that accrue to firms engaged in the production of ethanol. Moreover, foreign purchasers are included in the demand function shown in Figure 2.1. If they are not considered part of the welfare calculations, their losses due to higher prices for corn should be excluded. But there are other factors that work in the opposite direction. The production of ethanol yields feed byproducts and these compete with soybean meal and other feeds. Increased ethanol production will lower the price of these other feeds. The potential for these types of interaction suggests that a partial equilibrium analysis will likely miss significant market interactions and that a general equilibrium approach is required to assess the overall benefits and costs of the ethanol subsidy. Moreover, any environmental benefit must be accounted for. Clearly, a fully fledged cost–benefit analysis would require an enormous amount of information and faith in the modeling of these complex interactions.[46] As we show, in an environment of political information obfuscation, the challenge of completing such a study would be even more difficult. Because any results would have important implications for corn growers, the studies were unlikely to be done without political intervention to control the information released.

Information Obfuscation in the Absence of Competing Interest Groups: 1978–1986

In the early 1980s, congressional hearings and other sources of information were enthusiastic about the potential contribution of alternative fuels, such as ethanol, methanol, and liquified natural gas to energy independence, cleaner air and rural development.[47] Because no cohesive constituency was disadvantaged by the transfer, the claims made on behalf of ethanol were not seriously disputed by outside parties. The most damaging challenge came from an internal 1986 US Department of Agriculture (USDA) cost–benefit analysis of the subsidy.

The 1986 USDA study was headed by career civil service employee and Director of the USDA's Office of Energy, Earle Gavett. It was undertaken specifically to address the question of whether a positive trade-off existed between price support program costs and the ethanol subsidy.[48] The 1986 study was also a prerequisite to further programs regarding the feasibility of a strategic ethanol reserve as required by Section 1774 of the Food Security Act of 1985. When the report was issued, however, its findings came as a shock to ethanol proponents.

While falling short of a full cost–benefit analysis, the 1986 USDA study utilized a general equilibrium approach to estimate the non-environmental benefits and costs of the subsidy to ethanol. The report concluded that the industry could not survive through 1995 without 'massive Government subsidies, given the outlook for petroleum prices'.[49] Further it suggested that '[i]f the principle argument for subsidizing ethanol is to boost farm income, we conclude from this analysis that it would be more economical to burn straight gasoline in our automobiles and pay corn growers a direct subsidy equal to the amount they would receive as a result of ethanol production'.[50]

The response from ethanol subsidy advocates was quick. Industry representatives asked the Secretary of Agriculture to repudiate the report's findings and to fire Gavett.[51] Secretary of Agriculture Richard Lyng agreed to have another study performed, ostensibly to examine the costs of state-of-the-art plants, to determine whether new technology would reduce the cost of ethanol production, and to determine whether commodity program cost savings, largely corn deficiency payment savings, might exceed federal ethanol subsidies. The Gavett report had already concluded that any program savings would not offset the costs of the ethanol subsidy. Accordingly, the charge to the new study was to determine whether or not that outcome might be reversed. Senator Robert Dole of Kansas added an amendment (Section 13) to the Farm Disaster Assistance Act of 1987 (P.L. 100–45), which required that the Secretary of Agriculture establish a seven-member panel to conduct a study of the cost-effectiveness of ethanol production, the likelihood of new cost-saving technology, and the impact on agriculture and government farm programs. Dole sought specifically to dilute the input of USDA researchers with ethanol industry representatives:

> There has been one study done by the USDA, showing a rather distorted view because the study was done solely by USDA. Under this amendment there would be other representatives who would be part of the seven-member panel that would make the study: feedgrain producers, feedgrain processors, members of associations involved in the production and marketing of ethanol, and other industry or university related authorities. The panel would consist of four members representative of the ethanol industry, and then two members shall be employed by the Federal Government. I believe this seven-member panel would present a more objective study.[52]

The 'bias' of concern to Dole was clearly the relatively neutral position presented in Earle Gavett's study. Ultimately, the panel members included the Executive Vice-President of the Ohio Farm Bureau Federation, the Energy Chairman for Women Involved in Farm Economics, the Vice-President for Government Relations for the National Corn Growers Association, the Administrator for the Nebraska Gasohol Committee, the Staff Vice-President for the American Soybean Association, the Director of the Office of Mobile Sources, (Environmental Protection Agency: EPA) and, in what may have been an attempt to show that everybody was now on board, Earle Gavett of the USDA.[53] The Department of Agriculture, feeling the political heat from the Gavett report, decided to conduct another study of its own, but this time it would be conducted by the Economic Research Service, rather than the Office of Energy.[54]

Before any of the new reports were released, however, ethanol proponents were already discrediting the Gavett report. For example, in June 1987 Representative Richard Stallings of Idaho speaking in support of HR 2052 to mandate ethanol blending requirements in gasoline, stated: 'Incidentally, the USDA has acknowledged that a previous study done of the viability of ethanol as an alternative fuel was *seriously flawed* and will conduct a new study as required by recently passed legislation'.[55] The USDA had made no such assessment of the Gavett report, but this is but one case where claims were made by politicians that did not fit with the facts.

The panel report was issued in November 1987, but it did not provide the cost-effectiveness analysis as mandated. Rather, the report's conclusions were optimistic generalizations, including the statements that innovation would likely lower ethanol production costs, that there were environmental benefits, and that ethanol production would raise corn prices and farm incomes. The study did not determine whether or not any fall in farm program costs and other benefits would offset the cost of the ethanol subsidy, the point of contention raised by the 1986 Gavett report.[56]

The conclusions of the 1986 USDA study were clearly a blow to ethanol supporters and their congressional backers. The emphasis of further studies was not to be on the benefits and costs of the ethanol subsidy, but rather on reductions in deficiency payments and increases in farm incomes. The ethanol subsidy provided a convenient cover for rising corn deficiency payments in the late 1980s, and corn-state politicians were not about to lose or weaken that cover from publication of critical new information by a reputable government team of researchers. The flurry of reports that followed and subsequent repeated emphasis of the environmental and rural development benefits of ethanol by politicians successfully blunted the effects of the 1986 report.[57] Finally, a 1988 USDA report argued that with ethanol production reaching 2.7 billion gallons by 1995, corn prices would increase substantially, reducing deficiency payments to such an extent that there would be a net saving to the government.[58]

Ethanol supporters viewed the Gavett report as a threat, and acted quickly to reduce the potential damage it could cause. There is no evidence that the report caused lasting damage. It was successfully glossed over, in part, because there was no competing powerful interest group to take advantage of it. This episode reveals the extent politicians, backed by a powerful interest group, will go to mold the information the public holds about the benefits and costs of a transfer program.

Competing Constituencies and the Generation of Information about the Ethanol Subsidy: 1987–1998

Despite tax exemptions and loan guarantees, ethanol did not become the major fuel proponents claimed it would be in 1980. Moreover, ethanol did not become the predominate oxygenate additive. Less costly MTBE, made from natural gas, became more common with about two-thirds of the oxygenate market. By 1992, despite predictions of new technological breakthroughs, the ratio of the cost of producing a gallon of ethanol to a gallon of gasoline had changed little since 1980 so that without the subsidy, ethanol was not competitive with gasoline.[59] In 1997, ethanol accounted for less than one percent of transportation fuels consumed in the US, clearly a minuscule amount in terms of providing security against foreign oil interruptions.[60]

Amendments to the Clean Air Act, introduced in 1987 and adopted in 1990, required the use of gasoline blended with oxygenates, reformulated gasoline or RFG, to reduce volatile organic compounds (VOCs) and air toxic emissions in regions where air quality was low. These amendments provided an opportunity for proponents to extend demand for ethanol. They did so through legislative and administrative mandates for ethanol use at the expense of MTBE.[61] With MTBE and natural gas producers largely concentrated in states outside the corn belt, for the first time there were incentives for a cohesive interest group to challenge ethanol.[62] This competition among interest groups would generate more data to general voters about the costs and benefits of ethanol. Any environmental benefits of oxygenated fuels came through reduced carbon monoxide (CO) emissions. Ethanol or MTBE could be added to gasoline to reduce those emissions.[63] To insure that ethanol secured a larger share of the oxygenate market, legislation was introduced mandating that 'renewable' (ethanol) sources be included in reformulated gasoline: HR 2031, Clean Air Act Amendments of 1987, required that one half of all US gasoline have at least 10 percent ethanol and the other half have 5 percent methanol and 1.5 percent ethanol and HR 2052, the Ethanol Motor Fuel Act of 1987, required that 10 percent of all gasoline sold in 1988 be gasohol, 15 percent in 1989, 25 percent in 1990, 35 percent in 1991, and 50 percent by 1992.[64] This legislation was introduced by Representative Richard Durbin of Illinois and 71 co-sponsors, 43 of whom came from major corn-growing states.[65] Hearing testimony from Representatives William Alexander (Arkansas), Edward Madigan (Illinois), Durbin (Illinois), Richard Stallings (Idaho), Daniel Glickman (Kansas), and Eric Vaughn, President of the Renewable Fuels Association stressed the environmental benefits of ethanol and the desirability of reducing US dependence on foreign oil.[66]

Opposing testimony was provided by officials from Conoco, Chevron, ARCO, Marathon, UNOCAL, Amoco, National LP-Gas Association, Service Station Dealers of America, National Petroleum Refiners Association, and other groups.[67] Dixon Smith, General Manager of Operations for Chevron, representing the American Petroleum Institute, argued that the ethanol mandates would involve high investment costs with little gain in energy security or clean air advantages.[68]

Until these debates, there had been no serious challenge to the environmental claims made on behalf of ethanol. The bills were not enacted. Legislation was passed to promote both ethanol- and methanol-based fuels through government purchase of vehicles using alternative fuels, creation of an Interagency Commission on Alternative Motor Fuels, and raising the Department of Transport corporate average fuel economy rating of automobiles using alternative fuels.[69]

The Clean Air Act Amendments of 1990 provided another opportunity for ethanol producers. To reduce emissions of VOCs by 15 percent, gasoline sold in 39 CO non-attainment areas was required to contain 2.7 percent oxygen. Additionally, only RFG could be sold in the nine worst ozone non-attainment areas.[70]

In promoting ethanol use, proponents had to get around new problems regarding the environmental impact of ethanol that were surfacing.[71] New information indicated that ethanol, when mixed with gasoline, did not reduce emissions of VOCs to the same extent as did MTBE. Further, the use of ethanol could also increase emissions of nitrogen oxide and other pollutants such as carcinogenic aldehydes. Finally, any alcohol additive increased the volatility of the gasoline blend, making it difficult to meet the newly established VOC standards unless the base gasoline were made less volatile or the rules changed. Despite all the claims made that ethanol was good for the environment, VOC standards would have to be relaxed to encourage its use.

Given their earlier legislative defeats, ethanol proponents used more obscure administrative rulings rather than the more open legislative process. This action made it more difficult for methanol/MTBE supporters to counter and it raised the costs to voters of monitoring the costs and benefits of the ethanol subsidy. In 1994, the EPA issued a renewable oxygenate rule (ROR) that required at least 30 percent of the oxygenates used in RFG to come from *renewable* sources.[72] The rule was clearly aimed at expanding ethanol or its derivative ETBE's market share of oxygenate additives. Carol Browner, the EPA Administrator, emphasized the gains to farmers from the ethanol program as well as its ability to reduce oil imports and to provide environmental benefits, particularly reduced emissions of greenhouse gasses.[73] The Clinton administration was applauded by corn-state senators for initiating the 30 percent mandate.

The ROR led to another round of congressional hearings on ethanol. The farm program and the environment were again emphasized by leading advocate, Senator Thomas Daschle of South Dakota: 'If successfully implemented, the RFG program has the potential to reduce air pollution, reduce our dependence on foreign imports and petroleum and create domestic jobs'.[74] Senator Richard Kerrey of Nebraska added that

> [E]thanol production currently raises the price of corn by about 15 cents a bushel, and is expected to raise the price even more by the year 2000. Not only ... would this give vital financial help to our Nation's farmers, but it will also help to reduce the Federal farm outlays. Each one-cent increase in the price of corn saves the taxpayers $55 million in lower corn program costs. Thus, the current benefits of ethanol production saves about $825 million in annual USDA expenditures.[75]

Senator Thomas Harkin of Iowa dismissed questions about ethanol and ETBE's environmental effects as 'misinformation and misrepresentations', and claimed that: 'Without the renewable oxygenate rule, it is clear that the reformulated gasoline market would be monopolized by MTBE'.[76] Similar statements were submitted by Senators Charles Grassley of Iowa, James Exon of Nebraska, Richard Lugar of Indiana, and Paul Wellstone of Minnesota.[77] John McClelland of the USDA Office of Energy testified that the 30 percent mandate would save $3 billion in farm program outlays between 1995 and 2000, largely through lower deficiency payments.[78]

In other hearings, methanol proponents, such as Senator John Johnston of Louisiana, challenged the EPA's action. He argued that 'a 54 cent a gallon Federal tax subsidy seems a sufficient boost for market penetration [for ethanol]', disputed assertions that MTBE use involved significant foreign sources of supply, and denied there were air quality benefits from 'the use of ethanol over MTBE'.[79] Other rebuttals were provided by representatives of the Methanol Institute, the Natural Gas Council, and the National Petroleum Refiners Association.[80] Steven Berlin, Senior Vice-President of CITGO Petroleum, called for an open congressional debate on oxygenate policy rather than a 'crisis of implementation by EPA'.[81]

During the policy debates over ROR, environmental groups became actively involved in the ethanol subsidy for the first time, and they opposed the oxygenate mandates. Representatives of the Sierra Club, the Environmental Defense Fund, and Resources for the Future, argued that neither the alleged benefits nor the environmental and health costs were sufficiently established to justify the EPA's action.[82] A. Blakeman Early, Washington Director for Environmental Quality Programs of the Sierra Club, argued that greater ethanol production could increase the release of global warming gases, such as nitrous oxide.[83]

The EPA's 30 percent renewable oxygenate rule was challenged in the United States Court of Appeals for the District of Columbia by the American Petroleum Institute and National Petroleum Refiners Association in February 1995. The administrative ruling was reversed by the court as exceeding the EPA's authority.[84] During this time, the debate over the relative merits of ethanol, ETBE, methanol, and MTBE led to scientific studies by the EPA, the National Academy of Sciences, the White House National Science and Technology Council, and the Committee on the Environment and Natural Resources of the National Science and Technology Council. None of these or other studies found conclusive air quality benefits from the use of *any* oxygenate additive.[85] The GAO reported in 1997 that removal of ethanol subsidies (and hence, the end of costly ethanol production) would have little environmental impact or little effect on petroleum imports.[86] Hence, these and other studies, based on the best available data, provided no basis for the strong claims and fervent advocacy of ethanol and ETBE's air quality benefits made by corn-state politicians.

Although the EPA's renewable oxygenate rule was rejected in 1995, efforts by proponents to advance ethanol through regulation have continued.[87] Further, in May 1998, Congress overwhelmingly agreed to extend the ethanol tax incentive through 2007 as part of the six-year federal highway re-authorization bill.[88]

The competition between supporters of MTBE and ethanol has recently shifted to the debate over the health and water quality effects of MTBE in California. In March 1996, the California Air Resources Board implemented Phase II RFG and required that all gasoline be oxygenated during the four or five winter months. MTBE has been by far the most common oxygenate used in Phase II reformulated gasoline in California. Reformulated gasoline with ethanol could not meet the state's restrictions on oxygen content and volatility (VOC limits). In December 1997, the EPA issued a drinking water advisory regarding MTBE for its possible contamination of groundwater.[89] In November 1998, the EPA announced the creation of a Blue-Ribbon Panel to review use of MTBE and other oxygenates.[90] Taking advantage of these groundwater concerns, ethanol supporters such as the Renewable Fuels Association lobbied for legislation in Sacramento that would lift California's volatility limits and allow for ethanol's use in Phase II RFG.[91] More broadly, Senator Durbin of Illinois called on President Bill Clinton to change Phase II rules for RFG nationwide to open the market for ethanol:

> As you know, ethanol's most important market is as an oxygenate in RFG. Unfortunately, the federal RFG program has become an MTBE-dominated market. As a consequence, the RFG program is now under attack. From consumers to water quality officials to refiners Americans are expressing serious concerns about the health effects and safety of MTBE.[92]

Concerns about MTBE, however, also raised questions about the need for *any* oxygenates to meet the requirements of the Clean Air Act. HR 630 was introduced in the 105th Congress in 1998 to allow for the implementation of Phase II RFG without the use of oxygenates.[93] John Dunlap, Chairman of the California Air Resources Board, argued that no oxygenate was required to meet air quality standards. He was supported by some environmental groups.[94] But both MTBE supporter, Marvin Schlanger of ARCO, and ethanol supporter, Eric Vaughn of the Renewable Fuels Association, objected to rules that would allow elimination of oxygenate use.[95] Because of growing environmental concerns pertaining to groundwater, however, in March of 1999 Governor Gray Davis ordered the phaseout of MTBE from California's gasoline supply.[96] It remains uncertain whether there will be sufficient supplies of ethanol to replace MTBE or whether ethanol will become the oxygenate of choice. Californian RFG regulations allow refiners to produce complying fuel without any oxygenates, but it is a costly process.

With all of the claims and counter claims about the environmental benefits or costs of ethanol and MTBE generated by the competing interest groups, it would be very difficult for voters to sort through the material. Indeed, this debate raises questions as to how much useful information is presented to voters even when there are competing interests. The information is provided by parties with biased points of view, and in this case, the issues are complex. Because of the scientific nature of the material and the mixed incentives of MTBE and ethanol producers to protect oxygenate use, much of the information released has been difficult for voters to assess, as there is little in the way of impartial bodies to weigh the conflicting claims and promote their findings.

As we have shown, federal agencies, such as the EPA and the Department of Agriculture are subject to extreme political pressure when much is at stake.

For the most part, the EPA and the USDA have become proponents of ethanol. When potentially damaging and apparently neutral information was released in 1986, corn-state politicians were able to suppress the results and have them countered with updated studies. Recent scientific studies by the National Academy of Sciences and other bodies have suggested that the clean air contributions of ethanol are likely small at best. Yet, those studies have remained obscure, largely out of the debate, and have not prevented corn-state politicians from repeating the claims in congressional hearings that ethanol is good for the environment and good for energy security. The emphasis on these externalities by ethanol's political advocates has provided an appealing cloak for regulations and subsidies among the public. Given the value of the ethanol subsidy to corn growers, over the years advocates have actively and successfully resisted challenges to the externality argument.

CONCLUDING REMARKS

The history of the ethanol program reveals that politicians took advantage of energy concerns in the 1970s to put transfers and favorable regulations in place and since then have engaged in deliberate attempts to distort information flows and to obfuscate the underlying objective of the ethanol program in order to sustain it.[97] Ethanol is an example of special-interest transfers that are promoted by claims of positive spillover effects. The ethanol subsidy was first used to camouflage farm program costs and facilitate the channeling of funds to corn producers. Today, under the FAIR Act, the objective is relatively more conspicuous and direct: to increase the demand for corn. Corn-state politicians remain intense proponents, and they continue to stress broad benefits of ethanol beyond what the evidence would warrant.

No penalty will be placed upon members of the corn-state congressional delegations by their voters for obfuscating the benefits and costs of ethanol, and no challenger in those states will gain through exposure of new evidence counter to the claims of ethanol supporters. Other than politicians from oil-producing states there is not much incentive for members of Congress from other states, where the impacts of the program are small and dispersed, to expend resources to uncover more accurate information about the underlying benefits and costs of the ethanol program. Even among MTBE producers, oxygenate programs are beneficial, only preferential treatment of ethanol is opposed. Transfers are sought by all elected officials and to attack, or even demand closer scrutiny of some other member's program, would only invite retaliation. Indeed, these transfers are the glue that helps hold political coalitions together.

The systematic distortion of information available to voters by sponsoring politicians raises the transaction costs facing general voters in assessing the true benefits of regulations and other transfer programs. These actions add to the information costs that general voters face. Although competition among relatively powerful interest groups will provide an expanded information set to voters, that set will be characterized by conflicting claims aimed at offsetting or discrediting the information advanced by the opposing group. This process may provide useful information if voters can evaluate the competing claims, but the sources are not neutral. Our analysis indicates that there may be no unbiased sources of information that would allow voters to evaluate the claims and counter claims of the competing parties. Hence, even when there is competition among interest groups, there is information obfuscation in the political arena, and that activity can be interpreted as a costly rent seeking.

Once it is recognized that the competitive market analogy to politics is misplaced by its proponents, the notion that there is an automatic, corrective mechanism seems far too sanguine. Nor should a program's endurance be taken as justification for labeling the transfer as 'efficient'. Indeed, doing so not only confuses the standard meaning of the term, but diverts attention away from useful research on the origins, promotion, and magnitude of regulations and transfer programs in a democracy.

There is a tendency to presume that programs that survive over time must be reasonably efficient, given the transaction costs of changing them. Otherwise, it would be in the interest of politicians and constituent groups to adopt institutional changes and capture the resulting rents saved.[98] But, the endurance of the ethanol subsidy is not evidence that the program is in some sense 'efficient'.

An economy with rent seeking will have resource allocation patterns that do not fit with an idealized 'optimal' standard. Criticizing the alleged wastes of existing government policies and institutions by comparing them to hypothetical, transaction cost-free alternatives, however, is viewed as engaging in a 'nirvana' fallacy. According to this line of reasoning, the transaction costs of institutional change must be considered before labeling a particular program as wasteful or inefficient.[99] But, once transaction costs are introduced, the standard concept of Pareto efficiency loses meaning. The notion becomes tautological because, by definition, all observed arrangements will be 'efficient' if all of the transaction costs of adjustment are properly accounted for.[100]

Proponents of the efficient redistribution hypothesis could avoid this tautology trap if they were to describe how their efficiency assertions could be tested and falsified, but little progress has been made in that area.

Clearly, transaction costs in politics are positive and we should not expect outcomes in either the marketplace or the political arena to lie along the same frontier as they would in the absence of these costs.[101] But once transaction costs are considered, it becomes imperative that we examine the extent and basis of the information endowments possessed by voters before passing judgment on the efficiency of a government program. The question is not whether competition exists within the political arena, but whether the underlying institutions in which it takes place foster the production and release of sufficient information to allow voters to make informed decisions about the efficacy of a particular program. Only then can we assess whether or not the program promotes general welfare in a representative democracy.

NOTES

1. Acknowledgments: We have benefitted from able research assistance provided by Joseph Bial; support from the International Center for Economic Research (ICER), Turin, Italy; and comments from David Weimer, Oliver Williamson, Bruce Gardner, other colleagues, and participants at workshops at the Western Economics Association Meetings, 1998, the University of Chicago, 1999, the University of Texas, 1999, and the Conference on Regulation, Stockholm, June 12–15, 1999.
2. For example, P.L. 74–461, February 29, 1936, 'An Act to provide for the protection of land resources against soil erosion and for other purposes'; P.L. 74–835, June 29, 1936, 'An Act to further the development and maintenance of an adequate and well-balanced American merchant marine, to promote the commerce of the United States, to aid in the national defense'; P.L. 84–44, May 23, 1958, 'An Act to promote the national defense by authorizing the construction of aeronautical research facilities by the National Advisory Committee for Aeronautics necessary to the effective prosecution of aeronautical research'; or P.L. 95–501, October 21, 1978, 'An Act to strengthen the economy of the United States through increased sales abroad of United States agricultural commodities'.
3. Major contributions to that view are Buchanan and Tullock (1962); Stigler (1971, pp. 3–21); Krueger (1974, pp. 291–303; and Tullock (1967, pp. 224–32).
4. Representative is Wittman (1995) who claims that democratic politics are inherently efficient. Wittman's argument is an extension of Becker's (1983, pp. 371–400) claim that the political process will favor the most efficient policy instruments for affecting a transfer. Becker's point is a natural application of the standard Pareto conditions: if a given wealth transfer to a special-interest group can be obtained under different policies, then the policy instrument that imposed the least costs on the general electorate would be chosen. Although Becker does not claim that redistribution enhances aggregate wealth, his argument is the cornerstone for Wittman's, and others', more general assertion that political institutions in a representative democracy work as well as markets.
5. In a recent book, Lupia and McCubbins (1997), challenge conventional claims about voter ignorance. Although they concede that there is ignorance about many issues, Lupia and McCubbins argue that voters can and do make sufficiently reasoned choices and that delegation works.
6. In his various writings, Douglass North also has doubted that the institutional structure of government encourages the type of competition that maximizes welfare. For example, 'The point is that formal political rules, like formal economic rules, are designed to facilitate exchange but democracy in the polity is not to be equated with competitive markets in the economy. The distinction is important with respect to the efficiency of property rights' (North 1990, p. 51). Also see Dixit (1996, pp. 50–51). While Dixit comments that the 'analogy between political contracts and equity contracts may be worth further exploration', he does not equate the two.
7. Tullock (1989, p. 19).
8. While Becker focusses on competition among pressure groups and downplays the role of voters, Wittman (1995, pp. 20–30) focusses mainly on competition in the electoral market and downplays the influence of pressure groups (pp. 76–86).
9. The political selling of the US oil import quota in the 1960s as providing national energy security instead of primarily benefitting high-cost domestic producers and the justification

of the subsidized space shuttle program with emphasis on technology spinoffs, many of which were subsequently not realized, are two examples. See Cohen and Noll (1991) for analysis of government subsidies for R&D programs for the private sector. Banks et al. (1991, pp. 53–76) discuss allegations of important technological spillovers from government-assisted R&D programs have been a vital element in the political process underlying them. Banks (1991, pp. 179–215) discusses the externality arguments for and subsequent assessments of the space shuttle. With regard to the politics of the oil import quota, see Isser (1996, pp. 73–126); Burrows and Domencich (1970, pp. 1–6, 212–13); Bohi and Russell (1978, pp. 10–66, 268–99); Barzel and Hall (1977, pp. 7–10, 72–4).

10. Links to speeches and excerpts by legislators supporting the subsidy for ethanol can be found at the home page of the Renewable Fuels Association, http://www.ethanolRFA.org/.

11. Wittman (1995, ch. 2). In a recent book, Lupia and McCubbins (1997), also challenge conventional claims about voter ignorance. Although they concede that there is ignorance about many issues, Lupia and McCubbins argue that voters can and do make sufficiently reasoned choices and that delegation works.

12. Certain forms of advertising are similar to posting a performance bond. See Klein and Leffler (1981, pp. 615–41).

13. This point was emphasized by Alchian (1965, pp. 816–28).

14. On this point, we examined the 1996 House elections in 71 districts where either the incumbent lost or did not run. In 20 districts the incumbent lost. In none of these cases is there evidence of a damaging scandal involving distortion of information about the benefits and costs of a program designed for local constituents. Indeed of the 71 elections, ethics in general appears as a campaign issue in only six races and none of those involve unsuccessful incumbents. The ethical issues include campaign sources and inappropriate use of campaign funds, involvement in the House Post Office scandal, and sex. The reasons for retirement or electoral upsets of the incumbents range from old age, birth of twins, ideology (conservatives replacing liberals and vice versa), and insufficient funds to compete effectively with challenger. Electoral data for 1996 are from Congressional Quarterly Alert, www.Voter96.cqalert.com and the *Almanac of American Politics* (1998). Upsets occurred in CA # 10, 22; CT 5; IL 5; KY 3; ME 1; MA 3, 6; MI 8; MO 9; NJ 8; NY 4; NC 2, 4; OH 6, 10; OR 5; UT 3; WA 9; TX 14. Open elections (where no incumbent ran) occurred in AL 3; AR 1, 2, 3; CA 24, 27; CO 1, 4; FL 2, 11, 19; IL 7, 20; IN 7, 10; IA 3; KS 1, 2, 3; LA 5, 7; MA 10; MT 1; MS 3; MO 7, 8; MI 15; NV 2; NH 1; NJ 9, 12; NC 7; OK 3; OR 2; PA 5, 16; RI 2; SD 1; TN 1, 9; TX 1, 2, 5, 8, 12, 15, 16; UT 2; VA 5; and WI 3, 8. Ethical issues were raised in IL 9; LA 7; MI 15; NJ 9; OR 2; PA 5.

15. One of the classic articles on rent dissipation in the fishery industry is Gordon (1954, pp. 124–42). For a general discussion of the relationship between the lack of property rights and rent dissipation, see Cheung (1974, pp. 53–72).

16. Levitt and Snyder (1997, pp. 30–53) provide empirical evidence that pork barrel projects enhance re-election chances. Transportation and Infrastructure Committee Chairman Bud Schuster, for example, is considered one of the top pork getters in Congress and is popular in his home district. See Del Valle (1995, pp. 86–7).

17. Coate and Morris (1995, pp. 1210–35) also examine the impact of imperfect information on policy choice.

18. In assuming that elected officials attempt to maximize votes, we are following the lead of Mayhew (1974); Peltzman (1976, pp. 211–40); and others.

19. This result is similar to Peltzman's (1976, p. 211) point that politicians will not serve a single economic interest exclusively.

20. For a discussion of the benefits of as well as the problems with environmental risk assessment, see Hahn (1996).

21. There are some notable exceptions such as where stockholders own shares in numerous firms. In that case, they may be interested in joint maximization of profits rather than the performance of just one firm. See Hansen and Lott (1996, pp. 43–68).

22. The Freedom of Information Act or FOIA (5 U.S.C. Sec. 552, 1966) would seemingly provide voters with the opportunity to defend themselves against obfuscation. Analysis of the administration of the FOIA, however, suggests that the law provides little real access to

information on policy making and details essential to benefit/cost analysis. For example, see Katz (1970, pp. 1261–84); Miles (1989, pp. 1326–41); Sobczak (1989, pp. 181–213); Andrussier (1991, pp. 753–801); and O'Reilly (1994, pp. 415–68).

23. Legislation was enacted in Congress to promote the use of liquified natural gas and methanol in public transportation and in government agency fleets. Other legislation was enacted to promote the use of alternative fuels, such as methanol and ethanol, in private vehicles by relaxing mileage requirements and through other means. See US Senate, 'Rollback of CAFÉ Standards and Methanol Vehicle Incentives Act of 1985', Hearings Before the Committee on Commerce, Science, and Transportation, 99th Congress, 1st Sess., June 20, July 17, 1985 and US House of Representatives, 'Methanol as an Automotive Fuel', Staff Report, Subcommittee on Fossil and Synthetic Fuels of the Committee on Energy and Commerce, 98th Congress, February 1984.

24. US Senate, See 'Clean Air Act Amendments of 1987', Hearings before the Subcommittee of the Committee on Energy and Public Works, 100th Congress, 1st Sess., June 16, 17, 1987 and June 19, 1987 and July 22, 23, 1987.

25. As an example of the studies emphasizing the role of ethanol as a means of reducing energy dependence on foreign sources, see Bolet et al. (1983).

26. US National Alcohol Fuels Commission (1980) and Schnittker Associates and US National Alcohol Fuels Commission (1980, p. iv). See also US General Accounting Office (1990).

27. Members included Senators Birch Bayh of Indiana, Henry Bellman of Oklahoma, Robert Dole of Kansas, and George McGovern of South Dakota; Representatives Bill Alexander of Arkansas, Dan Glickman and Keith Sebelius of Kansas, and Toby Roth of Wisconsin; as well as Phil French of the Indiana Farm Bureau and Sharon Peterson of Women Involved in Farm Economics from Montana (US National Alcohol Fuels Commission 1981, p. iii).

28. See, for example, US National Alcohol Fuels Commission (1980).

29. Quoted in, Renewable Fuels Association, *Ethanol Report*, May 7, 1998, p. 2.

30. The loan guarantees of more than $482 million were administered by the Department of Energy and the USDA, Farmers Home Administration. See *New York Times*, January 12, 1980, p. 27; October 11, 1980, p. 37; October 13, 1980, p. 2. The Energy Security Act of 1980 authorized loan guarantees of $1 billion. By 1989, six of ten guarantees were in default. For a chronology of events and discussion of loan guarantees, see US Senate, Hearings Before the Committee on Energy and Natural Resources, Environmental Protection Agency's Proposed Renewable Oxygenate Standard, 103rd Congress, 2nd Sess., Washington, DC: Government Printing Office, 1994, pp. 5–8. For a general discussion of the relevancy of ethanol tax incentives to agriculture, see Kane and Le Blanc (1989).

31. This figure represents the loss in federal motor fuel excise tax revenues, which are waived for ethanol and ethanol-based fuels. See US General Accounting Office (1997b).

32. See ibid.

33. The FAIR Act largely removed the link between income support programs and farm prices and provided instead, direct payments to farmers. The current ethanol subsidy increases the demand for corn and that action increases the price received by farmers. Thus, the ethanol subsidy continues to provide clear benefit to corn producers.

34. For a discussion of farm programs, see Gardner (1987); and Hallberg (1992). Gisser (1993, pp. 584–611) argues that the use of acreage controls along with a price support leads to a more efficient scheme of redistribution than use of a price support alone.

35. Eligibility also allowed farmers access to Commodity Credit Corporation (CCC) nonrecourse commodity loans whereby their crop could be placed as collateral. If the market price rose above the loan rate, farmers could pay off the loan plus accrued interest and sell the corn at the market price. If the market price fell below the loan rate the farmers would simply forfeit their crop plus interest; farmers did not have to repay the full dollar amount of the loan. Upon default, the government assumed ownership of the corn. In years when the loan rate was above the market rate, stocks typically expanded. Since the 1985 farm bill, the average market price has generally been above the loan rate (but below the target price). Accordingly, in the analysis that follows, the complexities added by the presence of the nonrecourse loan program will be ignored.

36. There is an ongoing debate as to whether agricultural programs increase or restrict output, thus the outcome depicted is arbitrary. Whether the program expands or contracts output, however, is largely irrelevant to the key points developed here.
37. Although other input suppliers may benefit to some extent, it is a long-established principle in agriculture that the bulk of net returns go to land. See Rosin and Helmberger (1974, pp. 717–29).
38. LeBlanc and Reilly (1988, p. 37) comment that '[s]ignificant changes in aggregate income for grain producers who participated in farm programs occur only when the market price for their commodity approaches and then exceeds the target price'. Also see Kane and Reilly (1989).
39. Paarlberg (1988, pp. 109–10). Government stockpiles of corn grew to 1443 million bushels in 1986/87 as farmers chose to release corn held by the CCC as collateral in lieu of paying off their nonrecourse loans. CCC outlays for corn jumped from $2.1 billion in 1980 to $10.1 in 1986, adding to pressures to reduce output through acreage reduction as encouraged by the availability of deficiency payments. See Lin et al. (1995, pp. 20, 32–40) and Hoffman et al. (1990, p. 21).
40. Congressional Budget Office (1981, pp. 51–2; 1984a, pp. 42–3).
41. Congressional Budget Office (1985a, p. 159; 1981, p. 104). Congressional Budget Office (1984b, pp. xiii, 1, 30–43) outlined other modifications of farm policy including changes in deficiency payments as a means of reducing program costs. For annual recommendations to reduce or eliminate commodity deficiency payments, see Congressional Budget Office (1985b; 1985, p. 159; 1986, pp. 130–32; 1987, pp. 115–23; 1988, pp. 161–5; 1989, pp. 161–8; 1990, pp. 181–8). US General Accounting Office (1990). Lipton (1989, p. 10).
42. US General Accounting Office (1984).
43. See Tyner and Bottum (1979); Meekhof et al. (1980, pp. 408–15); and US General Accounting Office (1997b, p. 10). Most USDA studies have, in one way or another, also admitted that without the subsidy the market for ethanol would be very small. See, for example, LeBlanc and Reilly (1988, p. v).
44. There is little indication that the price for methanol or MTBE would rise significantly if the ethanol subsidy were eliminated. US General Accounting Office (1997b, p. 12).
45. For the zero ethanol industry rent outcome to hold, it is assumed that the only factor price that is bid up as ethanol production expands is the market price of corn. It is also assumed that given the existence of methanol and MTBE, ethanol producers are price takers in both the alternatives fuels market and the market for oxygenates.
46. Gardner (1995) presents results showing conditions under which a fuel ethanol subsidy would be preferable to a target price support program.
47. See US Senate, 'Effect of Alcohol Fuels Development on Agricultural Production, Price Support Programs and Commodity Reserves', Hearings before the Subcommittee on Agricultural Production, Marketing, and Stabilization of Prices of the Committee on Agriculture, Nutrition, and Forestry, 96th Congress, 2nd Sess., March 4, 1980; US House of Representatives, 'Methanol as Transportation Fuel', Hearings before the Subcommittee on Fossil and Synthetic Fuels and the Subcommittee on Energy Conservation and Power of the Committee on Energy and Commerce, 98th Congress, 2nd Sess., April 4, 25, 1984; and US House of Representatives, 'Developments in the Production and Use of Ethanol Fuels', Hearings before the Subcommittee on Investigations and Oversight of the Committee on Science, Space and Technology, and the Subcommittee on Wheat, Soybeans, and Feed Grains of the Committee on Agriculture, 98th Congress, 2nd Sess., July 6, August 14, 1984. Other support was voiced in US National Alcohol Fuels Commission (1980, 1981); and US Department of Energy (1980).
48. Gavett et al. (1986).
49. Ibid., p. iv.
50. Ibid., p. 45.
51. Gavett (1988). Firing a career civil servant is no easy matter, although they may be reassigned to less interesting or favorable projects or locations. See Johnson and Libecap (1994).
52. US Senate, *Congressional Record*, April 23, 1987, p. 9394.
53. National Advisory Panel on Cost-Effectiveness of Fuel Ethanol Production (1987).

54. The report produced an Economic Research Service study by LeBlanc and Reilly (1988).
55. US Congress, House of Representatives, Subcommittee on Energy and Power of the Committee on Energy and Commerce, Hearings on Bills to Encourage the Replacement of Gasoline with Alternative Fuels, 100th Congress, 1st Sess., 1987, p. 138. Emphasis added.
56. National Advisory Panel (1987, pp. xv–xxii).
57. Other potentially negative government studies were also sharply criticized. See Associated Press (1994). At the same time, government reports that emphasize the specific gains of ethanol to a particular sector have been released. For instance, see House et al. (1993), and Petrulis et al. (1993).
58. LeBlanc and Reilly (1988, p. 39). But despite the continuation of the ethanol subsidy, production barely reach 1.4 billion gallons in 1995, substantially less than the 2.7 billion gallon figure used in the 1988 USDA study to estimate the benefits of reduced program costs. US Department of Energy (1996, p. 20), reports ethanol consumption not production. Their figure, however, is very close to the Renewable Fuels Association (http://www.ethanolRFA.org) production figures for 1995. Since each bushel of corn yields about 2.5 gallons of ethanol, ethanol production accounted for about 7 percent of US corn production in 1995.
59. The cost of a gallon of ethanol ranged from $0.90 and $1.50; a gallon of gasoline was approximately $0.55 to produce. See US General Accounting Office (1997b).
60. Ibid., p. 36.
61. US Senate, 'Clean Air Act Amendments of 1987', Hearings before the Subcommittee on Energy Production of the Committee on Energy and Public Works', 100th Congress, 1st Sess., June 16, 17, 1987, and June 19 and July 22, 23, 1987.
62. MTBE is generally derived from methanol and 87 percent of methanol production came from plants in Texas and Louisiana with the rest coming from Florida, Wyoming, Delaware, Oklahoma, Colorado and Tennessee. See American Methanol Institute at AmMethInst@aol.com.
63. US Environmental Protection Agency (1995); US General Accounting Office (1996).
64. See US House of Representatives, 'Alternative Automotive Fuels', Hearings on HR 168, HR 1595, HR 2031, and HR 2052, Bills to Encourage the Replacement of Gasoline with Alternative Fuels, Hearings before the Subcommittee on Energy and Power of the Committee on Energy and Commerce, 100th Congress, 1st Sess., June 17, 24 and July 9, 1987. Referred to below as House Hearings (1987).
65. Iowa, Illinois, North and South Dakota, Minnesota, Missouri, Michigan, Ohio, Nebraska, Kansas, Indiana, Wisconsin, and Arkansas. The other representatives were from a scattering of states: New York, Pennsylvania, California, Virginia, Washington, New Mexico, North Carolina, Georgia, New Jersey, South Carolina, Florida, Massachusetts, Montana, Arizona, Tennessee, and Louisiana. Only Holloway of Louisiana and Jones of Tennessee came from states with methanol production.
66. US House, Hearings (1987, pp. 105, 118, 127–8, 140–55, 161).
67. Ibid. (pp. III, IV, 154, 350, 385, 388, 451–66, 490) for critical discussion of ethanol.
68. Ibid. (pp. 305–486).
69. Alternative Motor Fuels Act of 1988, P.L. 100–494.
70. The nine were areas within and surrounding, Los Angeles, San Diego, Hartford, New York, Philadelphia, Chicago, Baltimore, Houston, and Milwaukee. Numerous other areas have since 'opted in'. A number of other areas like Denver have their own gasohol programs.
71. For discussion of the politics behind the 1990 Clean Air Act Amendments, see Adler (1992, pp. 116–31).
72. 59 *Federal Register* 39258, 1994. See also, National Research Council (1996, p. 4).
73. Adler (1994). See the chronology in Hearings on the Environmental Protection Agency's Proposed Renewable Oxygenate Standard (1994, p. 8). Also in 1993, the Clinton administration exempted ethanol from its proposed BTU tax.
74. US Senate, 'Alternative Transportation Fuels', Hearing before the Subcommittee on Energy and Agricultural Taxation of the Committee on Finance, 103rd Congress, 1st Sess., September 29, 1993, p. 2. Referred to as US Senate, Hearings (1993).

75. Ibid., p. 11. David Gushee of the Congressional Research Service estimated that ETBE would cost blenders 10 to 15 cents more per gallon than MTBE because of the higher costs of ethanol relative to methanol, even with existing subsidies. See US Senate, Hearings (1993, pp. 23–25). With sufficient supplies of ethanol, production of ETBE and conversion of refineries that blended gasoline with MTBE to ETBE could be accomplished relatively easily according to William Piel of ARCO, ibid., pp. 20–22. Indeed, California saw production of ETBE as way of using southern California refineries and creating new jobs during the recession of 1992–94 in California. See, Leo McCarthy, Lt. Governor, ibid., pp. 3–9.

76. US Senate, Subcommittee on Nutrition and Investigations of the Committee on Agriculture, Nutrition, and Forestry, Hearings on Renewable Oxygenate Rules in the Reformulated Gasoline Program, 103rd Congress, 2nd Sess., Washington, DC: Government Printing Office, May 27, 1994, pp. 1–2. Hereafter referred to as US Senate, Agriculture Hearings (1994).

77. Ibid., pp. 8–16.

78. Ibid., pp. 19–22. During the presidential campaign of 1994, George Bush and Bill Clinton competed in farm states around a theme of an expanded ethanol role (ibid., p. 18).

79. US Senate, 'EPA's Proposed Renewable Oxygenate Standard', Hearings before the Committee on Energy and Natural Resources, on the Environmental Protection Agency's Proposed Renewable Oxygenate Standard, 103rd Congress, 2nd Sess., May 12, 1994, pp. 1–3. Hereafter, US Senate, Energy Hearings (1994).

80. Ibid., pp. 35–40.

81. Ibid., pp. 45–51.

82. Ibid., pp. 69–80; Blakeman Early (1994); Miller (1994); Stagliano (1994).

83. US Senate, Energy Hearings (1994, pp. 69–75).

84. *American Petroleum Institute and National Petroleum Refiners Association v United States Environmental Protection Agency and Carol M. Browner, Administrator, United States Environmental Protection Agency*, United States Court of Appeals for the District of Columbia, April 28, 1994, 94–1502.

85. For study results, see US Environmental Protection Agency (1993); National Science and Technology Council (1997, p. iii); Tennessee Valley Authority (1985, pp. 1, 6, 55–6); National Research Council (1991, pp. 1, 4, 13; 1996, pp. vi, 4, 24, 32); Mannino and Etzel (1996, pp. 20–24). See also Mayotte et al. (1994a, 1994b); Kirchstetter et al. (1996, pp. 661–70); Anderson et al. (1995, pp. 75–101).

86. US General Accounting Office (1997b).

87. See US Senate, 'Ethanol, Clean Air, and Farm Economy', Hearing before the Committee on Agriculture, Nutrition, and Forestry, 104th Congress, 1st Sess., September 28, 1995, p. 2, and US Senate, 'Renewable Fuels and the Future Security of U.S. Energy Supplies', Hearings before the Committee on Agriculture, Nutrition, and Forestry, 104th Congress, 2nd Sess., October 2, 1996.

88. The vote was 297 to 86 in the House, 88 to 5 in the Senate. *Congressional Quarterly*, http://www.cq.com. The bill voted on was HR 2400 (H Rept 105–467; S Rept 105–95). The bill contains some modest reductions in the excise tax exemption from the current 5.6 cents per gallon of blended gasoline to 5.3 cents in 2001, 5.2 cents in 2003, and 5.1 cents in 2005.

89. EPA-822-F097–009, December 1997, 'Drinking Water Advisory: Consumer Acceptability Advice and Health Effects Analysis on Methyl Tertiary-Butyl Ether (MTBE)'.

90. Clean Air Advisory Committee, Panel on Oxygenate Use in Gasoline.

91. See Renewable Fuels Association, Press Release, September 29, 1999, 'Ethanol industry vows to continue fight to open California gasoline market to ethanol'.

92. Renewable Fuels Association (1999).

93. US House of Representatives, 'Implementation of the Reformulated Gasoline Program in California', Hearings before the Committee on Commerce, 105th Congress, 2nd Sess., April 22, 1998 on HR 630. Referred to as US House Hearings (1998).

94. See http://www.oxybusters.com/casehist.htm.

95. US House Hearings (1998, pp. 28–589).

96. California Energy Commission, Fuel Resource Office (1999).

97. The point that programs often develop a life of their own is a cornerstone of Anne Krueger's (1990) analysis of the US sugar program.
98. For discussion of the efficiency of long-standing government transfer programs, in the context of the US sugar subsidy, see Stigler (1992, pp. 455–68). The argument that institutional change will occur whenever there are net gains from taking such action is described by Demsetz (1967, pp. 347–59).
99. For discussion, see Demsetz (1969, pp. 1–22).
100. The problems raised by expanding the Pareto efficiency concept to include transactions costs have not gone unrecognized. See, for example, Cheung (1982); De Alessi (1983, pp. 64–81); and Furubotn and Richter (1997, pp. 458–62, 475–7).
101. For discussion of some of the key issues regarding transactions costs and redistribution in politics, see Williamson (1996, pp. 195–213). Williamson attempts to resolve some of the conflicting issues regarding the efficiency of government policies by introducing a remediableness criterion for evaluating programs. See Williamson (1998, pp. 11–16). Dixit (1996) makes a very similar argument.

3. Bursting through state limits. Lessons from American railroad history

Colleen A. Dunlavy

> One fact must be accepted ... the railroad system has burst through State limits. (Charles F. Adams, Jr., 1871)

INTRODUCTION[1]

As the twenty-first century opens, the significance of 'nationality' in the economic world has become exceedingly fuzzy. Although experts on globalization disagree on the finer points of definition and evidence,[2] indicators point to financial markets as the seedbed of revolutionary change. Driven by liberalization of markets and electronic networks, world financial markets have expanded at an astounding pace. Cross-border transactions in bonds and equities involving US residents grew from 4 percent of American GDP in 1975 to 213 percent in 1997, with corresponding rates even higher in European countries.[3] Meanwhile, currency market turnover *per day* rose from $150 billion in 1985 to $1.26 trillion in 1995. As Andreas Busch concludes in a recent survey, 'changes [in some financial markets] have taken place at breathtaking speed and of a spectacular magnitude'.[4] As the 1990s came to a close, border-crossing seemed to reach even deeper into national economies. Between 1991 and 1998, the value of cross-border mergers and acquisitions in Organization for Economic Cooperation and Development (OECD) countries increased more than sixfold.[5] In the space of two years – 1996 to 1998 – direct investment inflows in OECD countries more than doubled.[6] As national borders have become increasingly porous, the largest firms have also come to rival whole nations in capitalization – Microsoft's market capitalization in late 1999, for example, equaled the entire annual GDP of Spain.[7]

When border-crossing becomes the norm and firms rival governments in size, what happens to the power of national governments to regulate business? This question has bedeviled scholars at least since the rapid growth of multinationals in 1970s, and in the last decade the literature on 'globalization' has mushroomed. But the scholarship on the regulation of global business focuses almost exclusively on twentieth-century developments.[8] The full dimensions of the political dilemma facing nation-states today can be seen with special clarity, this chapter suggests, in the American experience with railroad regulation in the nineteenth century. American corporations were – and still are – the creations of the state governments,[9] and the long-distance railroads chartered in the 1830s and 1840s constituted the nation's first 'big businesses'.[10] Commanding unprecedented amount of capital, they became the first truly interstate businesses in the US – the first to cross state borders routinely and frequently. Their novel character, in the words of one observer, brought 'a constant succession of surprises' – not least of which was a fundamental challenge to a long tradition of state-government regulation of transportation rates.[11]

This chapter explores the decades-long conflict over railroad regulation – especially rate regulation – in the United States. It shows how and why that conflict propelled US business regulation from the state to the national level between the 1830s and the 1880s. Understanding the political dynamics underlying the shift from state to federal regulation in the American past provides important insights into the prospects for a corresponding global shift from national to international regulation in the twenty-first century. In a nutshell, the prospects are exceedingly dim.

THE NINETEENTH-CENTURY AMERICAN EXPERIENCE

The starting-point of the American story lies in the decades before the Civil War. This was not – as many mistakenly think – an era of *'laissez-faire'*.[12] It is true that the first federal regulatory commission, the Interstate Commerce Commission (ICC), was not created until 1887. But business regulation in the US did not suddenly begin with the birth of the ICC. Because of federalism – that is, decentralization of power in the state governments – much of the action in the nineteenth century actually took place at the state, not the national, level and therefore has tended to be overlooked.[13] At the state level, a remarkably vibrant tradition of government activism prevailed.

Not hamstrung by the constitutional debates that the federal government's initiatives inevitably sparked, the antebellum state governments promoted and regulated economic activity with great energy. Several generations of scholars have now deepened and enriched our understanding of this critical aspect of American history. Best-documented are the states' promotional efforts. '[I]n no other period of American history', in the words of George Rogers Taylor, 'has the government been so active in financing and actually promoting, owning, and controlling banks and public works including turnpike, bridges, canals, and railroads'. Equally energetic, though nearly forgotten, were the states' regulatory efforts, often delegated to local governments. As William J. Novak argues in a recent study, 'a plethora of bylaws, ordinances, statutes, and common law restrictions regulat[ed] nearly every aspect of early American economy and society'.[14]

Among their traditional powers, the states' right to regulate common carriers was one of the most important, widely exercised, and well established.[15] Here the public interest was regarded as inherent, even when a firm's capital lay in private hands. In traditional forms of transportation – turnpikes and canals – public policy distinguished between *tolls* paid for use of the road- or waterway and *carrying charges* for transporting passengers and freight. On turnpike and canals, a multiplicity of stagecoach operators and canal boat owners transported passengers and freight. Thus competition among multiple carriers could be relied upon to keep carrying charges within bounds. But those who owned the roadway or canal itself usually enjoyed a monopoly. The state legislatures, therefore, took care to regulate their behavior, usually by setting maximum tolls for use of the road- or waterway. The states' right to do so went unquestioned. They also had the means to do so in the corporate charter itself. Companies were normally incorporated individually in special acts passed by the legislature, so it was generally in the provisions of that legislation – the corporate charter – that the legislature regulated companies. The states' jurisdiction was adequate to the task, finally, since enterprise remained relatively small in scale.

This tradition of state regulation ran abruptly into trouble, however, in the face of technological change. Railroad construction began in earnest in the US in the 1830s. By the end of the decade, American railroads totaled some 4500 kilometers; by 1850, they had more than tripled in length to 14 400 km. Total railroad investment, meanwhile, climbed from an estimated $96 million in 1839 to $301 million in 1850. The density of track was greatest in New England, but railroad development proceeded apace in all parts of the country. The largest firms soon commanded capital in the tens of millions of dollars. Then suddenly, between 1851 and 1854, four great trunkline railroads, linking eastern cities with the western hinterlands, reached completion. As the trunklines extended their reach westward, the 1850s experienced a railroad-building boom without precedent. By 1860, the combined length of American railroads had more than tripled again to 49 000 km, while investment soared to $1.15 billion. The railroads had become the first billion-dollar industry in American history. By 1880 American railroad track totaled nearly 150 000 km, representing an investment of some $4.7 billion dollars.[16]

Almost as soon as railroad construction began, it brought a rapid succession of unprecedented problems. One was the sheer physical size of their operations. As had become apparent by the late 1840s and unmistakable by the early 1850s, the new long-distance roads increasingly crossed state lines, thus literally exceeding the states' reach. Further growth in the 1850s and 1860s only compounded the problems. Charles Francis Adams, Jr., stated the matter baldly in 1871, as he weighed solutions to the problem: 'One fact must be accepted ... the railroad system has burst through State limits'.[17] By that time no one could dispute the fact.

But the problems ran deeper, for the new technology also upset prevailing legal norms regarding competition. Many railroad experts initially assumed that freight and passengers would be transported on the railroads by many competing carriers, as they had on canals and roadways. But safety considerations quickly ruled this out. As British railroad expert Dionysius Lardner explained in 1850:

> It soon became apparent ... that this new means of transport was attended with qualities which must exclude every indiscriminate exercise of the carrying business. A railway, like a vast machine, the wheels of which are all connected with each other, and whose movement requires a certain harmony, cannot be worked by a number of independent agents. Such a system would speedily be attended with self-destruction.[18]

Thus competition among carriers could no longer be relied upon to keep carrying charges to a minimum, as they traditionally had. As the railroad network expanded and filled in, moreover, the long-distance railroads inevitably began to compete directly with one another. In their annual report to the shareholders in 1851, the directors of the Baltimore and Ohio Railroad, one of the trunklines, expressed surprise to find themselves suddenly in competition with lines as far away as Boston.[19] This, too, was exactly the opposite of what had characterized canals and turnpikes. Where carriers had traditionally competed among themselves to offer service on monopolistic roadways, in other words, the long-distance railroads now monopolized carriage on their own routes but competed against each other for traffic. The assumptions underlying traditional regulation had been completed upturned. As one observer later put it, 'The law was thus brought face to face with a most perplexing problem'.[20]

Compounding regulatory problems, the railroads were also the first to engage in rampant rate discrimination – that is, they offered different rates to different shippers. Rate discrimination was a competitive tool spawned largely by their unprecedented cost structure. Railroads were very capital-intensive enterprises, and many of the costs entailed in running a railroad – for example, maintenance of depots and track, administrative expenses, insurance, interest, even staffing – did not change appreciably with an increase in the volume of traffic or the distance it traveled. In the language of economics, they enjoyed increasing returns to scale.[21] As early as 1840, the directors of the Boston and Worcester Railroad reported that they were charging higher rates per mile for shorter trips because the 'freight once loaded in the cars ... might be carried to the termination of the line at as little cost at least, as it can be delivered at any of the intervening stations'.[22] High fixed costs created extraordinary pressure to lower unit costs by increasing the total volume of traffic or the distance it traveled, for this had the salutary effect of spreading fixed costs over larger and larger quantities of goods or passengers. Thus the railroads offered special, low rates to large-scale shippers, to long-distance shippers, and to those located at points where different companies competed for traffic. This was exactly the opposite of the pricing strategy upon which the legislatures' traditional chartering policy as well as the common law had been predicated. Both were oriented to the problem of unfairly high rates, not unfairly *low* rates.

In short, the railroads – the 'high technology' of their day – put the American states in difficult straits: their jurisdiction no longer matched the scale of enterprise, while the novel competitive behavior of the railroads threw into question the basic principles underlying traditional regulation of transportation rates. In these new circumstances, their right to regulate at all became a matter of bitter political dispute for the first time.

In the ensuing, decades-long battles over railroad regulation, the locus of power – and, therefore, the site of conflict – shifted around the American political structure numerous times before finally moving to the national level in the 1880s. In tracking these moves, it is helpful to think of the American political structure as a matrix (Figure 3.1) defined by the separate levels and branches of government. Unlike a unitary, bureaucratic structure, the American

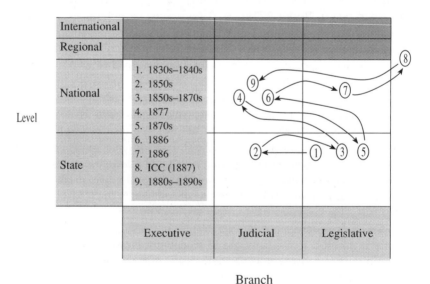

Branch

Figure 3.1   Sites of conflict in the American political structure: railroad regulation, 1830s to 1880s

political structure was fragmented both by federalism, which split power between two levels of government, and by separation of powers, which divided it among branches. As the history of American railroad regulation amply demonstrates, a fragmented structure has the desired effect of diffusing power, but it also ratchets up the overall level of overt political conflict. Political issues remain perpetually unsettled as long as the possibility exists of pursuing a more favorable resolution in another branch or at another level of government.

In the nineteenth century, the fractures designed into the American political structure gave business interests, in Harry Scheiber's words, alternative 'routes of escape' from hostile state legislation.[23] In conflicts over railroad rate regulation, these tactical moves took three forms: what might be termed *jurisdiction jumping*, that is, shifting the site of conflict to a more favorable geographical jurisdiction; *branch jumping*, that is, seeking a favorable resolution in another branch of government; and *level jumping*, that is, moving the conflict to a different level of government.

Until the late 1840s, competitive conditions in the railroad industry were subdued, and regulatory power remained firmly in the hands of state legislators – see '1' in Figure 3.1. But, when competition among long-distance lines heated up and rate discrimination increased abruptly in the late 1840s and in the early 1850s, shippers who experienced unfavorable rate discrimination turned to the state courts ($1\rightarrow2$) for a remedy. Their complaints centered on the special, low rates that the railroads offered certain shippers to increase the volume of traffic or the distance it traveled. But the state courts could offer little help, for the legislatures, as noted, had followed tradition in specifying only maximum rates. Neither could the common law provide relief, for it, too, was oriented to the problem of high rates, not rate-cutting. Thus conflict necessarily shifted back to the state legislatures ($2\rightarrow3$) in the 1850s and intensified, as the traditional understanding of rate regulation completely unraveled.

In political battles in the 1850s and again from the late 1860s into the 1880s, railroad interests sought to fend off regulation by adroitly exploiting the fractures in the American political structure. One means of escaping hostile legislation was to shift jurisdictions by moving to a more benign political environment. Of course, existing companies were well anchored by their physical capital, so railroads and their defenders normally invoked the specter of capital flight in other ways. Regulation would scare off additional investment in railroads, they argued, thereby inhibiting further development of a state's transportation network. One B.B. Taylor, an opponent of railroad regulation, put the threat bluntly in 1874: 'Such legislation will, of course, stop all further improvement by associated capital'.[24] In a different formulation, critics of regulation warned that railroad traffic would be diverted around the regulating state, thus depriving it of valuable commercial ties and trans-shipment business. Such arguments were heard as early as 1850 in Rhode Island, a small state and thus particularly vulnerable to the diversion argument. But even the most extreme of threats – the physical removal of an existing company – was not unheard of. Political economist Richard T. Ely reported in 1900 that Chicago railroads had once 'proposed ... to leave Chicago and build another city in adjacent territory to escape what [they] regarded ... as oppression on the part of the city'.[25] During the last half of the century, the threat of jurisdiction jumping became generalized in the US. The prospect that corporations would flee to more lenient states tended to hold the states' regulatory impulses in check, giving rise to a dynamic that has become known as a 'race to the bottom'.[26] In a report on trusts at the turn of the century, the US Industrial Commission summed it up neatly: 'whenever any State has put conservative restrictions upon corporations ... other States have taken advantage of the situation and enacted such liberal laws that corporations have removed to them from other States'.[27]

As an alternative to jurisdiction jumping, railroad interests could pursue one of the other two tactics, depending on the circumstances. They could try to shift the level of conflict upward from the state to the national level or to shift it from one branch of government to another. In the early 1870s, four midwestern states passed so-called Granger laws to regulate railroad and warehouse rates. In their battles against the Granger laws, the railroads combined the two tactics by challenging state legislation in federal courts (3→4). Other industries soon adopted both tactics, level and branch jumping, as tactical weapons in their efforts to fend off adverse regulation. Speaking, in effect, of repeated level jumping within the judicial branch, Democratic presidential candidate William Jennings Bryan expressed his frustration with it in 1899: 'When you prosecute a trust in the United States court it hides behind state sovereignty', he complained, 'and when you prosecute it in the state court it rushes to cover under federal jurisdiction'.[28]

In the 1870s, the site of conflict over railroad rate regulation shifted again between the federal courts and state legislatures. Beset by declining prices and intensified competition, especially after the panic of 1873, the railroads found themselves embroiled in political conflict on all sides. The large midwestern railroads lost their initial bid to have the federal courts declare the Granger laws unconstitutional. In the spring of 1877, the US Supreme Court upheld the states' rights to regulate rates. Battles over rate regulation continued unabated, therefore, in the state legislatures (4→5), as several more states responded by passing Granger laws. This, in turn, prompted railroad companies to combine branch and level jumping, once again, by seeking aid in federal courts (5→6). By the late 1870s, Congress had also begun to look seriously at the option of national regulation.

Meanwhile, from the 1870s on, the railroads also did their best to privatize regulation by putting their own house in order. Various groups of railroads sought to end ruinous competition by setting common rates and dividing up their business in voluntary 'pools'. The discriminatory nature of the common rate structures they periodically hammered out added fuel to the political fires, as did the special rebates they offered to selected shippers. But self-regulation of rates proved impossible, since the companies' agreements were not enforceable in court. Intensive rate wars broke out repeatedly. Transportation rates fluctuated wildly. The disastrous war of 1876–77, for example, drove down rates on the trunklines between the Midwest and the Northeast by as much as 85 percent. The railroads did reach a collective agreement to cut wages in the summer of 1877, but this move unexpectedly precipitated the 'Great Strike', the most extensive labor unrest the country had seen, quelled only when federal troops stepped in.[29]

As political conflict and rate wars accelerated in the 1880s, the railroads launched a new, two-pronged initiative to regulate themselves. Increasing pressure in the state legislatures as well as in Congress galvanized railroads nationwide to form an effective national association, which they organized in 1886 after nearly 40 years of failed efforts. The new American Railway Association did not tackle rates but moved quickly to standardize equipment and operations across state lines. Designed to head off impending legislation at the state and national levels, these initiatives produced, among other things, the United States' standard time zones. Meanwhile, even as efforts at collective rate-making continued, the trunklines developed an alternative strategy – 'system-building'. Where the railroads had earlier developed regional alliances with adjacent railroads, this was a defensive move that entailed buying up adjacent lines and building new ones over a much larger area. The result was self-contained, interterritorial monopolies. In the 1870s, the Pennsylvania Railroad built the first such 'megacorp', in Alfred Chandler's words, and others followed suit in all regions of the country in the 1880s.[30]

Abruptly, however, the seemingly interminable political battles over the state legislatures' regulation of interstate rates came to an end. In the fall of 1886, the Supreme Court reversed itself, declaring in *Wabash v. Illinois* that the states could not regulate traffic across state lines. Once again, this shifted the site of conflict over rate regulation, now lodging it squarely in Congress (6→7). If Congress failed to legislate, interstate rates would not be subject to any regulation at all. Conditions in the industry undoubtedly encouraged the Court's change of view, for the new systems under construction clearly outsized the state governments. In fact, by the mid-1880s, almost everyone – the railroads included – agreed on the need for national regulation of the industry, though they differed on the specifics.[31]

Thus spurred to action, Congress quickly forged a compromise after more than a decade of hearings and debates. Within months, it passed the Interstate Commerce Act, creating the United States' first independent regulatory commission (7→8), its ostensible 'independence' denoted by its position to the side of the traditional American political structure. Railroad rates were to be 'reasonable', companies had to publicize their rates, and personal discrimination was prohibited. The act outlawed pooling, which the railroads would have preferred to have legalized, but it did not prohibit collective rate-making and its provisions regarding distance-based discrimination (long- and short-haul rates) were vaguely worded, thus open to widely different interpretation. ICC commissioners, five in number and appointed by the president to six-year terms, had subpoena power and could initiate proceedings. If a company resisted its rulings, the ICC could call on a US circuit court for help.[32]

But it was too little, too late. The first ICC commissioners tread carefully, and even then the inevitable legal challenges came, for the wording of the act provided great leeway for reinterpretation in the courts. At every turn, the Supreme Court favored a narrow interpretation of its power that, in Stephen Skowronek's words, 'reduced the ICC to a mere statistics-gathering agency'. Thus regulatory power in the 1890s effectively shifted back to the federal courts (8→9), where the prevailing judicial sentiment and machinations on the part of the railroads hobbled the ICC for years.[33]

In the late 1880s, meanwhile, conditions in the railroad industry deteriorated. The strategy of system-building – undertaken largely at the urging of speculators, according to Chandler – proved very expensive and promoted extravagant overconstruction. This made the industry's traditionally precarious condition even worse by increasing fixed costs (above all, interest on debt) beyond the ordinarily high levels that had characterized the railroads from the beginning. As a result, the roads became even more vulnerable to economic downturns and rate cutting than they traditionally had been. The results of system-building were twofold: on the one hand, construction of 75 000 miles of railroad in the 1880s alone; on the other, foreclosure sales during the economic depression in the mid-1890s of some 40 000 miles of road – in Chandler's words, 'the most massive set of receiverships in American history'. It took concerted intervention by J.P. Morgan and other Wall Street bankers to reorganize the industry on a firmer footing.[34]

Thus, over the middle decades of the nineteenth century, conflict over rate regulation shifted repeatedly between branches and levels of government. The *form* that regulation of interstate rates should take remained hotly contested as the century came to a close. But what had been settled was the *level* at which it would be hammered out. Henceforth, it was a matter for the national, not the state governments, to determine. Creation of the ICC thus signaled not the end of *laissez-faire* but a new era in business regulation, one in which the reach of the law again – ineffectual though it was – at least matched the reach of enterprise. As large-scale, capital-intensive firms became common in other sectors of the economy, passage of the Sherman Anti-Trust Act in 1890 reinforced and generalized the upward shift in regulatory power that conflict over railroad rates had set in motion decades earlier.

But even settling the question whether the federal government would regulate an industry that had clearly come to exceed the boundaries of the states took a remarkable length of time. More than 30 years elapsed from completion of the first trunkline railroads in the early 1850s to passage of the Interstate Commerce Act in 1887. Because it offered conflicting interests multiple avenues of redress, the American political structure, in effect, facilitated and encouraged adversarial relations, both between government and business and among business interests themselves.[35] It also protracted the inherently difficult process of addressing the novel and perplexing competitive problems that the railroads introduced.

Over those 30 years – and well beyond – the lack of effective regulation of railroad rates worked to the advantage of some and to the disadvantage of many others. The principal winners seem to have been those, whether shippers or consumers, who benefitted from the special, low rates that the trunkline railroads offered in their scramble to attract traffic. The speculators involved in system-building, if they gambled right, also reaped benefits. But the roster of losers was much larger. It surely includes those shippers and passengers who were located at points where the trunklines did not compete, and those who traveled or shipped locally, all of whom paid higher rates. It includes investors who lost out in the turbulence that repeatedly beset the railroad industry – not to mention the railroad companies themselves. 'System-building proved costly to individual roads', Chandler concludes, 'and to some extent to the national economy as well'.[36] Among the losers in the 1880s and 1890s must be counted the vast number of stakeholders in the railroads that went bankrupt in the 1880s and 1890s – not only investors but employees and customers as well.

More intangible social costs, though difficult to measure, might at least be noted. The low rates that prevailed for long-distance transportation, as Gerald Berk suggests, surely spurred a centralization of economic activity in a relatively small number of urban areas.[37] Had non-discriminatory rates prevailed, the American economy might have entered the twentieth century with a more decentralized economic landscape. The low rates offered to large shippers, according to observers at the time, also exacted a cost by promoting the growth of abnormally large firms – the largest in the world by the turn of the century. This view was expressed both at the Chicago Conference on Trusts in 1899 and before the US Industrial Commission, which conducted hearings on the 'the subject of "Trusts," or Industrial Combinations' in 1899–1900. A number of witnesses attributed the rise of excessively large firms such as Standard Oil to discriminatory railroad rates. In the words of one observer, 'It is in the railroad companies that the greatest danger lies', for their discriminatory rates formed the basis on which 'the large trusts or combinations' accumulated 'their wealth and power'.[38] Although it is impossible to tally up the costs precisely, it seems quite likely that the United States paid a very high price for its lengthy failure to regulate railroad rates.

LESSONS FROM THE AMERICAN EXPERIENCE

Are national governments today any better positioned to regulate global business than the American state governments were when business first 'burst through State limits' in the nineteenth century? As a template for understanding contemporary dilemmas, the railroad experience helps to pinpoint the special problems that national governments confront today – ones that are likely to prove their undoing as well. First of all, the political dynamics to which the global political structure gives rise today are very much like those that characterized the nineteenth-century US. The difference is mainly in the mix of defensive tactics available to business interests. Because political institutions at the international level are even weaker than those at the national level in the nineteenth-century US, branch and level jumping as 'avenues of escape' from hostile legislation are less of a factor today. The most useful – and widely used – tactic is jurisdiction jumping, now among nations rather than states.

Like nineteenth-century firms threatening to move to another American state, present-day firms have made good use of this threat in lobbying for more favorable legislation. In Britain, where the tactic is known as 'flagging out', trucking companies threaten to move to the Netherlands to escape increases in fuel prices and license fees.[39] The Swedish company, Ericsson, recently announced plans to move its headquarters to London to escape high income taxes at home. Meanwhile, four large German firms are threatening to leave if the government goes through with planned tax changes.[40] In the United States, the National Foreign Trade Council, representing hundreds of American multinationals, is lobbying for changes in the US tax code. In 1962, it reported, 18 of the world's 20 largest corporations were headquartered in the US, but now only eight remain – 'mainly because of companies moving abroad', according to a news report. Several executives also testified before a US Senate Finance Committee hearing in 1999 on 'International tax issues relating to globalization'. An Intel official maintained that his company would probably not have incorporated itself in the US, if it had had a better understanding of US tax laws.[41] Undertaken internationally, jurisdiction jumping – or, in today's parlance, engaging in 'regulatory arbitrage'[42] – takes on special potency, even if only threatened.

The opportunities for jurisdiction jumping, moreover, seem even greater now than they were for nineteenth-century railroads. The most dynamic sectors of the global economy – finance, computers, communications technology –

are not tied as closely to physical place as nineteenth-century railroads and manufacturing firms were. As a recent report on debates about capital flight in Sweden put it, 'the problem for Sweden is that many of its new industrialists ... feel less committed to their country. Their assets are not factories or famous brands but highly mobile professionals'.[43] In the so-called 'new economy' of the twenty-first century, in other words, international jurisdiction jumping takes on added potency and, as many fear, may well result in a global 'race to the bottom'.[44]

To be sure, at least one scholar has argued, to the contrary, that trade liberalization does not necessarily undercut national regulatory standards and can even strengthen them. In political scientist David Vogel's language, it is possible for nations to 'trade up'. The ensuing 'race to the top' he dubs the 'California effect', in contrast to the 'Delaware effect', his metaphor for the race to the bottom. But his argument offers very limited grounds for optimism. As he notes, it applies only to the regulation of products, for the costs of producing environmentally- or consumer-friendly products are relatively small and can give their producers a comparative advantage in the regulated market. But it does not apply to the regulation of production, since labor standards, for example, would impose higher costs. And whether it translates well to financial regulation is not obvious. Even more discouraging, trading up depends for its success on strong international institutions that enable rich and powerful members of a trading group to raise the standards of other groups.[45] This is precisely what is missing at the international level. Rampant jurisdiction jumping today, therefore, is much more likely to result in the traditional 'trading down' of regulatory standards that occurred in the nineteenth-century US.

By analogy with the railroad experience, secondly, national governments today are also facing the kind of momentous technological changes that heighten political conflict. The new technology of the railroad proved so unsettling in its time not merely because company operations quickly transcended state borders, but because they also turned upside down the traditional assumptions on which rate regulation had been based. With the stunning development of new communications and computer technologies in the last decade, border-crossing increasingly occurs by electronic means – the analog of the railroads' discriminatory rates.

For regulation, the novelty of this new technology centers on the placelessness of transactions in cyberspace. Regulation of all kinds has always been tied firmly to physical space – to geographically-defined jurisdictions. But interaction in cyberspace is not tied firmly to place. The server with which a web browser interacts could be located anywhere. As legal scholars David R. Johnson and David Post write, 'The rise of an electronic medium that disregards geographical boundaries throws the law into disarray by creating entirely new phenomena that need to become the subject of clear legal rules but that cannot be governed, satisfactorily, by any current territorially based sovereign'.[46] Cyberspace thus threatens to subvert traditional conceptions of regulation at least as much as the peculiar competitive behavior of the railroads did in the nineteenth century. As the basic principles underlying regulation come up for grabs, national governments grappling with the thorny jurisdictional issues raised by electronic enterprise, like the American states when they first confronted interstate business, are likely to find their basic right to regulate challenged as never before.

What, then, are the prospects that political conflict will force a shift in regulation from the national to the international level, as it did from the state to the national level in late nineteenth-century America? When the shift occurred in the US, two factors worked in tandem. Most railroad companies had finally aligned themselves with other economic interests in favor of national regulation; then the US Supreme Court foreclosed jurisdiction and level jumping by declaring regulatory power to lie uniquely in the hands of Congress. What are the prospects that similar developments will smooth the way for a shift to international regulation?

Widespread interest in creating some kind of international regulatory framework certainly exists today, as it did in the nineteenth century. Despite the views of free-market enthusiasts, market participants realize that a healthy capitalist economy requires a stable legal framework or economic life quickly takes on Hobbesian qualities: 'nasty, brutish, and short'. The interstate railroads caught vivid glimpses of the disorder into which an under-regulated economy could rapidly descend during the tumultuous rate wars of the late nineteenth century, just as the global financial sector did in the 1990s during the Asian and Russian financial crises. Like late nineteenth-century railroad men, who came to favor some kind of national regulation, a number of top executives today are urging concerted action to strengthen the legal framework governing international financial markets. In early 1997 Thomas A. Russo, managing director and legal counsel of Lehman Brothers, issued a resounding call for global financial guidelines. They are sorely needed, he argues, because 'trillions of dollars chang[e] hands daily in the global financial arena without a universal gatekeeper'.[47] Later that year, the Group of 30, a self-described private organization of 'very senior representatives of the private and public sectors and academia',[48] published a study calling both for more effective self-regulation by core financial institutions and for more co-ordination of national policies. 'There is an inherent contradiction in the national supervision of global firms in global markets', said the group's co-chair, John G. Heimann of Merrill Lynch & Co. The Group of 30's study group concluded that 'the global operations of major financial institutions and markets have outgrown the national accounting, legal and supervisory systems on which the safety and soundness of individual institutions and the financial system rely'.[49] Speaking of accounting standards, General Electric's comptroller takes a similar view: 'Global standards are inevitable', says Philip Ameen. 'We, like every multinational, have an incentive and we will certainly embrace them' (Waters 1999). Meanwhile, the G-7 countries have moved to strengthen supervision of global markets, while the OECD is seeking to develop international standards of corporate governance.[50] Thus, one indispensable ingredient – an alignment of public and private interests in favor of some kind of international regulation – seems to be emerging.

But if a consensus is emerging, it is aimed largely at self-regulation and at the harmonization of national policies, not at building an international regulatory structure. The Group of 30's study envisaged corporate and government officials engaging in a co-operative endeavor. The accounting standards praised by General Electric are being developed by the International Accounting Standards Committee, an umbrella association representing two million accountants around the world. And when Thomas Russo of Lehman Brothers called for global financial standards, he regarded self-regulation as imperative: 'Because there is no omnipresent regulator in the sky (because none has worldwide jurisdiction), there is only one viable solution to firms' flying under the regulatory radar: We should develop universally applicable voluntary standards'. Legislative regulation has been difficult to harmonize within nations, let alone across nations, he argues, while 'the task of revamping global financial regulation has proved insurmountable' (Russo 1997). Instead, he advocates extending worldwide the model of the Derivatives Policy Group, a voluntary initiative of the six largest US investment banks. Whether the voluntary model can indeed be extended successfully across national borders remains to be seen, of course, since the structures and byways of banking differ dramatically from country to country.

The crux of the matter, as Russo suggests, is the absence of an 'omnipresent regulator in the sky' (Russo 1997). Nothing comparable to the US federal government in the nineteenth century exists on an international scale today. By present-day standards, of course, the federal government was relatively weak in the 1880s. But the basic governmental structure nonetheless existed, as did, more importantly, the written constitution on which rested the Supreme Court's decision to lay regulation of interstate business at the door of Congress. Although a variety of international agencies have been created and recreated since the Second World War, refashioning them into an international structure comparable in strength even to the US federal government in the 1880s is a formidable task. The prospects of institution building on this scale are dim, indeed. Thus, as national governments struggle with problems very similar to those that confronted the American states in the nineteenth century – jurisdiction shifting and subversive technological change – global businesses will be forced to rely on self-regulation for the foreseeable future. If the financial crises of the 1990s should recur, competitive stresses will make voluntary initiatives as difficult to sustain now as they were when American railroads tried self-regulation in the 1880s. Perhaps then the political will can be mustered to create a sturdy framework of regulation on an international scale. Until then, if the American experience offers a reliable guide, the losers will far outnumber the winners worldwide.

NOTES

1. This is a revised and expanded version of Dunlavy (1999).
2. For a sampling of the multidisciplinary literature, see Busch (2000). On the growth of American multinationals, see Wilkins (1974).
3. Bank for International Settlements (1998), Table VI.1. Percentage increases for German, French, Italian, and Canadian residents, measured against their home country's GDP, were even higher, ranging from 253 percent (Germany) to 672 percent (Italy).
4. Busch (2000), pp. 40–41 and Table 6.
5. OECD, 'New patterns of industrial globalisation: cross-border mergers and acquisitions', http://www.oecd.org//dsti/sti/industry/indcomp/act/mergers.htm.
6. OECD (1999), Table 1. Direct investment outflows advanced by 76 percent.
7. Morgenson (1999).
8. An early, influential work on the regulation of multinationals was Barnet and Müller (1974). For the recent literature, a good starting-point is Busch.
9. Exceptions were the first Bank of the United States and its successor, the second BUS. Otherwise, Congress did not charter corporations until the Civil War.
10. See Chandler (1965); Chandler (1977), pp. 81–121.
11. Nimmo (1881).
12. For two recent arguments to this effect, see Dunlavy (1994a), pp. 18–19, 97, 126–27, and Novak (1996), pp. 2–8.
13. Local governments also promoted and regulated business, but they did so only under powers granted them by the state governments. The principal division of power was between the state governments and the federal government.
14. Taylor (1951), p. 383; Novak (1996), p. 1; Dunlavy (1994a), pp. 45–144. For an overview of the literatures, see John (1997), pp. 347–80.
15. This paragraph and the characterization of shifts in regulatory power in the following paragraphs are based largely on Dunlavy (1994a). Additional footnotes are used only for sources not found there or for quotations. My understanding of the political dynamics at work was strongly informed by Miller (1971) and Scheiber (1975). 'Common carriers' were transportation providers who offered their services to the general public.
16. Data for 1880 are from US Bureau of the Census (1960), Q15, Q33.
17. Adams (1871), p. 34. Thanks to Eric Morser for bringing this source to my attention.
18. Lardner (1850), p. 503.
19. *Twenty-Fifth Annual Report ...* (1851), pp. 3–4, 18–23.
20. Hadley (1886), p. 31.
21. See Hadley (1886), p. 40; Ely (1887), pp. 261–2. Both cite Henry C. Adams for his classification of industries by returns to scale.
22. *Report of the Directors of the Boston & Worcester Rail Road ...* (1840), pp. 7–8.
23. Scheiber (1975), pp. 115–16.
24. Taylor (1874), p. 502.
25. Ely (1900), pp. 260–61.
26. See especially Grandy (1993).

27. Quoted in Grandy (1993), p. 14.
28. *Chicago Conference on Trusts ...* (1900), pp. 502–3.
29. Kolko (1965), pp. 7–20; Chandler (1977), pp. 133–43.
30. Chandler (1977), pp. 145–71.
31. Kolko (1965), pp. 34–41. Kolko's argument that railroad interests dominated the ICC has been much disputed, but his narrower point that the railroads generally supported federal regulation of some kind by the mid-1880s stands. For a sensible discussion of the economic interests at stake, see Skowronek (1982), pp. 125–31. As early as 1850, railroad men in New England would have preferred to have government aid in dealing with industry problems – at that time, the aid of the state legislatures – but, again, only if they could have it on their terms. See Dunlavy (1994a), pp. 175–6.
32. Hoogenboom and Hoogenboom (1976), pp. 12–18; Skowronek (1982), pp. 148–9.
33. Skowronek (1982), pp. 150–60 (quotation from p. 151). On the ICC's fate from 1887 to the 1970s, see Hoogenboom and Hoogenboom (1976).
34. Chandler (1977), pp. 171–85 (quotation from p. 171); Berk (1994), pp. 47–72. Berk tends to equate fixed costs with debt, which has some validity for his period but not earlier. On the novel problems generated by corporate debt, see 'The borrowing power of corporations', *The Nation*, June 8, 1871, p. 398.
35. Scholars have largely overlooked these structural origins of the adversarial pattern of government–business relations in the US. Instead, the conventional explanation locates their adversarial character in the notion that the growth of big business in the US, unlike in Europe, preceded the growth of the state. See Thomas K. McCraw (1984), 'Business and Government: The Origins of the Adversary Relationship', *California Management Review*, **26**, 33–52.
36. Chandler (1977), p. 147.
37. Berk (1994), pp. 75–149.
38. Industrial Commission, *Preliminary Report on Trusts and Industrial Combinations, Together with Testimony ...* , House Doc. No. 476, Part 1, 56th Congress, 1st sess., p. 1190. For further examples, see Dunlavy (1994b), pp. 41–9. About the same time, the political economist Richard T. Ely noted the following observation in a German newspaper (the *Frankfurter Allgemeine*): 'the reason why private monopolies like those in the United States did not exist to a great extent in Germany was that the railways there were State railways, and that all producers and dealers were treated impartially'. Ely (1900), p. 234.
39. Cowell (1999), p. C4.
40. 'European taxes: excise exiles', *The Economist*, March 6, 1999, p. 59.
41. 'Congress attacked over "uncompetitive" tax rules', *Financial Times* (US edition), March 26, 1999, p. 22.
42. See, for example, Russo (1997), sec. 3, p. 14.
43. Burt (1999), p. 20.
44. On the traditional, negative view of the 'race to the bottom', as well as more recent, positive assessments, see Grandy (1993), pp. 98–103; and Mark (1995), pp. 69–73. As both authors note, hardly anyone disputes the general dynamic in American history. Scholarly controversy centers on whether its consequences were (and are) harmful or beneficial. Among those who take a positive view is economist Roberta Romano, who cites 'the benefits produced by state competition for corporate charters – a responsive legal regime that has tended to maximize share value'. She advocates a system of 'competitive federalism' in securities regulation today, which entails 'a menu-approach to securities regulation under which firms elect whether to be covered by federal law or the securities law of a specified states, such as their state of incorporation'. She would extend the menu to foreign issuers, who could choose among not only American federal or state laws but also the laws of other nations (Romano 1998, pp. 143–217; quotations from pp. 145–6). This would indeed 'empower investors' (or at least some of them), but at the expense of other stakeholders. Underlying such approaches is a conviction that markets necessarily produce socially optimal outcomes, which is a matter of dispute.
45. Vogel (1995), pp. 1–8.
46. Johnson and Post (1996), pp. 1367–78 (quotation from p. 1375). Legal scholars and lawmakers are just beginning to grapple with this new challenge. For insights, see the web page

(http://www.abanet.org/buslaw/cyber/) of the 'Committee on the Law of Cyberspace', which the American Bar Association's Section on Business Law established in late 1995.
47. Russo (1997).
48. See http://www.group30.org/about.htm.
49. Group of 30 (1997).
50. Schlesinger (1997).

4. Origins of the myth of neo-liberalism: regulation in the first century of US railroading*

Timothy Dowd and Frank Dobbin

Laissez faire ... has taken an exaggerated hold on the public imagination, and has been regarded as a fundamental axiom of economic science, when it is in fact only a practical maxim of political wisdom, subject to all the limitations which experience may afford. (Arthur Twining Hadley 1903 p. 14)

INTRODUCTION

Neo-liberalism has two components. One is historical, and it revolves around the idea that advanced economies – particularly those of Britain and the US – developed under conditions that are best characterized as *laissez-faire*. The other is definitional, and it revolves around the idea that one group of industrial policies can be defined as 'non-interventionist' (that is, those that reinforce the unabated competition of free markets) while another group can only be defined as 'meddlesome' (that is, those that contravene free markets). Neo-liberalism combines these components as follows: Britain and the US became economic giants by allowing free markets to build their respective economies and by embracing non-interventionist policies. Other nations have obtained – or will obtain – similar results by following the examples of Britain and the US. Put another way, neo-liberalism posits that economic reality conforms to transcendent laws and policies that reinforce such laws lead to growth and prosperity. This position has gained staunch support in segments of academia and government (see Adams and Brock 1991; Eisner 1991; Sciulli 1999; Shonfield 1965; Yonay 1998).

Much scholarship reveals that neo-liberalism is at odds with the reality that it describes. Classic analyses reveal that the initial burgeoning of the British and US economies occurred under policies that were antithetical to free markets (see Goodrich 1960; Handlin and Handlin 1947; Polanyi 1944). Comparative research finds that nations have attained advanced economies and prosperity under a variety of policies, including those that neo-liberals would clearly label as 'meddlesome' (Hall 1986; Hicks and Kenworthy 1998; Katzenstein 1984). Finally, a growing literature demonstrates that markets do not conform to transcendent laws but, instead, vary widely by social and historical context (see Zelizer 1988; Zukin and DiMaggio 1990); industrial policy is perhaps the most salient source of this variation (Fligstein 1996; Lindberg and Campbell 1991; Zysman 1983). Neo-liberalism thus offers a myth, for its rhetoric diverges from the practices that it purports to explain (see Meyer and Rowan 1977).

In the present chapter, we extend the critique of neo-liberalism by making two arguments. The first is simple. The exceptional industrial policies found in the US emerged for identifiable political reasons, and they spawned the business rhetoric that now undergirds the neo-liberal myth. We show this by demonstrating how such policies dramatically altered business strategy and how these policies were later recast as conforming to overarching economic laws. Our second argument is only a bit more complex. US industrial policies were indeterminate because they did not stipulate the strategies that firms should adopt. Consequently, the resulting strategies were neither obvious nor inevitable but were drawn from viable alternatives. We show this by demonstrating how firms responded to policy shifts in different ways before powerful actors led them to converge in practice. Both arguments thus turn the neo-liberal myth on its head and reveal that economic activity is driven by the interplay between public policy and private interests rather than by transcendent laws.

Our arguments draw on a theoretical tradition that extends from the seminal work of Max Weber (1946, 1978) to the current neo-institutional paradigm found in organizational analysis (see Scott 1995). This tradition suggests that the neo-liberal myth is emblematic of modern times, wherein actors tend toward explanatory accounts that bear the imprint of rationality and science. That is, actors – be they academics or practitioners – portray various social realms (for example, business) as governed by natural laws just as the physical realm is. While these social laws need not be empirically accurate, and they often are not, they have very real consequences.

The Weberian tradition suggests that the neo-liberal myth parallels, and builds on, tendencies found in the realm of business. Indeed, neo-institutionalists find that business personnel glean 'laws' from experience and invoke those laws to guide their subsequent actions. Because these economic laws are cast as 'natural', they orient the tacit assumptions of managers and thereby escape empirical scrutiny. However, severe challenges to the status quo bring these tacit assumptions to the fore and force an articulation of new economic laws. Policy shifts, for example, initiate this process when business personnel must devise strategies that comply with new laws and regulations. Given the modern tendencies described by Weber and others, managers elide the impetus of policy shifts and, instead, frame their new strategies as an inevitable response to natural economic laws (see Edelman 1990, 1992). We demonstrate this articulation and re-articulation of economic laws by focussing on early US railroading. In the process, we hope to show how the myth neo-liberalism took root in the US.

Policy Regimes and Strategies in Early US Railroading

Early US railroading provides an important case for assessing neo-liberalism. The first modern industry, railroading accounts for much of the dramatic growth of the US economy in the 1800s (Atack and Passell 1994; Dunlavy 1993). Moreover, it was arguably the industry in which current ideas about markets and management first developed (Chandler 1977; Dunlavy 1993). As Roy (1997:79) summarizes, 'If the railroad had not developed in the form that it did, modern enterprise would not have taken the institutional forms we know as corporate capitalism'.

For our purposes, what is perhaps most important is that railroading developed under two divergent policy regimes before experiencing antitrust as a mature industry (Dobbin 1994). During the public capitalization regime that reigned from 1825 to 1870, competition for capital and customers was often absent. During the pro-cartel regime that reigned from 1871 to 1897, competition for capital emerged and competition for customers was eventually quashed. During the antitrust regime that reigned after 1897, competition for capital was sustained while competition for customers became common. Note that railroaders fought these new policy regimes. Regulation was won by rail customers who feared the specter of European baronial tyranny: hence, the progression of policy regimes was essentially exogenous to the system of railroad economics (Hartz 1948; Lipset 1963).

We pursue our case via historical and quantitative analyses. In historical analysis, we show that each new policy regime produced a similar pattern among railroaders. They initially objected to each policy shift as a meddlesome intervention in the private economy. They next experimented with new strategies so as to cope with each policy shift. Finally, they settled on new strategies, and in the process, they came to view the newly adopted strategies – and the respective policy shifts that spawned them – as conforming to newly articulated economic laws. In sum, railroaders came to describe *divergent* policy regimes and strategies as 'natural'. The disjuncture between the rhetoric and practice of early railroaders presaged the disjuncture currently found in neo-liberalism.

In quantitative analysis, we further demonstrate that, rhetoric aside, the US did not pursue *laissez-faire*, and what it did pursue mattered a great deal to this first of modern industries. We do so by focussing on the founding and acquisition of firms. Using time-series data on some three hundred railroads, we show the palpable effects of policy regimes while controlling for profitability, demand, and other factors. The public capitalization and pro-cartel regimes both spurred foundings and limited acquisitions, while the antitrust regimes virtually eliminated foundings and unleashed acquisitions. Thus while antitrust was later recast as a means for enforcing competition, its initial impact led to severe consolidation in the railroad industry. In subsequent years, antitrust formed the core of US industrial policy, and it provided the template for neo-liberalism (Fligstein 1990; Roy 1997; Adams and Brock 1991; Eisner 1991).

The Relevance of Policy Regimes

Understanding the effects of policy regimes on American railroading is an important task in itself, but understanding their effects is more broadly relevant because all three are empirically common. The public capitalization regime has been common in French history, from the time of Louis XIV's canal policies to François Mitterrand's high-technology policies (Dobbin 1992; Shonfield 1965); it also was used to promote early American banks, canals, turnpikes, shipyards, and textile factories (Callendar 1902; Hartz 1948; Roy 1997). The pro-cartel regime has been in force in different British and German industries since the late nineteenth century (Chandler 1990; Florence 1953). More recently, public capitalization and pro-cartel regimes have played roles in the flourishing of Pacific Rim economies (Hamilton and Biggart 1988; Johnson 1982; Wade 1990). Of course, the antitrust regime operates in most US industries today and has diffused, in some form, to other nations (Fligstein 1990; McCraw 1997). In short, our findings about business strategy under these policy regimes are potentially generalizable to many other industries, countries, and periods.

The policy regimes are also relevant because it reminds the reader that the US economy did not emerge under the *laissez-faire* regime that neo-liberals tout. Indeed, early US railroading underscores how 'un-liberal' the early American state was. The public capitalization and pro-cartel regimes were each, for a time, seen as the way of the future, and they were each cast as non-interventionist. The third regime, antitrust, is the foundation for the neo-liberal myth that now appeals to the global community. Had the largest economy in the world retained one of its earlier policy regimes, instead of enforcing the antitrust regime, we might today define '*laissez-faire*', 'non-intervention', and 'liberalism' in quite different terms.

POLICY REGIMES, RAILROAD STRATEGIES, AND ECONOMIC LAWS

In this historical section, we begin by outlining the industrial policy and business strategies that prevailed in railroading between 1825 and 1870; we then examine how policy shocks in 1871 and 1897 altered both the strategies and economic laws espoused by railroaders. To document such changes, we draw on the letters of industry leaders compiled by Thomas Cochran (1965), the writings of state railroad commissioners, and the voluminous literature on railroading. Our story suggests hypotheses about railroad foundings and acquisitions. We spell out those hypotheses as we proceed, and then in the quantitative section, we test those hypotheses with time-series analyses of data that span nearly a century of Massachusetts railroading. In the historical section, then, we pay particular attention to state policies in Massachusetts, which were typical.

We emphasize one state because states established the relevant legal constraints for the early time period and because detailed national data do not exist before 1887. However, we heed national events and trends that affected this state. We chose Massachusetts because it was where railroading first emerged in the US, in 1825, and because it published the most complete railroad data of any state. We end in 1922 because Massachusetts ceased publishing its railroad reports.

The Public Capitalization Policy Regime, 1825–1870

Policy environment

When railroading technology came to the US in the mid-1820s, American industrial policy was marked by the following arrangement: the federal government played a small and contested role in commercial activity, while state and municipal governments played major and accepted roles (Dunlavy 1993; Scheiber 1975). This arrangement had nothing to do with notions of *laissez-faire* and everything to do with notions of democracy (Dobbin 1994). Americans feared that federal involvement in commercial activity could lead to a concentration of power that undermined democracy (Sciulli 1999), while they viewed the involvement of local governments as the incarnation of democratic self-rule (Lipset 1963; Tocqueville 1945). Such local involvement occurred as state and municipal governments, in efforts to build their respective economies, used public monies to stimulate a wide range of commercial enterprises (Handlin and Handlin 1947; Kennedy 1961). Local governments proffered loans, stock subscriptions, land grants, and public bonds to railroads (Cleveland and Powell 1909; Dunlavy 1993; Ripley 1912).

Two factors reinforced the proffering of public monies to railroads. The first entailed the competition between locales. State legislatures pursued economic vitality by promoting competition *against* other states rather than competition *within* their respective states; as a result, they did not want to fall behind in railroad construction (Goodrich 1949; Scheiber 1981). Massachusetts politicians, for example, were determined to build railroads westward so as to compete with the railroads sponsored by New York, Pennsylvania, Maryland,

Virginia, the Carolinas, and Georgia (Massachusetts, General Court 1828). Municipalities were equally sensitive to competition: 'No ambitious town could stand idly by and see a new railroad go to a rival place. There was no option but to vote bonds' (Ripley 1912:38). The second factor was the initial lack of private capital. Investors hesitated to fund railroads because lines were often built in anticipation of demand and, hence, did not guarantee profits (Cleveland and Powell 1909; Hadley 1903). State and municipal governments, by contrast, expected that public monies would stimulate demand for railroads and would spur subsequent economic growth (Adams1893; see also Massachusetts, General Court, 1828). Consequently, local governments were generous in their funding; they provided capital for establishment and for operational costs. State governments were equally generous with railroad charters; they granted companies exclusive monopolies over their tracks (Dobbin 1994), and they sometimes granted temporary monopolies over geographic areas (Cleveland and Powell 1909).

US railroading emerged and expanded under a policy regime that embraced public capitalization of private companies. States and municipalities were the primary architects of this regime, as both focussed on stimulating rather than regulating commercial activity (Shonfield 1965). Railroaders responded to this regime with founding and acquisition strategies oriented toward the public trough and with pricing strategies that exploited monopolies and minimal regulation. The public capitalization regime found in the United States, however, was not inevitable. Vibrant railroad industries likewise developed in countries that eschewed public capitalization, such as Britain and Prussia, and in countries that lacked privately owned railroads, such as Belgium and France (Dobbin 1994; Dunlavy 1993; Roy 1997).

Railroading strategies

Railroaders prescribed a founding strategy based on the availability of public capitalization, thereby curtailing competition for private capital (Hartz 1948; Stover 1970). Because most locales sought to capitalize only one railroad, railroaders identified those locales that lacked service and they sought aid from each one (Cleveland and Powell 1909). Sometimes they even initiated bidding wars between locales that desired rail service (Roy 1997). Fortunately for railroaders, numerous locales were willing to fund the establishment and operation of railroads (Goodrich 1960; Ripley 1912). By 1871, Massachusetts and its municipalities provided railroaders with nearly 14 million dollars (Cleveland and Powell 1909). Over a comparable period, states and municipalities in every region of the country accounted for at least one-half of US railroad capital. The vast majority of railroads benefitted from public capital, and all major railroads had done so (Dunlavy 1993; Goodrich 1960, 1968). Given such efforts to stimulate railroads, we expect the following:

Hypothesis 1: The availability of public capital will greatly boost the founding of railroads between 1825 and 1871.

Railroaders prescribed a delimited acquisition strategy that likewise was attuned to public capitalization. On the one hand, state and municipal governments viewed the local railroads that they capitalized as integral parts of their respective economies, and they resisted the control of these lines by distant railroads that might not heed local interests (Ripley 1912; Cleveland and Powell 1909). Rather than expand their existing lines via acquisition, railroaders typically established new railroads that remained independent so that each could return to local government for capital infusions to cover losses (Goodrich 1960; Roy 1997). Small wonder that the average Massachusetts railroad operated less than 40 miles of track in 1870, nearly 50 years after the genesis of US railroading (Massachusetts, Board of Railroad Commissioners 1871). On the other hand, local governments welcomed acquisitions under certain circumstances. For instance, they would encourage prospering railroads to buy and operate failing railroads, thereby preventing the disruption of local rail service. Some local governments went so far as accepting little or no remuneration for the purchase of their stake in a failing railroad (see Handlin and Handlin 1947). Railroaders thus advocated the purchase of failing railroads as a low-cost means of acquiring new routes. The following hypothesis may seem trivial, but below we suggest that under the antitrust regime, railroads that performed poorly were *not* more likely to be acquired.

Hypothesis 2: Between 1825 and 1871, railroads that performed poorly were more likely than others to be acquired.

In the wake of government largesse, railroaders adopted pricing strategies that responded to minimal regulation rather than competition. Given that most locales – apart from large cities – capitalized only one line, most railroads held service monopolies before 1850. Pricing strategies at this time, then, were likewise monopolistic. The potential for competition emerged during the 1850s as the tracks of various railroads began to cross (Dunlavy 1993). This meant that customers could now reach destinations via a number of different railroad firms. The situation, however, did not lead to an unabated competition for customers.

The absence of pricing regulations enabled two strategies that curtailed competition for customers. First, railroads practiced 'rate discrimination': they charged low rates for transport between the large cities at their endpoints, which were served by multiple railroads, and high rates for transport to isolated towns along their routes, which were typically served by one railroad (Adams 1893; Ripley 1912). That is, they discriminated against passengers and freight that traveled *short distances* on monopoly routes, and they discriminated in favor of those that traveled *long distances* on competitive routes. 'It has long been a favorite object with me', wrote the director of Massachusetts' Western Railroad, 'to attract passengers from greater distances ... by ticketing [them] through at reduced rates' (from Cochran 1965:263). Second, railroaders co-operated to ensure that rates on competitive routes did not drop too low. In the 1850s, for example, freight agents for Massachusetts railroads held meetings to fix prices (Adams 1893; Dunlavy 1993). Their efforts were indicative of a general tendency. As one railroader surmised, in 1863, 'it has come to be the fashion in these days ... to strike hands to prevent and swallow up competition' (from Cochran 1965:471). Thus competition for customers was offset by rate discrimination, which subsidized competitive routes with revenues from monopoly routes, and it was contained by cooperative agreements between railroads and their agents.

Naturalization of policy and strategy
In the earliest years of railroading, *laissez-faire* had yet to appear in the lexicon of state and municipal governments (Dunlavy 1991; Lipset 1963). Local governments embraced 'meddlesome' policies in order to stimulate their respective economies. Such policies, furthermore, had widespread public support. Pennsylvania's Chief Justice epitomized this when he wrote, 'To aid, encourage, and stimulate, commerce ... is a duty of the [states] as plain and as universally recognized as any other' (quoted in Hartz 1948:304).

US railroading emerged amidst a policy regime that made public funding and monopoly privileges commonplace (Cleveland and Powell 1909). Railroaders operated on the assumptions that they could routinely turn to governments for capital and that they would not compete directly with other railroads (Cochran 1965). When the potential for customer competition emerged, they embraced strategies that mitigated competition. Thus, railroaders – like local governments – did not have an idealized view of free markets. They instead saw extant policies and strategies as natural. Albert Fink (1979 [1876]:57) encapsulated such a view when he wrote about rate discrimination, 'the nature of things make them necessary ... It can not be maintained that it is the duty of the common carrier to equalize these existing inequalities at his own expense'.

The Rate Regulation/Pro-cartel Regime, 1872–1896

Policy environment
American railroad policy underwent two dramatic changes that culminated around 1871. First, public capitalization of railroads ended because of widespread graft (Henry 1945; Skowronek 1982). Scores of railroaders misappropriated public funds, and by 1870, 14 states passed amendments that

prohibited government aid to all commercial enterprises. Massachusetts, for example, limited municipal railway aid to 5 percent of a railroad's total cost, and it soon foreswore state aid to new projects (Cleveland and Powell 1909; Goodrich 1960). Second, customer complaints about rate inequities prompted states to impose rate regulation. In 1867, Massachusetts responded by requiring that railroads give 'reasonable and equal terms, facilities, and accommodations' to all customers; in 1869 they created a board of commissioners to oversee disputes (Kennedy 1961:17). In 1871, Massachusetts passed the 'short haul' law, which made rate discrimination illegal. Rate regulation by state commission quickly became common across the US (Massachusetts, Board of Railroad Commissioners 1881; Sanders 1981; Wilcox 1960).

The end of public capitalization and the introduction of rate regulation produced a financial crisis for railroaders: they could no longer rely on public monies for costs of establishment and operation, and they could no longer charge high rates on exclusive routes to offset low rates on competitive routes (Goodrich 1960). Railroaders responded in two notable ways. First, they resisted the policy shift and charged that rate regulation was unconstitutional. The Massachusetts Supreme Court would render that response ineffective; it ruled that, because of the benefits associated with their state-granted charters, railroaders were subject to rate regulation (Massachusetts, Board of Railroad Commissioners 1881). Second, they experimented with new strategies – initially emphasizing predatory strategies before settling on cooperative strategies. Their eventual reliance on cooperation marked the end of their crisis.

US railroading eventually thrived under a policy regime that enforced rate regulation and, as shown below, tolerated collusion. Financiers and public officials shaped the response of railroaders by discouraging cutthroat competition and by encouraging reliance on cartels. Besides their cooperative pricing strategy, railroaders would respond to this regime with founding and acquisition strategies that were also attuned to cartels. The rise of this new regime, however, was not inevitable. In the face of graft, the US government could have expanded its control of railroads, as the French state had done, rather than reducing its fiscal involvement (Dobbin 1994).

Railroad strategies

Railroaders experimented with business strategies designed to overcome the financial crisis wrought by the policy shift. We outline how they responded with several types of strategies before converging on one. In the process, we show that policy did not overdetermine railroad strategy.

First, railroaders responded with pricing strategies that were meant to damage, if not eliminate, competitors. William H. Vanderbilt offered rebates to firms that shipped large amounts of goods (for example, oil companies), thereby enticing large shippers away from competing railroads. Such rebates soon became commonplace, as other railroads reluctantly followed suit (Cochran 1965). In Massachusetts, competition for large shippers occurred 'through well-understood systems of agencies, rebates, drawbacks, underbilling, etc.' (Massachusetts, Board of Railroad Commissioners 1878:40). Jay Gould of the Erie devised another form of predatory pricing. His railroad would offer below-cost rates; this would force less-endowed competitors to follow suit and, in turn, likely expire. Many railroads imitated Gould's strategy, fearing that the growing number of competitors left them little choice (Adams 1893; Bruchey 1990).

Strategies of predatory pricing eventually waned because of the reticence of railroaders and the ardent opposition of financiers. While some railroaders embraced predatory pricing with enthusiasm – particularly those with resources to weather rebates and below-cost rates – others looked askance at such strategies (Cochran 1965). The latter group noted that predatory pricing could indeed drive competitors to bankruptcy, but it did not drive them out of business. Bankrupt firms continued to operate because their primary asset – the road itself – could not be transferred to other uses (Cochran 1965; Hadley 1903; Chandler 1977; Roy 1997); furthermore, these desperate companies would offer rock-bottom prices to win business (Adams 1893). 'The New York Central is undoubtedly powerful enough to push both the Pennsylvania Co. and the Balt. & Ohio to bankruptcy', observed one railroad president in 1878, 'but if they do so, they will have a still worse competitor in insolvent companies' (Cochran 1965). While railroaders were split on the utility of predatory pricing, financiers were united in their opposition. They saw it as inimical to their interests because their holdings in small railroads would be wiped out (Cochran 1965). Their opposition would prove influential because the end of public capitalization made railroaders dependent on private funds. Indeed, financiers only backed railroads whose strategies were compatible with the interests of finance (Roy 1997).

Second, railroaders responded with strategies to gain control of competing lines. On the one hand, Gould, Vanderbilt, and others sought control by leasing and acquiring lines that connected with their respective roads (Berk 1994). They typically did so for reasons other than expansion: 'We bought the Road merely to get rid of competition', wrote a railroad chairman in 1878, 'and not with the view of adding a first class Road to our line' (from Cochran 1965:346). On the other hand, Vanderbilt and others sought control by 'parallel building'. They built tracks adjacent to those of their competitors. They did so in hopes of winning business for that locale and in turn damaging, if not destroying, their competitors. When discussing a bothersome road that had invaded its territory, for example, one director wrote, 'I believe that I can stop this business immediately if the Board will authorize me to say … that for every mile of road that they construct hereafter … we will build a mile parallel with their main line' (from Cochran 1965:243).

Reticent railroaders and ardent financiers once again quelled the predatory strategies that Gould, Vanderbilt and others devised. Some railroaders questioned the utility of controlling competing lines. Given that competitors served overlapping locales, the leasing and acquiring of such lines meant that railroads were duplicating service that they already addressed (see Fink 1979 [1880]. Other railroaders questioned the wisdom of parallel building. One president surmised that, 'I cannot conceive it to be a wise policy to build a Road which at the outset competes with a line already constructed and thoroughly equipped and organized' (from Cochran 1965:423). Financiers uniformly decried the intent of such predatory strategies: they would destroy small railroads, which was contrary to national interests and to the interests of financiers with diversified rail holdings. J.P. Morgan warned that the key banking houses were 'prepared to say that they will not negotiate, and will do all in their power to prevent negotiation of any securities for construction of parallel lines' (quoted in Chandler 1977:171). Railroaders heeded his warning.

Third, railroads responded by creating formal cartels, which were designed to circumvent rate regulations by buoying rates. Amasa Stone, who ran railroads in Massachusetts, Connecticut, and the Midwest, outlined the emerging view of railroad interests in 1874: 'the time will come when there will be little value in railroad property without general cooperation of competing lines' (from Cochran 1965:469). The three leading railroads in the US – the Pennsylvania, the Erie, and the New York Central – created a railroad pool that would standardize rates, and they created a central organization to enforce the rates (Massachusetts, Board of Railroad Commissioners 1878). Cartels spread quickly. Some were simple price-fixing clubs. Others pooled profits, or traffic, to guarantee that each member received its fair share of revenues (Chandler 1977; Massachusetts, Board of Railroad Commissioners 1878; McCraw 1984).

Public officials encouraged railroads to join cartels and eschew predatory strategies. Officials argued that it was not in the public interest to see railroads ruined, especially when public monies had helped build them. The courts had long found written agreements between competitors to be legal – although they would not enforce them. The US Congress had edged toward the position of the courts in 1866, when it passed a law that facilitated the sharing of rolling stock and track by railroaders; it tolerated such agreements but passed no laws that penalized railroads for breaking their written agreements (Kennedy 1991; McCraw 1984). State governments also would tolerate, if not tout, cartels. In 1875, Massachusetts' Board of Railroad Commissioners (1875:41) advocated co-operation and combined rate-making: 'an open and reasonable combination would probably be found far less fruitful in abuses than a secret and irresponsible one'. Its commissioners (1878:80) later argued that 'uncontrolled competition is but one phase in railroad development and must result in some form of regulated competition', and they encouraged railroads to establish formal price-setting arrangements in the open. Railroaders followed such encouragement: cartels became the dominant strategy in railroading (Cochran 1965; Massachusetts, Board of Railroad Commissioners 1881).

The proliferation of cartel strategies held implication for railroad foundings. To be sure, the level would not be as high as it was under the previous policy regime; the end of public capitalization now meant that a prospective railroad had to convince financiers about its potential for profit (Bruchey 1990). Nevertheless, the security of cartels should result in a moderate level of foundings. As Albert Fink (1979 [1880]:23) explained before Congress, cartels could guarantee 'the separate existence of a great number of competing roads' by stabilizing the income of new and small railroads. We thus expect the following:

Hypothesis 3: The security of cartels will boost foundings moderately between 1872 and 1896.

The proliferation of cartel strategies likewise held implications for railroad acquisitions. Industry leaders touted acquisition as a means to police maverick railroads that broke cartel agreements. Their counsel, however, had certain qualifications. On the one hand, business writers and economists such as Henry Carter Adams (1954 [1886]) advised that railroads should pay attention to the size of capital investments when buying railroads. Asset specificity and high fixed costs would make it difficult for railroads with high capitalization to operate as effectively as railroads with low capitalization. On the other hand, Charles Francis Adams (1893) advised that a railroad that had wiped out its capital obligations through bankruptcy could be more profitable than a railroad that had not done so. The implication of the two qualifications was clear: acquire failing railroads for bargain prices and use the low marginal cost of operation to make money in cartelized regions. We expect the following hypothesis to hold. While the business rationales that inform this hypothesis differ from those found in the public capitalization regime, the predicted outcome is the same.

Hypothesis 4: Between 1872 and 1896, railroads that performed poorly were more likely than others to be acquired.

Naturalization of policy and strategy
The rhetoric of *laissez-faire* entered the lexicon of local governments, as they withdrew public capitalization and forced railroaders to compete for private capital (see Lipset 1963; Roy 1997). The rise of *laissez-faire* rhetoric belied another notable development: local governments increased their regulation of railroads via railroad commissions and 'short haul' laws. The political establishment and citizenry saw the end of public capitalization and the onset of rate

regulation as natural responses to the graft of railroaders and to their abuses of monopoly privileges (Dobbin 1994).

Railroaders initially objected to the new policy regime, but after embracing cartel strategies, they viewed it as reinforcing natural laws of railroad economics. Albert Fink once deemed rate discrimination as natural and hence resisted rate regulation (1979 [1876]); he *now* represented conventional wisdom when he argued that no justification existed for rate discrimination (1979 [1880]). Others concurred and heralded the naturalness of railroad co-operation and unnaturalness of railroad competition. The benefit of competition, wrote one president in 1877, 'applies to most business but it does not apply to Railroads' (from Cochran 1965:161). Charles Francis Adams (1893:80) would likewise write in 1877 that, for railroads, 'the recognized laws of trade operate but imperfectly'. Another president wrote, 'There cannot be permanent competition between Railroads. Legislation can no more establish permanent competition … than it can nullify the laws of gravitation' (from Cochran 1965:342). Such comments were typical of both the rhetoric and practice of railroaders.

In sum, by cutting off railroads from the public trough and by regulating rate inequities, local governments undermined the tacit assumptions of railroaders and forced them to articulate new economic 'laws'. Railroaders responded with three types of strategies, and for political reasons they settled on cartel strategies as resonating with the economic laws of railroading. Moreover, they argued that the extant policy regime naturally followed from these natural laws.

The Antitrust Policy Regime, 1897–1922

Policy environment
Two federal acts threatened cartels: the Interstate Commerce Act of 1887, which governed railroading, and the Sherman Antitrust Act of 1890, which governed industry more widely. Both were adopted to protect the economic liberties of small enterprises and consumers by preventing the 'restraint of trade'. The impetus for both acts was not, as some have since suggested, to create competition. The idea was to curtail the power of large firms and their combinations, which Americans feared as undemocratic (McCraw 1984; Wilson 1980). In the words of Senator Sherman: 'If we will not endure a king as political power we should not endure a king over the production, transportation, and sale of any necessities of life. If we would not submit to an emperor we should not submit to an autocrat of trade' (quoted in Eisner 1991:49). Together the Commerce and the Sherman acts outlawed the co-operative arrangements that railroaders used to stabilize their industry.

The end of the pro-cartel regime and the onset of antitrust produced a managerial crisis for railroaders: they could not collude to manage competition (Chandler 1990). Railroaders responded in two notable ways. First, they maintained that cartels were still appropriate and legal. Indeed, some railroaders lambasted the *meddlesome* character of these policies. 'Railroads either are or are not business enterprises. If they are ... it seems obvious that Government must leave them alone commercially' (from Cochran 1965:440). In 1897, the US Supreme Court went against this position and ruled that collusion was indeed illegal (Binder 1988). Second, they experimented with a range of strategies – exploring both predatory and co-operative strategies before settling on consolidation strategies. The triumph of consolidation strategies marked the end of the managerial crisis.

The rail industry continued to expand under a policy regime that outlawed cartels and, as a result, heightened competition for customers. The federal government was the architect of this regime, as individual states were in no position to regulate railroads that spanned numerous states (see McCraw 1984). Financiers shaped the response of railroaders by continuing to discourage cutthroat competition. The consolidation strategies that they would embrace had other ramifications: foundings came to a virtual halt, while the largest railroads acquired railroads representing the range of profitability. The rise of the antitrust regime, however, was not inevitable. Rather than dismantling co-operation between railroads, the federal government could have strengthened cartels by legally enforcing their agreements – as US railroaders had requested and as the British government had done with its expanding railroad industry (Dobbin 1994; Fink 1979 [1880]).

Railroading strategies
Railroaders experimented with strategies in order to overcome the managerial crisis that first materialized with the Commerce Act and later came to fruition with the Supreme Court enforcement of antitrust in 1897. We outline how they responded with three types of strategies before converging on one. Once again, we show that policy did not overdetermine the strategies of railroaders

First, railroads responded with dramatic rate reductions designed to drive competitors out of the market. 'The Interstate Law is responsible for the existing rate war', surmised a railroad president in an open letter, 'Pooling ... has been prohibited and nothing provided to take its place' (from Cochran 1965:447). The rationale for the rate war hearkened back to the 1870s: hardy firms might prosper by driving their competitors out of the market to create a monopoly. However, the lessons from the 1870s still held. Rate wars did not clear out competitors because, in the words of one economist, a railroad can 'be used for one narrowly defined purpose, and for no other. The capital, once invested, must remain' (Hadley 1903:192). As in the 1870s, then, most bankrupt roads did not abandon operation. Instead, they became more competitive after bankruptcy wiped out their capital obligations (see Roy 1997). Meanwhile financiers with diversified railroad holdings opposed rate wars that would bankrupt many of the firms in which they held stock, and they coerced railroaders to abandon such cutthroat competition (see Chandler 1977; Roy 1997).

Second, railroaders responded by continuing their reliance on cartels, particularly those involving the collective fixing of rates. J.P. Morgan, for example, responded to the Commerce Act by restructuring the Southwestern pool into a rate-fixing club and proclaiming the club legal (Chandler 1977; Cochran 1965). Railroaders across the country followed Morgan's lead. While various rate-fixing systems emerged, perhaps the most common was to designate a weak railroad to set prices on a route (Hilton 1966; MacAvoy 1965; Ripley 1915).

Railroaders initially continued their cartel strategies because of the ambiguities of antitrust policies and because of their successes in courts. Regarding the Commerce Act, many railroaders were not certain that it actually undermined cooperative arrangements. As one railroad president wrote to another, 'Kindly advise me whether or not in your opinion the passage of the Inter-State Commerce Bill will ... abrogate the existing arrangements between the various lines working between Boston and New York' (from Cochran 1965:290). Railroaders also fought the Commerce Act in court for a decade and won 15 of 16 cases that reached the US Supreme Court. They had hopes, then, that the act would be struck down (Stover 1970). Regarding the Sherman Act, railroaders and others considered the vague language and absence of a means of enforcement (no funds were allocated) to be auspicious (Eisner 1991). Thus between 1887 and 1897, many railroads remained in cartels of some sort, albeit in unstable ones because the federal government continued its refusal to enforce inter-firm agreements (Bittlingmayer 1985). But in 1897, the US Supreme Court's Trans-Missouri decision reversed the tide by upholding the central tenets of both the Commerce and the Sherman acts. It explicitly outlawed pooling and price fixing (Binder 1988). Cartels of all sorts thereby met their demise.

Finally, railroaders responded by steering a middle course between co-operative strategies, which were now illegal, and cutthroat strategies, which raised the ire of financiers. The largest railroads avoided rate-wars by acquiring roads, even when those railroads were geographically distant from their current roads (see McCraw 1984). Many of the remaining railroads likewise avoided rate-wars by selling out before ruinous competition began. As would be the case for manufacturers, the mere possibility of pricing battles prompted many railroads to exit rather than fight (Roy 1997). Ironically, consolidation strategies followed the letter of antitrust law. After the Supreme Court enforced the Commerce and the Sherman acts, railroaders could not manage competition via co-operative arrangements; they could do so, however, via merger and acquisitions. It was only in the wake of later antitrust law that mergers became problematic (Fligstein 1990). Consolidation strategies thus appeased the concerns of both public officials and private financiers.

Consolidation strategies had a notable impact on railroading foundings. Incumbent railroads, rather than new ones, were typically responsible for the expansion of railroad service. As one railroad president advised, 'it is wiser to buy existing Roads than to build new ones' (Cochran 1965:320). The annual reports of Massachusetts indicate that others concurred with the logic of such advice. Figure 4.1 shows that the foundings of new railroads came to a virtual halt, while Figure 4.2 shows that the mileage of Massachusetts railroads continued to climb while the number of railroads declined. This suggests the following hypothesis:

Hypothesis 5: The rise of consolidation strategies will dampen foundings after 1896.

Consolidation strategies likewise had a notable impact on acquisitions. In the 1890s, railroads representing one-eighth of all US mileage (25 000 miles) merged (Ripley 1915). New England railroads were little affected by these mergers, in which competitors for business between the East Coast and the Mid-West combined (Ripley 1915). Figure 4.3 shows, for example, that Massachusetts did not have a rash of mergers following the Supreme Court ruling of 1897. Nevertheless, the Court's enforcement of antitrust changed the logic of mergers for all railroads, even those located in New England. On the one

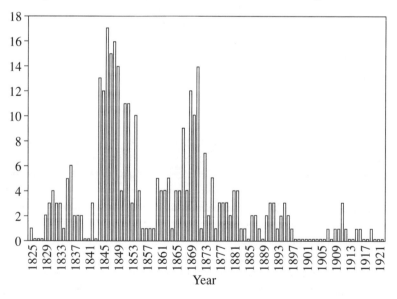

Figure 4.1   Railroad foundings

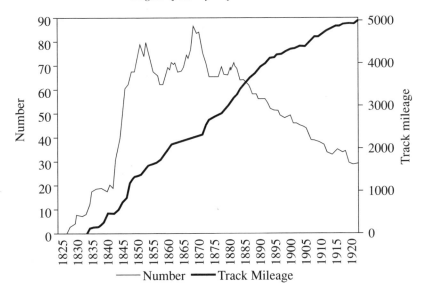

Figure 4.2   Number of railroads and track mileage in Massachusetts, 1825–1922

hand, railroads now bought railroads to build and expand their systems (McCraw 1984). The performance of the acquired road, then, had little bearing in their acquisition calculus. On the other hand, industry dominance and acquisition now went hand in hand. A declining number of firms dominated the industry, in part, by acquiring an expanding number of railroads (see Bittlingmayer 1985). These developments suggest the following hypotheses:

Hypothesis 6: Between 1897 and 1922, the performance of a railroad will not affect the likelihood of its acquisition.

Hypothesis 7: Between 1897 and 1992, rising concentration (that is, the extent to which a few firms dominate the industry) will increase the likelihood that a given railroad will be acquired.

Naturalization of policy and strategies

Railroaders had carefully monitored the political maneuverings that preceded the Supreme Court ruling of 1897. As legislation moved from state governments to the federal government (Eisner 1991), concern was rampant among railroaders (Dobbin 1994). When the Commerce Act neared its passage, for example, one railroader lamented that it was a 'cross between socialism and

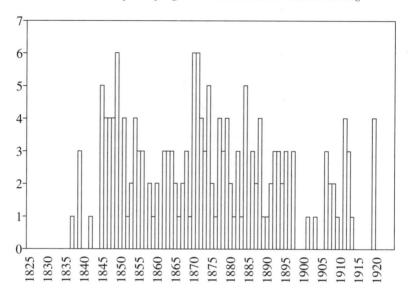

Figure 4.3   Massachusetts railroad acquisitions, 1825–1922 (n = 167)

paternalism ... this assumption of the right to manage private property by Government Officials' (from Cochran 1965:342). Others feared that the Commerce Act departed 'from well known and natural laws of trade' (from Cochran 1965:301) and that it would reap the 'danger of meddling with commerce' (from Cochran 1965:401).

The concern of railroaders regarding the Commerce and Sherman acts eventually gave way to acceptance, particularly after the Supreme Court ruling of 1897. C.F. Adams, Henry Carter Adams, Albert Fink and others had long suspected that railroading would consolidate if co-operative arrangements were prevented or ignored (Fink 1979 [1880]; McCraw 1984; Skowronek 1982). As their suspicions were borne out, railroaders went a step further and viewed their industry as both inherently competitive and naturally monopolistic. Because of these conditions, wrote Adams (1893:121), 'the effect of competition is ... to bring about combination and closer monopoly. The law is invariable. It knows no exception'. Consolidation strategies, then, were merely a natural response. One president wrote that the 'law of Railroad nature, namely that each line must own its own feeders. This law, like other natural laws may work slowly, but it is the law nevertheless' (from Cochran 1965:433). The idea of a natural monopoly, in effect, emerged as a corollary to the notion of the 'free market'. It supported the general idea that competition is natural but it explained why it could be lacking in railroading.

In sum, the outlawing of cartels by the federal government undermined the tacit assumptions of railroaders regarding the naturalness of cooperation. Railroaders responded with three types of strategies, before public officials and financiers winnowed this range to one type: consolidation strategies. While initially resisting the 'meddlesome' intervention of antitrust, railroaders developed new tacit assumptions: antitrust and consolidation reflected the natural condition of railroading. Thus it was through this naturalizing process that railroaders and others came to view antitrust – which was adopted for political reasons rather reasons of economic efficiency – became part of the *laissez-faire* lexicon (see Eisner 1991; Wilson 1980).

TESTING THE EFFECTS OF POLICY ON FOUNDINGS AND ACQUISITIONS

We have argued that under each policy regime, railroaders settled on one broad type of strategy and they articulated economic laws to explain extant policy and strategy. The third policy regime that they addressed, antitrust, was especially important: it became the foundation of the modern American economy (Fligstein 1990; McCraw 1997) and it shaped modern economic theory (see Adams and Brock 1991; Eisner 1991; Skowronek 1982). To demonstrate that the strategies that railroaders advocated were more than rhetoric, we quantitatively test the hypotheses detailed above. We bolster our analysis by deriving control variables from the research of population ecologists and industrial organization (IO) economists.

Control Variables

The work of ecologists and IO economists has import for our analysis. Both groups make clear predictions about factors that spur the proliferation of new firms. Ecologists make explicit predictions about factors that affect organizational failures of all kinds. Below we examine one class of failure: acquisitions. IO theorists make explicit predictions about factors that predict acquisitions.

Ecologists have found that sheer numbers shape both foundings and acquisitions. First, the total number of firms in the industry (density) has an inverted-U-shaped effect on foundings. As the number of firms rises, the legitimacy of the industry is established and new firms gain access to customers and capital. As density continues to rise, competition kicks in and fewer firms are founded. Second, density likewise has an inverted-U-shaped effect on failures. Third, the number of foundings shows an inverted-U-shaped effect on the subsequent number of both foundings and failures. This occurs as rising numbers signal a hospitable environment, but very high numbers signal a crowded industry. Finally, the prior number of failures shows an inverted-U shaped effect on current foundings; rising numbers make room for future entrants but excessively high numbers denote a volatile industry (Carroll and Huo 1986; Delacroix and Carroll 1983; Delacroix and Solt 1988; Hannan and Freeman 1989; Tucker et al. 1990).

Ecologists have also found that resource availability and industry composition have an impact on foundings. First, capital availability and the health of the economy each show a positive effect on foundings, as both facilitate access to resources (Hannan and Freeman 1989). Second, in industries where a firm's success depends on the size of its total network (for example, telephones, railroads), industry size has a positive effect on foundings (Barnett and Amburgey 1990; Barnett and Carroll 1987; Hannan and Carroll 1992). Finally, ecologists find that when a few firms dominate an industry, new firms proliferate to meet the peripheral demand that dominant firms ignore. That is, industry concentration has a positive effect on foundings (Carroll 1985; Hannan and Carroll 1992).

Ecologists have also found that the age of a firm affects its likelihood of failure. New firms are susceptible to failure because they lack resources, experience, and stable connections to customers and suppliers (Baum 1998).

IO economists have considered the effects of competitive processes on market entry and acquisitions (Bain 1956; Stigler 1968). First, in industries characterized by high fixed costs, such as railroading, capital accumulation reduces production costs for incumbents, thereby making it difficult for new entrants to compete. They expect the opposite of what ecologists predict: capital accumulation will have a negative effect on foundings and a positive effect on acquisitions (Stackelberg 1952; Tirole 1988). Second, in industries with economies of scale, concentration is a threat to new firms because it means that their competitors enjoy economies of scale (Bain 1956; Shepherd 1979). Concentration will have a negative effect on foundings and a positive effect on acquisitions. Third, failing firms are most likely to sell out, so that their owners can reinvest the proceeds in profitable ventures. Profitability will be negatively associated with the likelihood of being acquired (see Marris 1964; Weir 1997). Finally, firms are at greater risk when the economy is faltering. Gross state product will be negatively associated with acquisition (Becketti 1986; Gort 1969).

Data

We have complete data on foundings and acquisitions from 1825, when the Granite Railway won the first US railroad charter, through 1922. We examined each of the state's annual railroad reports for evidence of foundings and acquisitions (Massachusetts, Committee on Railways and Canals, 1838–1856; Massachusetts, Secretary of the Commonwealth, 1857–1869; Massachusetts, Board of Railroad Commissioners 1869–1922). Next, we cross-checked founding and acquisition dates in the commonwealth's annual Acts and Resolves of the General Court (1825–1922), which contains copies of rail charters. Finally, we cross-checked once again for the early period in Henry Poor's *History of the Railroads and Canals of the United States of America* (1860). There were 318 railroads chartered between 1825 and 1922, excluding charters granted to local street car lines and those granted to incumbent firms when they acquired other firms or entered receivership. There were 167 acquisitions during the same period. We truncated the analysis in 1922 because Massachusetts ceased publishing annual reports in that year. Most covariates come from the same published Massachusetts sources.

Methods

We used negative binomial regression to model railway foundings. Although analysts commonly use Poisson regression to model annual event counts, Poisson regression depends on the assumption that the conditional variance and mean of the number of events are equal (Barron 1992; Cameron and Trivedi 1986). A *t*-test of the hypothesis that the overdispersion parameter, α, differs significantly from zero verified overdispersion in every equation we report below, confirming the need for negative binomial analysis (Barron 1992). We derived the negative binomial estimates by maximum likelihood estimation using the software package LIMDEP. Given that the first year of our series is constrained to have one founding (that is, that of the Granite in 1825), we begin the founding analysis in the subsequent year. We thus analyse the incidence of foundings from 1826 to 1922.

We used loglinear event-history models, estimated with SAS, to model railway acquisitions (Allison 1995). We modeled factors that predict the acquisition of a railroad. We interact binary variables representing periods with other variables to represent the effects of those variables within periods. The 318 railroads in our population of Massachusetts railroads experienced a total of 167 mergers and yield a total of 4818 annual spells. Because of missing values on net income, some analyses do not utilize the full 4818 spells.

Findings

In analysing both foundings and acquisitions, we entered the variables in blocks. First, we enter the variables representing the ecological controls. Then, we enter the variables representing the IO economic controls. Finally, for the sake of parsimony, we enter our policy variables along with all controls that remained significant; furthermore, this last block includes a time-trend variable, so as to demonstrate that the policy effects are not merely capturing secular trends. When we have alternative specifications for a given variable, we report the results from the specification that showed the strongest effects (see Table 4.1). When the results for alternative specifications were roughly identical, we report results for the specification most frequently used in previous studies.

Results of the negative binomial regression support our predictions about the effects of policy on railroad foundings (see Table 4.2). First, policy regimes show robust effects on railroad foundings, even in the presence of a time-trend variable. The public capitalization regime entailed the generous proffering of public monies; it has a large and positive effect on foundings. The pro-cartel regime dampened competition for customers and created a secure environment for small railroads; it has a moderate and positive effect on foundings. Second, policy regimes condition the impact of density. Only in the presence of the policy regimes does density show its expected impact: it initially boosts foundings by expanding resource availability and then it depresses foundings by expanding competition. Third, the effect of policy regimes persists in the presence of ecological controls, two of which were significant. State railroads, including those of Massachusetts, relied on Britain for capital (Heydinger 1954; Massachusetts, Committee on Railways and Canals 1839). The availability of British capital spurs railroad foundings. The previous number of railroad failures likewise affects current foundings, but in a linear fashion rather than an inverted-U fashion. Finally, the results do not support industrial organization arguments. While capital accumulation and concentration initially show the effects expected by IO economists, both effects disappear in the presence of other variables.

Results of the event-history analysis support our predictions about the impact of policy on acquisitions (see Table 4.3). First, policy regimes mitigate the relationship between a railroad's profitability and its likelihood of being bought. We hypothesized that the preferences of local governments, in the public capitalization regime, and the preferences of financiers, in the pro-cartel regime, led railroaders to favor the purchase of failing railroads; meanwhile, consolidation strategies in the antitrust regime led railroaders to buy *both* unprofitable and profitable railroads. The interaction between the time period and profitability variables strongly supports these hypotheses, as poor profitability only mattered from 1825 to 1896. Second, policy regimes mitigate the relationship between industry concentration and acquisition. We hypothesized that concentration would only have an affect in the wake of the antitrust regime, as dominant railroads now eschewed co-operative arrangements and embraced consolidation strategies. The interaction between the time period and concentration variables strongly supports this hypothesis, as the impact of concentration occurs from 1897 onward.

Table 4.1   Independent variables

Variable	Definition
Log density	Natural logarithm of the number of railroads in existence at the beginning of the year
Density^2	Square of simple density
Foundings	Number of railroads chartered in previous year
Foundings^2	Square of foundings
Failures	Number of railroads that failed in previous year
Failures^2	Square of failures
Log capital accumulation	Log of total railroad capitalization in Massachusetts, in constant dollars
Concentration	Herfindahl concentration index; sum of squares of market shares of operating firms
Public capitalization, 1825–71	Binary variable for public capitalization regime
Pro-cartel policy, 1872–96	Binary variable for pro-cartel regime
Antitrust policy, 1897–1922	Antitrust regime
Profitability	Return on revenues
Demand	GSP in constant dollars
Prior-year acquisitions (in state)	Number of Massachusetts railroads acquired in prior year
Previous acquisitions (cumulative for ego)	Sum of focal firm's previous acquisitions
Size	Track operated, in miles
Age (log)	Log of years since charter was granted
Age^2	Age*age
Number of firms	Number of railroads in existence
Time trend	1–97
Capital availability (UK)	Months British economy held steady or grew in t–1, with years of US war activity set to zero

Specifications omitted from reported results

Variable	Definition
Log independent density	Log of number of non-leased railroads operating at beginning of the year
Independent density^2	Square of independent density
Log population	Population of Commonwealth of Massachusetts
Log gross state product	Gross product of Massachusetts
Log mileage mass	Log of total working rail mileage in Massachusetts
Log revenue mass	Log of total railroad revenues in Massachusetts, in constant dollars
4-firm concentration	Combined market share of four largest firms
8-firm concentration	Combined market share of eight largest firms
Capital availability (US)	Months US economy held steady or grew in t–1, with years of US war activity set to zero

Table 4.2   Negative binomial regression estimates of factors affecting foundings, 1826–1922

	Equation		
	(1)	(2)	(3)
Variables			
Intercept	0.265	13.937**	−2.778*
	(0.583)	(2.230)	(1.409)
Log density	−0.242		1.087**
	(0.487)		(0.440)
Density^2/1000	0.039		−0.172*
	(0.116)		(0.100)
Foundings	0.230		0.094**
	(0.106)		(0.038)
Foundings^2/1000	−8.064		
	(6.817)		
Failures	0.170		
	(0.128)		
Failures^2/1000	−7.447		
	(11.000)		
Log capital accumulation		−1.545**	
		(0.277)	
Concentration		−3.064**	
		(0.450)	
Capital availability (UK)			0.038**
			(0.018)
Public capital, 1826–1871			2.556*
			(1.265)
Pro-cartel, 1872–1896			1.689*
			(0.885)
Time trend			−0.001
			(0.019)
α^2	0.519**	0.754**	0.250*
	(0.147)	(0.202)	(0.106)
Log likelihood	−200.55	−207.74	−182.32
N (years)	97	97	97

Notes: Standard errors in parentheses; * $p < 0.05$; ** $p < 0.01$; one-tailed tests.

Table 4.3   *Event history analysis estimates of factors affecting acquisitions, 1825–1922*

	Equation		
	(1)	(2)	(3)
Variables			
Intercept	-3.225^{**}	-22.213^{**}	-16.444
	(0.545)	(7.357)	(10.012)
Age	-0.024^{*}		-0.012^{*}
	(0.005)		(0.007)
Foundings	0.051		
	(0.075)		
Foundings^2/1000	-0.003		
	(0.005)		
Log Density	-0.091		
	(0.078)		
Density^2/1000	0.009		
	(0.005)		
Failures	0.025		
	(0.027)		
Failures^2/1000	$-3e^{-3}$		
	$(3e^{-3})$		
GSP		-0.101^{**}	-0.075
		(0.036)	(0.041)
Log capital accumulation		2.430^{**}	1.287
		(0.945)	(1.387)
Net income		-0.267^{**}	-0.152
		(0.084)	(0.219)
Concentration		1.617	7.772^{**}
		(1.132)	(2.942)
Pre-antitrust			2.831^{*}
1825–1896			(1.228)
Net Income*			-3.367^{**}
1825–1896			(1.172)
Concentration*			-7.702^{*}
1825–1896			(3.371)
Time trend			0.018
			(0.014)
χ^2	-702.99	-554.47	-540.40
N (spells)	4695	4288	4288
N (events)	167	124	124

Notes: Standard errors in parentheses; * $p < 0.05$; ** $p < 0.01$; one-tailed tests.

Our policy findings obtain in the presence of ecological controls, with only age of firm showing a significant effect. Foundings, density, and failures do not show significant effects. They also failed to show significant effects when modeled separately. As population ecologists have generally collapsed all sorts of failures – bankruptcy and acquisition – into a single outcome variable, it may be that acquisitions are driven by different dynamics than are other forms of failure. Our policy findings also obtain in the presence of IO economic controls, three of which are significant. Gross state product (GSP) shows a negative effect, suggesting that in periods of economic decline acquisitions are more frequent. Industry capital accumulation shows a positive effect, suggesting that capital accumulation makes it difficult for firms to survive and increases the likelihood of acquisition. Net income shows a negative effect, in support of the failing firm hypothesis: firms with lower income are more likely to be acquired.

CONCLUSION

Our central argument has been driven by the Weberian notion that modern actors describe various social realms in terms of natural law. In particular, we have sought to show how under three historically specific industrial policy regimes between 1825 and 1925, railroaders prescribed three different types of strategy and that they depicted each as conforming to economic laws rather than to a particular policy regime. They thus divined three different sets of economic laws in the first century of US railroading.

These policy regimes produced different prescriptions for founding and acquiring railroads. The first policy regime, of public capitalization, led railroaders to describe railroads as enterprises designed to serve local producers and consumers and as permanently attached to local economies. This suggested that all railroads would succeed, and hence that railroads should be founded wherever possible and that thriving firms should acquire faltering railroads. The second policy regime, which favored cartels, led railroaders to describe the industry as naturally co-operative and to describe joint operation and pricing as inevitable. This suggested that cartelized railroads would prosper, and hence that prospective entrepreneurs should found railroads freely and that existing railroads should acquire faltering firms. The third policy regime, of antitrust, led railroaders to describe the industry as naturally predatory and monopolistic. This suggested that only monopolies would prosper, and hence that new track should be built only by existing railroads (that is, no new railroads should be founded) and that railroads should acquire their successful competitors as the industry became concentrated and should not acquire faltering firms.

We have shown, in quantitative analyses of railroad foundings and acquisitions, that railroads in fact behaved as railroad leaders prescribed. In the case of foundings, the first policy regime has a strong positive effect on foundings; the second a considerable positive effect; the third a negative effect by comparison. In the case of acquisitions, we find that the fact that a firm was failing predicted acquisition only before the antitrust policy regime was enforced, and that the concentration of the industry predicted acquisition only after the antitrust policy regime was enforced. These results, furthermore, remain robust in the presence of numerous controls.

Social scientists of many stripes treat economic behavior as driven by laws that make such behavior predictable across a wide range of settings. Many pay little attention to institutional conditions, assuming that they have relatively modest effects on behavior. We have shown at the very least that railroad foundings and acquisitions were influenced palpably by changes in public policy. By showing that after each policy shift railroaders experimented with at least three quite different business strategies, we hope to have shown that business strategy was worked out in political negotiations and was not over-determined by the character of public policy.

The bigger story here concerns the origins of the myth of neo-liberalism. Our most simple goal was to remind readers of what economic historians have never forgotten: the American economy did not rise under the *laissez-faire* regime that neo-liberals tout. Our more ambitious goal was to trace the origins of neo-liberal thinking to the particular history of American industrial policy. The tendency to divine natural laws to explain social behavior is common among modern actors. We found the process at work under each of three very different policy regimes. Railroaders worked hard to come up with business practices that would allow them to prosper in each of three different kinds of environments. They then worked doubly hard to divine economic principles that would explain both the policy environments and the business strategies. The principles that they found to explain the final pair, antitrust and business practices oriented to price competition, became the foundation of the neo-liberal thought that now dominates global economic discourse.

Given that under each of these policy regimes, railroaders found natural economic laws to explain economic behavior, we suspect that had either of the earlier policy regimes survived, neo-liberalism would look quite different today. American economic thought came to dominate global thinking in large measure because the United States appeared to be the best example to follow. Americans themselves were largely responsible for refining and formalizing the theory they derived from their own success story, and their peculiar variety of provincialism ensured that they would seldom encounter evidence that would challenge their assumptions. Had the Supreme Court struck down the Sherman and the Interstate Commerce acts in 1897, as some had expected it would, neo-liberalism might now be defined by the pro-cartel policies that Britain continued to pursue into the twentieth century. The freedom to pursue production and pricing agreements with competing organizations might be the ultimate neo-liberal freedom. The idea that modern economies require interfirm co-ordination to prevent price competition that destroys productive firms might be the mantra of the World Bank.

*   We thank Jan Ottosson and Lars Magnusson for incisive comments on an earlier draft.

5. Taxation, redistribution and regulation: fiscal policy in a changing world economy

Sven Steinmo

INTRODUCTION

It is widely believed that the internationalization of the world economy must have some important effects on domestic politics. At one extreme, we find those who effectively argue that the state is dead and that corporations will dominate the world (Korten 1995; see also Rodrik 1997). Others, however, have argued that the effects of the global economy on domestic political choices have been relatively minor (Garret and Lange 1995; Garrett 1995).

Both of these extreme views are overstated. Instead, most analysts would agree with Johansson and Magnusson when they suggest that we are currently undergoing some kind of 'Third Industrial Revolution', which is bringing about 'thoroughgoing structural changes' which must affect the relationship between the nation-state and modern capital (Johansson and Magnusson 1998: 342; see also Magnusson 1996: 483–7). However, although this argument finds a lot of anecdotal support in the media and even from academic sources, there has not been a great deal of careful analysis of exactly how these macroeconomic changes are affecting specific policy arenas. This chapter offers just such an analysis. Specifically, I examine tax policy. The analysis shows that the internationalization of the world economy does indeed present policy makers with a new set of incentives and constraints as they address the problem of financing the state. The evidence does not support the thesis that the state is dead, nor do we find evidence that there is no room to maneuver for domestic policy makers: clearly differences in policy choices between countries like the United States and, say, Sweden, are significant and interesting. This chapter instead examines the pressures and responses presented by internationalization on tax policy makers across the Organization for Economic Cooperation and Development (OECD).

A number of fiscal economists have commented on the relationship between globalization and tax reform in the 1980s and 1990s (Giovannini 1990; Lee and McKenzie 1989; OECD 1997; Pechman 1987; Radaelli 1997; Sandford 1993; Tanzi 1995). These authors virtually unanimously hold that 'globalization' dramatically increases the ease and availability of the 'exit' option for those with mobile resources. In the context of this new or increased mobility, this argument holds, governments must redesign their tax systems – largely irrespective of the preferences or desires of the majority of citizens. The result, they argue, is that all nation-states must restructure their tax systems to fit more appropriately the political and economic realities of this new world economy. But beyond this general hypothetical shift, there have been few studies that have examined the actual changes introduced across countries as well as the context of tax policy in the modern era and certainly no studies have specifically compared the tax policy agenda of this current era with those of the past. The following chapter offers just such an analysis.

This chapter suggests that this new economic context has two major implications for the relationship between state and society as we enter the twenty-first century. First, modern states across the world are introducing tax reforms that generally imply a redistribution of the tax burden from higher-to lower-income groups. In short, tax policy is losing its redistributive functions as a consequence of globalization. Second, in line with the argument of this book as a whole, this analysis suggests that the nation-state is losing (or perhaps more accurately abandoning) its taxation as a *regulatory* instrument. Up until very recently it was widely accepted that governments could, and indeed should, manipulate their tax structures to encourage some types of economic activity and discourage others (for example, tax advantage for domestic capital investment). These tax 'distortions' are being removed in favor of more 'neutral' tax policies (that is, policies that do not favor any one type of economic activity over another – 'let the market decide'). The consequence is that governments are yielding control of a major policy instrument which they previously believed was an efficient and efficacious mechanism to regulate social and economic outcomes.

The argument will proceed in three stages. First, I shall provide a short history of taxation in the twentieth century. The point here will be to establish both major forces and trends that have characterized tax policy for most of the twentieth century so that the reader can better appreciate the changes in tax politics that have occurred in the last decade. The next section will provide a brief overview of the tax changes that have been introduced and/or proposed in several countries. I shall provide general overviews emphasizing the commonality of the various reforms in each of these countries.[1]

The final section suggests some implications of the empirical findings. Here I suggest that the changing incentives and constraints facing domestic policy makers are likely to provide incentives for policy makers to yield increasing authority over tax policy to supranational authorities.

TAXATION IN THE TWENTIETH CENTURY

Tax as a Redistributive Instrument

Before the dawn of the twentieth century, taxation was not a major instrument of social and economic regulation. On the contrary, it instead tended to comprise an enormous array of various levies on a myriad of specific items and services. Tax systems before the turn of the century were hardly 'systems' at all. For the most part, finance ministers saw collecting taxes as a necessary duty they had to perform in pursuit of the necessary revenues to finance the state (Levi 1988). 'The art of taxation', commented French Minister of Finance Jean Baptist Colbert, 'was to pluck the goose in such a way as to get the most amount of feathers with the least amount of hissing'. Indeed, it was widely recognized that taxes were mostly paid by those who lacked the political power to avoid them. In the pre-democratic world this, of course, meant the poor. The consequence was highly inefficient and highly regressive tax structures which rarely raised much revenue. Although there were an enormous number of different revenue sources – on everything from windows, to men's hair powder, to salt – the entire 'system' rarely collected more than 5 percent of GDP (Mitchell 1998a, 1998b; Steinmo 1993).

The turn of the century witnessed a major battlefront between the interests of the established economic elite and the mobilizing masses demanding more egalitarian public policies and democratic control of national political institutions (Magnusson 1996). The twin forces of industrialization and democratization thus brought about a dramatic change in the political context in which finance officials operated: as economies modernized monetary incomes grew, it became possible to tax both corporate and personal incomes. Moreover, as the working classes grew in strength, the demand for both 'progressive' taxes and redistributive spending programs grew at the same time. The previously disenfranchised citizens demanded new public programs to protect them against the ravages of the capitalist market and policies that would take some of the surplus profit from the capitalists and redistribute it to the poor. Taxation reform thus became a major focus of political demand across the democratizing world (Rodriguez 1980; Sabine 1980; Stein 1969). The result was a revolution in the 'Fiscal State'.[2]

These political and economic forces were matched by the development of new economic ideas – particularly with respect to taxation policy. Although it would be inaccurate to say that these ideas drove tax policy development, it is fair to say that the policies demanded in this era were supported by the new idea of 'ability to pay'. Ability to pay – which meant that tax loads should be related to the taxpayers' ability to bear the burden – provided a new theoretical justification for progressive income and corporate profits taxes. It is difficult to overemphasize how radical this concept was in tax policy thinking – the very idea that the wealthy *ought* to pay more than the poor was not yet accepted as a matter of principle. If the wealthy did in fact pay more, this was only because it was difficult to collect from the poor. Indeed, it was widely understood and accepted that landowners, for example, would simply pass the taxes down to their tenants.

It could hardly be said, however, that state bureaucracies were simply agents of the ruling class. Who, by the century's end, were 'the ruling class?' Whereas it may have been the case that the ruling class had shared more or less common economic interests in the feudal period, as modernization progressed, the ruling class itself became pluralized (Hobsbawm 1969).

The political reality was even simpler: progressive income and corporate profit taxes were initially popular because they were largely seen as punitive taxes on the rich. When introduced at the turn of the century, these taxes were in fact quite minor in revenue terms but were to be paid only by the very richest individuals. They were therefore accurately described as 'class taxes' (Rodriguez 1980; Stein 1969; Vallinder 1962; Waltman 1985; Weber and Wildavsky 1986).

As the First World War broke out, the principle of 'let the rich pay' was taken to some remarkable extremes. New 'excess profit taxes', 'war preparedness taxes', and 'national defense levies' were implemented everywhere.[3] For most belligerents, income taxes on the very wealthy were increased to historic levels. By 1918 the top marginal income tax in the US, for example, was 77 percent, while in Britain the top rate reached a somewhat more moderate 60 percent by 1920. In both cases, it was widely argued that it was unfair to have working-class men fight this 'rich man's war' while the rich stayed home and got even richer.[4] In many countries, these taxes quickly became the major sources of national government finance even though they were paid only by corporations and by fewer than 5 percent of citizens.[5]

From Class Taxes to Mass Taxes

The Second World War marks the next evolutionary step in the development of modern tax policy in the advancing capitalist world. The costs of fighting (or in Sweden's case, staying out of) this war were enormous, and it was clear to virtually all concerned that no one would be able to escape massive increases in their tax burden. Very high taxes on capital and capital income were once again reintroduced everywhere. There was a firm political commitment in all democratic nations to the principle that capitalists should not get rich supplying the instruments of war. In many cases the various profit taxes introduced in this period amounted to nearly 100 percent of net earnings. Wealthy individuals were also subjected to very steep increases in their tax burdens. In Britain, for example, the top marginal tax bracket was pushed up to 97.5 percent in 1941. In the US, the top bracket peaked at 94 percent in 1944. In Sweden, the top marginal tax rate of all taxes combined reached 80 percent. The fiscal problem, however, was that the rich and the corporations simply did not have enough money to tax to finance the costs of the war. Modern technology had once again advanced, and even more so than during the previous war, it was perfectly clear that those who would be victors would need more than simply lots of men who were willing to be slaughtered. The Second World War was to be a new kind of war, fought with new kinds of weapons. Unfortunately, this kind of war was *very* expensive. In short, new sources of revenue were necessary if the country was to have a fighting chance.

Here we see, once again, how the changing structure of modern capitalism offered new fiscal policy solutions (along with new demands). As capitalist economies advanced, an ever larger share of the populace left subsistence farming and moved to industrial work. These workers were becoming more organized and thus increasingly better able to champion their own political interests. But equally importantly, the workers were now getting *wage* incomes, and these incomes, of course, could be taxed. Thus revenue authorities in all democratic countries found the new source of revenue that they so desperately needed. Whereas up to this point income taxes had generally been considered as punitive, to be imposed on the wealthy, increasingly state authorities saw that tax could be paid by lower-paid workers as well. Therefore, along with increasing tax rates on the very rich, revenue authorities began to lower tax thresholds[6] and thereby could demand income tax even from those with lower incomes. Thus it was during the Second World War that income tax ceased being a 'class tax' and became a 'mass tax'. Whereas until the end of the 1930s income taxes were still paid by only the very richest in society, by the end of the war at least 60 percent of income earners were paying tax. These changes massively increased the revenue-raising capacity of central governments in Europe and America. Tax revenues as a share of GDP nearly doubled in most of these countries between 1930 and 1945.

Taken together, the revenue reforms of the 1930–45 era transformed the politics of taxation in all industrial democracies. By steeply increasing tax rates on companies and the very wealthy at the same time as they extended the income tax net downward, central/national governments became responsible for both redistributing wealth and income across classes and generations and, as we shall see, managing both the macro- and microeconomic outcomes.

Tax as a Regulatory Instrument

At the close of the war, most people expected governments to roll back taxes to somewhere near pre-war levels. This, of course, did not happen. Instead, all western democratic governments held on to the high levels of taxation that the war had made politically possible (Peacock and Weisman 1961). Even where conservative parties gained a majority in parliament, tax rates were not reduced substantially.[7] Unsurprisingly, huge conflicts were common. The traditional arguments used by capitalists and the political Right were evoked with new passion. Tax rates like the ones now in place would surely destroy the workers' and capitalists' willingness to work, save, and invest. Foreshadowing arguments we would hear voiced more than a generation later, it was often asserted that retaining these very high taxes would evoke massive capital flight (Rodriguez 1981; Sabine 1966; Steinmo 1993; Waltman 1985; Witte 1985). These arguments and threats did not work because of five related factors. First, the war had left these countries with massive public debts. Second, the majority of voters were hostile to capitalists and the very rich, and increasingly well enough organized to penalize any party or government that would propose cutting taxes on the rich significantly, while working-class taxes remained historically high. Third, the fiscal policy elite now believed in the principle of steeply progressive taxation. The following comment made in a 1937 US Treasury Report is illustrative of the thinking at the time: 'direct taxes levied at progressive rates best satisfy the present-day concept of equity in taxation, and in the further belief that such taxes result in a minimum of undesirable economic and social effects' (Haas 1937: para. 2). Fourth, commitments made before, during, and immediately after the war for social programs, social insurance, education, public health, housing and so on would clearly require substantial financial commitments. Finally, both political necessity and economic experience during the war had placed the state in a position of responsibility for the economic management of the economy (see Magnusson 1996: 410). Tax policy – through tax incentives – was seen as an especially important tool in this economic regulation model (Hansen 1969; Steinmo 1993).

The logic of 'Keynesian' economic management had by now become widely accepted in most advanced capitalist nations. The basic tenet of this economic idea was that governments had both the right and the ability to influence the macro economy (Hall 1989). It did not take a major intellectual leap, then, to conclude that the government might also be able to influence more microeconomic outcomes.[8] Tax policy was seen as the major instrument with which to accomplish this end. Modern governments discovered that, given the high marginal rates of taxation, the tax structure could be manipulated to provide incentives for a wide range of economic activities. In effect, governments were now in a position to impose a deal on capitalists: if you invest at a specified time in places or activities that we determine, you will pay lower taxes; if you choose to ignore our incentives, you will pay higher taxes.

Tax policy thus quickly became a major instrument of social and economic regulation. Tax incentives could be (and were) used to affect decisions about where to invest, when to invest, what to invest in and how much to invest. There were far too many complicated incentive mechanisms developed in various nations to discuss here (they ranged from general investment tax credits, to inventories, to reserve funds, to special depreciation allowances, to tax deductions for investments in particular regions, products, and companies). But it is important to note that all countries engaged in these micro-manipulations of the economy via the tax code, irrespective of party, ideology, and level of economic wealth. There was, moreover, a considerable amount of international sharing of ideas and specific policies over how to use the tax code most effectively to achieve the desired social and economic ends (Hansen 1969).[9]

Whatever the specific mechanisms used in different countries, and irrespective of whether they were always used effectively or efficiently (which they were not), there was widespread agreement that governments could and should use their tax systems as instruments of economic policy: that tax incentives could affect the timing, structure and shape of investment and other private economic decisions. Under this regime (high marginal taxes combined with generous tax incentives and strict capital controls regulating the export of capital) capitalists and their money could be used to promote the ends of society as a whole. At the same time this 'carrot and stick' approach helped reduce uncertainty in the marketplace and contributed to the postwar economic miracle. This regime was a centerpiece of the postwar compromise between capital and labor in all western industrial democracies (Steinmo 1993). The now dominant definition of a 'good' tax system was one that promoted social equity and allowed governments to influence private economic outcomes in publicly determined ways. Certainly there were those who continued to argue that high taxes damaged economic performance. But, as a number of empirical studies have indicated, there was very little empirical evidence that could be used to support this proposition (Barro 1991; Korpi 1996). For most of the postwar period there has simply been no correlation between tax burdens and economic performance.

Taxation and the Pursuit of Economic Growth

By the late 1970s and early 1980s, economic growth had become the dominant political issue throughout the democratic world. Unfortunately for these countries' governments, there were few real arrows in their quivers with which they could slay the double-headed demon of stagflation. Unquestionably, tax policy was one of these arrows. It is certainly not the case that taxes are the only thing that affect investment, economic growth, and employment. But few other variables affecting economic performance are under the direct control of the government. The cost of labor and materials, proximity to markets, management structures and decisions, the cost and availability of capital and technology are all undoubtedly more important factors shaping investment decisions and choices. But a government can have only limited impact on these variables. Taxes, however, can be changed.

Interestingly, the first tax policy response to the economic crisis was to accelerate the use of taxes and tax expenditures as instruments of economic management. Country after country – under both left and right governments – *increased* their use of a dizzying array of tax policy instruments. It would take volumes to simply catalogue the astonishing number of tax instruments enacted in the 1970s and early 1980s that were designed to promote or support different types of economic activity within the OECD (McDaniel and Surrey 1985; Reese 1980; Rodriguez 1981; Sandford 1993). To be sure, tax expenditures became far more than economic instruments; they were equally used as political plums whose intent was to satisfy particular constituencies.

Ironically, the very tax incentives introduced (at least in part) to promote economic growth tended to exacerbate the political dilemma facing virtually all OECD nations. Whether tax incentives had the general economic effects their sponsors claim or not, they clearly had the specific effects of complicating tax codes, making it easier for sophisticated taxpayers to avoid paying taxes and, finally, radically reducing taxes for *some* taxpayers. Consequently, reports of huge corporations and multimillionaires who paid little or no taxes became commonplace throughout the OECD. In short, tax policies justified with reference to the goal of promoting economic growth, had the direct effect of undermining another widely accepted goal for tax policy – equity. Taxes were increasingly felt to be 'unfair'.

To make matters worse, an increasing number of economic studies show little evidence that tax expenditures always have economic utility (Bergström and Södersten 1984; Surrey and Hellmuth 1969). It was more and more obvious that the extreme overuse and enormous accumulation of tax expenditures of the 1970s and early 1980s have become, at the very least, seriously questionable.

A NEW POLITICAL ECONOMY OF TAXATION

To understand tax policy in the last two decades one needs once again to appreciate the political economic context in which these policies are made. By the mid-1980s, advanced capitalist economies were undergoing what Magnusson calls a 'Third Industrial Revolution' which is changing the 'structural environment' of modern capitalism (Johansson and Magnusson 1998; see also Magnusson 1996). The basic point here is well known, though rarely specifically examined: the nature of modern capitalism is once again undergoing a transformation. As we saw in earlier epochs of capitalist development, these structural changes are restructuring the environment in which tax policy is made and, as a result, tax policy is changing as well. Before we go on to discuss the specific policy changes made in this new political economy, we shall examine the political context into which these structural changes fit.

First, there was growing dissatisfaction with extant tax structures. Not only had the thousands of tax manipulations introduced in recent years *not* worked to stimulate economic growth and investment as promised; they had also radically complicated tax codes and dramatically altered their incidence. In short, it was widely believed that even income tax was no longer progressive.

Second, inflation and economic growth had both pushed more and more workers into higher and higher income tax brackets. Indeed, the continued development of advanced capitalism has had the effect that more and more 'workers' were becoming middle class. With respect to taxation policy this has effectively meant that their *interests* have changed. By the mid-1980s an ever larger percentage of the electorate was now facing marginal tax rates in excess of 50 percent (Steinmo 1993). Moreover, an ever larger percentage of workers were abandoning traditional trade unions and/or joining unions who represented middle and upper-middle class interests (Johansson and Magnusson 1998). Bluntly, 'screw the rich' does not have the same emotional appeal to those who increasingly feel that they too are becoming rich.

Finally, a multitude of economic studies were published that suggested that taxes did affect investment, and thus jobs and economic performance.[10] The OECD survey *Taxing Profits in a Global Economy* suggested the following, for example:

> Taxation is, however, only one and in many cases not the most important determinant of investment and financing decisions. ... Nevertheless, the taxation of profits can and often does have an important impact on marginal investments and their financing, as well as on location decisions both within a country and across frontiers. Other taxes, such as those on payroll and social security contributions, may also affect costs and thus location of investment, particularly in the short to medium term. (OECD 1991: 12)

Morever, both anecdotal evidence and more systematic surveys began to support the conclusion that business executives did indeed consider taxes when deciding when and where to invest.[11] (see Table 5.1). These arguments against high taxes have changed remarkably little in the 80 years or so since progressive income and corporate profit taxes were first permanently introduced. But, concomitant changes in technology and public policies in the late 1970s and early 1980s effectively lent capitalist interests new resources in their battle to reduce their tax burden. The 'exit' was quickly becoming a more viable option and a more believable implicit threat. As Lee and McKenzie point out:

> The full impact of an increase in the capacity to move may not be revealed in actual capital movements. This is because the perception of increased capital mobility may

cause governments to adjust their tax policies toward capital, and/or income that can be earned from capital. (Lee and McKenzie 1989: 81)

The OECD described the effects of these new international pressures on tax policy makers in the following way:

> [Economic] liberalization, which has gone furthest with the EC [European Community] countries with their commitment to a single unified market, offers new opportunities for policy makers, but also implies new constraints. The importance of international considerations in the determination of national tax policies will increase, especially for small open economies ... The increased openness of national economies has, in practice, made it more difficult to separate out domestic and international tax issues. When changes to national tax systems are made attention has increasingly to be paid to the international implication of any proposed modifications. This, in turn, may mean that the traditional criteria used to evaluate tax reforms have to be reconsidered. Policies which may have been appropriate in economies where exchange controls and other limitations on international transactions were prevalent may be neither feasible nor desirable once these non-tax barriers are removed. (OECD 1991: 14)

In sum, policy makers throughout the OECD were thus under dual, and contradictory, pressures with respect to tax policy as their economies entered this third Industrial Revolution. On the one hand, there was growing disenchantment with specific tax incentives. On the other hand, it was becoming equally obvious that both technological and policy changes were making it possible for capital and capitalists to place their money and investment in areas where they received the highest possible *after tax* return.

Table 5.1   'Critical factors' in foreign investment decisions

Critical factors	Percentage rating
1. 'Projected market growth'	61
2. 'Host government tax policies'	60
3. 'Host pricing controls'	58
4. 'Foreign exchange rates and controls on transfers'	58
5. 'Competition'	56
6. 'US tax policy'	53

Source: Wallace (1990).

Redistribution?

Policy makers throughout the world have responded to these new incentives and constraints in broadly similar ways. First, they have cut marginal taxes on high-income earners. As Table 5.2 indicates, this trend has been followed almost universally. The revenues lost in these rate reductions are generally, but not always, replaced by increases in consumption taxes or social insurance fees. Taken together these moves have meant a downward redistribution of tax burdens. Vertical equity has virtually been taken off the agenda.[12] 'Common intellectual themes [of the tax reform movement]' reports Boskin in Boskin and McClure, *World Tax Reform*, 'included concern about the adverse incentive effects of high marginal tax rates and about distortions caused by differential tax treatment of economically similar activities, *and a downplaying of vertical equity as a central objective of tax policy*' (Boskin 1990: 3, my emphasis).

Table 5.2   *Top rates of central government personal income tax, 1976, 1986, 1992, 1997, selected OECD countries*

Country	1976	1986	1992	1997	Reduction 1997–76
Australia	65	57	47	47	18
Austria	62	62	50	50	12
Canada[1]	43	34	31	31	12
Finland[1]	51	51	39	39	12
France	60	65	57	57	3
Germany	56	56	53	53[*]	3
Ireland	77	58	52	48	29
Italy	72	62	51	51	21
Japan[1]	75	70	50	50	25
Netherlands[1]	72	72	60	50[*]	22
New Zealand	60	57	33	33	27
Norway[1]	48	40	23	23	25
Sweden[1]	57	50	20	25	32
United Kingdom	83	60	40	40	43
United States[1]	70	50	31	39	31
Unweighted average	63.4	56.3	40.4	42.4	21.0

Notes:
1. Countries with income tax at lower levels of government. Typical rates in 1992 being flat: Canada, 17; Finland, 16; Norway, 28; Sweden, 31; progressive: Japan, 5–14; United States, 2–14.
[*] The 'Steuerreform 2000' will reduce the top rate to 42 per cent by 2005.

Sources: Sandford (1993: 12); OECD Tax Database (1998).

It is, of course, not surprising that right-leaning governments, such as those in power in the US and the UK at the time should favor tax reductions for the rich. But, these views were increasingly shared by key policy makers throughout the democratic world (and beyond) of virtually all political persuasions. In the last five years, this author interviewed ministry of finance officials in seven OECD countries from Australia and Japan to Sweden and Denmark. *In every single case*, I have heard a remarkably similar argument. This view is best summarized in the following statement made by former Swedish Minister of Finance Kjell Olof Feldt: 'The very high level of progressive taxation just doesn't work'.[13]

As we saw in Table 5.1, the trend to cut top personal and corporate tax rates has been universal. It is possible that the cuts in tax rates are being distributed progressively, but I have found no evidence to suggest that this has happened. It appears instead, as Williams has noted in a survey of tax reforms in the EC conducted for the accounting firm Price Waterhouse, that

> At the same time as some disillusion was spreading about the efficacy of our main taxes, other pressures were building up ... Our objective now is to be [neutral], with taxes that do not penalize one person rather than another. They give equality of opportunity rather than equality of result ... A 'fair' tax is one which presents us with a 'level playing field' and does not concern itself with the quality of the teams ... This shifting appears to be occurring now to an extent few could have foretold a few years ago. As we move to the post-1992 Single European market ... [Western as well as Eastern European states] are adjusting to reflect these same ideas of neutrality rather than equity. (Williams 1991b: 24)

Unfortunately, the enormous complexity of both tax systems and the stunning number of specific tax reforms introduced over the past decade, make it impossible to provide a full accounting of the redistributive effects of all tax changes introduced. However, while there are some who may focus on a particular major piece of legislation (US 1986, Sweden 1991, Germany 1993) and argue that this specific reform was 'neutral' between income classes, virtually all analysts agree that the *cumulative* effects of the many tax policy changes introduced in OECD nations over the past decade and a half have made these tax systems less progressive (Aronsson and Palme 1994; Atkinson and Smeeding 1995; Björklund et al. 1995; Boskin and McLure Jr. 1990; Cowie 1993; Gravelle 1992; Palme 1993; Williams 1991b).

In sum, the last decade and a half has witnessed a remarkable transformation of both tax policies and attitudes towards tax systems (on the part of elites, at least). Whereas in the first seven decades of this century, there was a widespread consensus that taxes *should* be used as a social policy instrument that had an essential function in redistributing income and wealth in capitalist democracies, today there appears to be a growing consensus (especially among elites) that taxes *should not* be used for these purposes.

Regulation?

Many have suggested that corporate and capital taxes should fall in the context of the new structural environment facing modern states (see Lee and McKenzie 1989; Rodrik 1997). Interestingly, however, cross-national surveys have shown that this expectation has not (yet) been borne out by the statistical evidence (Swank 1996). The best way to explain this apparently curious outcome is to think more carefully both about the changing nature of corporate interests in the new global economy and to better understand the effects of corporate tax reform on the distribution of the burden *within* the corporate sector. We saw above that corporate taxes had become major instruments of domestic economic policy in all industrial states. What this effectively meant was that there were some types of firms and some types of investments that were tax advantaged while others were discriminated against. Obviously, there was considerable variation across countries and even over time as to who actually benefitted the most. But the general pattern was to yield tax incentives for domestic investment (particularly during economic slowdowns) in plant, equipment, and machinery. Due to these various tax programs domestic manufacturing, construction, and retailing tended to be tax advantaged over services and financial corporations. At the same time, domestic investment was advantaged over foreign investment.

By the 1980s, however, the structure of corporate enterprise had begun to change. Not only are modern corporations bigger in the global economy, they are also more interconnected and more interdependent. As Magnusson points out, the old Fordist model is in decline: 'Now growth comes from high technology, more differentiated and customer driven firms. Instead of standardizing, long production lines, and low prices [the third Industrial Revolution] favors flexibility, service and uniqueness' (Magnusson 1996: 485) This implies that tax policy interests have changed. Firms that formerly were quite content with tax incentive policies that released them from paying taxes as long as they invested in domestic plant and equipment, no longer find these kinds of incentive appealing. In a largely insulated economy, manufacturing firms would be quite happy with accelerated depreciation for capital investment, for example. But a global manufacturing firm, in contrast, prefers a lower tax rate with fewer incentives which 'lock in investment'. The growing internationalization of manufacturing in several industrial countries has led companies to prefer taxes that give an advantage to domestic suppliers and/or consumers over those beyond national frontiers (*The Economist* 2000; Porter 1990: 57; Sansonetti 1989).

In short, the third Industrial Revolution means that the needs of capital have changed: whereas a stable (and peaceful) domestic environment and labor market were sufficient for successful export-oriented firms, today the demands of modern flexible technology mean that these same companies must pursue different production strategies in order to survive in the global competitive environment. As their interests have changed, so too have the tax policies that have been applied to them. There are a huge number of other specific instances which could be cited to illustrate the general point that modern states are bowing to both domestic and international pressures and giving up their tax policy instruments (see, for example, Boskin 1990; Cowie 1993; Pechman 1988; Tanzi 1995; Williams 1991a). In every single case that I am aware of, at least, the official justification for these reforms is that they will make the tax system more efficient and more neutral to different economic activities. Although it is rarely stated explicitly, these governments are conceding that the tax system cannot and should not be used to manage or direct the domestic economy. In point of fact, however, these governments are giving away a major (and perhaps the major) instrument which they once had to manage and manipulate the private economy.

The pursuit of greater neutrality has been based on the growing acceptance that a proportional tax system is more likely to be optimal from an efficiency point of view than one which is graduated and selective. Also, the idea of minimizing the impact of the tax structure on economic behavior has been a distinctly unfamiliar one to many OECD governments until recently. Governments have often used the tax system deliberately to alter consumption or investment patterns (OECD 1989: 185).

It has long been argued that tax incentives do not create new activity, but simply give some economic actors rewards for doing what they might have done anyway. In previous decades fiscal economists and policy makers alike responded to these criticisms by arguing that the entire point of tax incentives was to produce distortions and to give tax advantages to those who are doing what we believe should be done. But in the past several years this view has been scarcely heard. How could it be that the consensus has shifted so dramatically in such a short time? The answer is clearly that governments believe they can no longer effectively manage or control private economic decision makers through the tax system. A 'good tax system' has moved from being one that explicitly introduced distortions into the capitalist marketplace to one that minimizes these distortions. In short, a good tax system, it is widely believed by the Left and the Right, keeps the government out of private economic decision making.

CONCLUSION: WHITHER THE STATE?

In a recent survey essay in *The Economist*, 'The vanishing taxpayer', Bishop commented:

> As globalization ebbed and flowed, the taxman's share of economic output went relentlessly up, despite warnings from politicians that globalization would make it

harder for governments to collect taxes and thus to provide public services. But now a new factor has entered the equation: the Internet. It epitomises borderlessness, and the irrelevance of being in a particular physical location. By being everywhere and nowhere at once, it seems certain to speed up globalization. And in doing so, according to the Organisation for Economic Co-operation and Development, it might damage tax systems so badly that it could lead to governments being unable to meet the legitimate demands of their citizens for public services. (Bishop 2000)

This chapter has shown that tax policy has always been made within a particular political and economic strategic context. In the current environment, globalization creates a new strategic context in which democratic capitalist states – no matter who holds the reins of power – face incentives to both cut taxes for the wealthy and for internationally mobile capital and retreat from using tax policy as an active instrument of economic management. They have also apparently decided that the market should be responsible for economic outcomes. Governments, even social democratic governments, are moving to get out of the way.

In short, tax reform means changing the character of the relationship between the state and the private economy: public authority is being yielded to private interests. Tanzi makes a similar point, but puts the issue in a slightly different light:

> Tax competition from other countries may force some countries into choosing tax structures (and, perhaps, tax levels) that their policy-makers might consider less desirable than the ones they would have chosen if their economies had remained closed. (Tanzi 1995: 134)

It is clearly the case that these pro-market and state-interventionist ideas are now dominant, but it is not true that they are new. Capitalists and the ideological Right have been making these same arguments since the turn of the century. But until recently, those who called for more socially and economically 'neutral' tax systems have been overwhelmed by those who saw it as the legitimate responsibility of the state to try to shape both the distribution of income/wealth in society and to encourage certain kinds of economic activity over others.

For a good part of the twentieth century workers, ordinary citizens, and thus political representatives demanded that taxes be used as instruments to change what they believed was the maldistribution of income and wealth in society. High taxes on capital and capitalists were clearly intended to be punitive. Certainly there were those who argued eloquently for principles and ideals. But as Adams rather bluntly pointed out: 'The dominating factor of economic interest in taxation determines to a large extent the role or place of idealism in taxation. Ideals are effective when they further the economic interest of powerful groups' (Adams 1928: 4). The fact that a new (or at least reawakened) set of ideals are increasingly dominant, speaks less of the intellectual power or rigor of these ideals and more of the economic and political power of the interests that they represent.

Nevertheless, the evidence presented in this chapter does not suggest that the economic arguments embedded in the recent spat of world tax reform are simply a wrongheaded conspiracy on the part of some kind of international capitalist elite. Quite the contrary. I do not argue that states can or should return to the kind of interventionist/redistributive tax systems prevalent only a few years ago. Instead, modern governments may be correct in their assessment that they have no alternative but to follow this new course. The key point here is that the modern world has changed dramatically and modern public policy will change with it. To be sure, there is, and will continue to be, considerable 'room for maneuver' on the part of various national governments. It would be banal to argue that 'the state is dead'. But it would be equally facile to argue that the new economic context surrounding policy makers in a globalizing world economy need not shape their policy choices (Garrett and Lange 1995). One should remember that along with the international or global economic context that is shaping and constraining tax policy makers' choices, domestic politics frame tax choices as well. The argument and evidence offered in this chapter in no way suggests that domestic political concerns and/or national political institutions are (or will be) irrelevant for tax policy making. Rather, the balance of power is clearly shifting. How each democratic government responds will, of course, vary.

Still, in an open global economy, high social welfare spending subsidizes domestic consumption and thus indirectly increases the cost of domestic production. But if this logic applies to the high-tax countries, should it not also apply to other countries? If so, do advanced welfare states run the risk of engaging in 'tax competition', evoking an international 'Tragedy of the Commons', with each country trying to undercut the other by offering lower taxes and lower costs of production? The answer is, clearly, yes. Moreover, policy elites are aware of this problem. In a recent survey of changes in economic policy evoked by global competition the OECD observed, for example:

> One clear lesson is the importance for countries of paying due attention to developments and policies abroad. The majority of situations considered were, or would if left untended have become, unsustainable in their own domestic terms – although it is hardly possible in today's world to visualize any national situation in purely closed-economy context. But many of the cases considered ... bear eloquent witness to the realities of interdependence: what is sustainable can depend upon what is happening abroad. This conclusion should not be thought of merely as expressing the constraints on national performance; it can, in principle be built on to devise internationally co-operative sets of policies for a better (and sustainable) global outcome. (OECD 1988: 11)

We are only now beginning to see this kind of argument applied to tax policy explicitly. But an obvious implication of much of the above is that a solution to limit the downward financial pressures on the welfare state due to tax competition is to yield taxing authority to supranational institutions like the EC. We can see substantial movement in this direction already. But whether this option is politically feasible – and in whose interests these supranational institutions will act – remain open questions.

NOTES

1. Another perhaps equally interesting analysis that could be explored here has to do with explaining the *differences* in tax reform outcomes among these countries. In my view, an institutional analysis would provide the most analytic leverage for such a study. I do not pursue such an analysis here largely due to space limitations, but a larger study will specifically attempt to integrate historical institutional analysis and macro structural analysis (see Steinmo 1993).
2. There were exceptions, however. In Sweden and Germany, for example, progressive taxes were introduced by the ruling bureaucratic oligarchy in advance of mass participation in politics. These rulers hoped that they could stem the tide of democratization by offering both social insurance and progressive taxation.
3. There were several different types of 'excess profits' taxes used in these years in these countries. They are far too complicated to explain here, but in each case an attempt was made to tax all, or nearly all, the profits made as a result of the hostilities.
4. In the US, income tax was called the 'rich man's conscription' (Waltman 1985: 45).
5. In 1918, income and profit taxes contributed 44.8 percent of total state and local government revenue in Sweden. In the same year, the income and profit taxes contributed 63.1 percent of the federal government's ordinary receipts in the US. In Britain these taxes contributed 64.9 percent of total tax revenue in 1920.
6. The income at which the individual begins to pay income tax.
7. In most cases the wartime 'excess profits' duties and taxes were scaled back and/or incorporated into more permanent corporate profit tax systems.
8. For a specific analysis of the evolution of this regulatory logic in economic affairs, see Magnusson (1996: 410–45). See also Lewin (1970).
9. Of course, the character and structure of these tax expenditures could differ quite dramatically between nations. The US, for example, tended to write very specific tax incentives designed to benefit specific (politically powerful) industries, firms and individuals. Other countries designed broader and less complicated) incentive mechanisms which could be used by anyone who invested in the ways determined by the government. Two of the countries which perfected these incentive mechanisms the most were Germany and Sweden (Steinmo 1986).
10. There is a very substantial debate over the quality of these analyses at this point. A thorough discussion of these arguments lies outside the scope of this chapter. A general conclusion, however, would be that while it was in no way *proven* that high taxes negatively affect economic growth, the dominant economic theories used for public policy recommendations suggested that high taxes *should* negatively affect economic performance (see, for example, Agell et al. 1995; Dowrick 1996; Henrekson 1996; Korpi 1996).
11. In my interviews with policy makers and business people alike, it has become clear that as capital becomes more mobile, capitalists become more sophisticated in their investment decisions. The following is typical: when I asked a chief executive officer of a large American automobile parts manufacturing corporation if his company considered taxes when deciding where to place new investment, he looked at me with obvious surprise and said, 'Are you kidding? Taxes affect my bottom line. Obviously, taxes aren't the only thing that we take

into account ... but they sure as hell matter' (Interview with author July 1996. Similar comments have been made in over 50 interviews I have conducted with multinational business executives over the past two years). See also, Magnusson (1996); Pontusson and Swenson (1996).

12. Vertical equity usually implies that those with greater incomes should pay a larger share of their income in taxes.

13. Interview with author, May 1988.

6. The role of path dependence in the history of regulation

Lars Magnusson

INTRODUCTION

For hundreds of years, visible hand regulation has been a common feature of the market economy. Hence, the dismantling of the dirigiste mercantilist state during the nineteenth century did not mean total deregulation. Rather a process of deregulation occurred which implied the replacement of old forms of regulation with new ones. Nor did this mean that the state's interference in market processes was seriously weakened. It is certainly possible to argue that the opposite occurred, namely that perhaps the most important precondition for the rise of a modern industrialized economy during the nineteenth century was the modern centralized state, which was able to create new rules of the game and had the ability to enforce them, to invest in new infrastructures including communication networks, to open and develop new markets, to invest in higher learning and education and so on (Magnusson 2000). Much of the same can be said of the last two decades which everywhere has implied a quest for new regulative orders and the renewal of governance. The disruption of the Keynesian state has certainly meant that governance in many markets have changed radically. However, to speak of unilateral deregulation is to neglect the importance – as, for example, Steven Vogel (1996), has reminded us – of all the new regulations which have appeared in the wake of the old ones. Hence in many cases – most pertinently perhaps with the communications industries – state monopolies have disappeared, which has led to much work to reconstruct these industries and to create a more competitive structure.

A major problem, however, has been – and still remain so – to understand the historical development of regulation. Which conditions create the development of governance and how do such orders change? A number of suggestions to understand such processes over time have been presented by different theoretical schools. However, as we mentioned in the introduction to this book, neither market failure nor rent seeking can satisfactorily explain all forms of governance and regulation change. Most certainly new transaction cost economics, by emphasizing the role of contractual hazards for under-standing the introduction of governance institutions, is certainly helpful to some extent (Williamson 1996, pp. 5ff.). Hence, by insisting on the importance of bounded rationality (farsighted contracting) and incomplete contracts by agents who are opportunistic or even open rent seekers, we can also acknowledge the existence and even survival of quite irrational forms of governance – in contrast to the 'old' market failure argument. The main problem with this modern 'new institutional' view is that it neglects the historical dimension of regulation. Hence, different modes of regulation are not only relatively stable institutions, but old ones seem to influence the establishment of new ones as well as the process by which they are implemented. This in its turn means that it is worthwhile studying the history of regulation, as we have done in this book. It is common among today's scholars to acknowledge the existence of different 'national' modes of regulation. This implies that to recognize the importance of some form of path dependence in this case is necessary and will bring new insights to the actual process of regulation over time.

The aim of this chapter is to discuss the often used concept of path dependency and analyse the possibility of using it in this context. As will become clear, the meaning of 'path dependence' is far from clearly stated in the discussion. This means that we shall have to devote some time to disentangling its different meanings before we end with a discussion on how it can be used to understand the historical paths of regulation.

PATH DEPENDENCE AND TECHNOLOGY

Lately the concept of 'path dependence' has been widely used in a number of different social sciences. Most pertinently, in the history of technology 'path dependence' is utilized in order to understand processes of technological change – often in explicit opposition to the standard (factor-substitution) economic explanatory model. One of the most influential proponents of such a view, Nathan Rosenberg, argues that: '[e]conomic forces powerfully influence the decision to undertake a search process, but they do so in ways that do not pre-determine the nature and the shape of the things that are found' (Rosenberg 1994, p. 10). Instead he offers an analytical framework which presupposes that 'ongoing technological research is shaped by what has gone before'. More specifically he argues that: '[m]uch technological progress at any given time, therefore, has to be understood as the attempt to extend and further explore certain trajectories of improvement that are made possible by the existing stock of technological knowledge' (ibid., p. 16). Hence, according to this view, the existing stock of technological knowledge is a powerful factor in limiting the number of technological choices that are available to historical actors. To this extent technological change is path dependent: that is, the path of technological development is closed at least to some extent and must largely be explained by decisions already taken. In order to illustrate his argument, Rosenberg uses well-known major innovations such as the electrical power plant, the transistor and the computer. Other examples which have been used in the literature are the standard gauge railway (4 feet 8½ inches) established in the first half of the nineteenth century (Kindleberger 1983, pp. 377ff.) and the gasoline engine used in cars.[1]

It is certainly possible to argue that 'path dependence' in technological processes not only limits the number of available choice-sets but that its influence is even more profound than that. Hence, in recent attempts to discuss technological change within a social-constructivist framework, Bruno Latour, Wiebe E. Bijker, Thomas Hughes and others have presented a 'strong' structural and determinist version of Rosenberg's 'weak' path-dependence argument (Bijker et al. 1987). In their world, certain technologies – as any social artefacts – carry purposeful meaning which not only limits the number of available choices but also has a determinative cognitive influence. Hence, unlike Rosenberg, they presuppose that the initial path chosen not only influences the 'nature of the shape of things that are found' but also predetermines the cognitive search process as such.

Perhaps the most famous example of technological path dependence was presented in a seminal paper by Paul David more than a decade ago, 'Clio and the economics of QWERTY'. In this article, David seek to demonstrate how the organization of letters on the keyboard of typewriters became standardized through a series of chance events and how this standard became permanent although there obviously existed a more efficient alternative, the August Dvorak machine (David 1985). The reason why the 'wrong' machine won out was, according to David, not only due to sunk investments but also because of imperfect markets (more of that later). In other articles David has followed up this observation and has in general terms argued that 'history matters': 'current phenomena sometimes cannot be adequately understood without a knowledge of how they have been shaped by past events, some situated in the remote past.' (David 1988, p. 16). His presupposition is that agents are 'sensitive to initial conditions' (ibid., p. 18). In a follow up paper, he has tried to specify more exactly the role of history in this context. More specifically, path dependency occurs in institutions and organizations for three main reasons, according to David. First, historical experience plays a role in 'the formation of structures of mutually consistent expectations that enable coordination to be achieved without centralized direction of the individual economic agents'. By this, David largely refers to different forms of cognitive selection which appear over time as 'shared historical experience'. Second, David points out that specific organizations such as firms have their own information channels and codes which often appear as sunk organizational costs; that is, the specific organization's capital which is built up over time. As Arrow has also pointed out, David argues that the (knowledge) basis of such an 'organizational capital' would include the capital stock, knowledge of market structures, the specific composition of the workforce and so on (Arrow 1974). Third, David points to the existence of 'strong complementarities or interrelatedness' which appear not only in the form of 'technical interrelatedness' but in any complex human organization. Certainly, these three factors which lead to path dependence – or a 'certain historical bias' – relate rather to the role of biased information and cognitive selection, as in the 'strong' version by the social constructivists, than to Rosenberg's 'weak' version. Hence David says that 'History is a mental construct, being a particular mode of understanding the world' (David 1988, p. 23). Moreover, it is clear that David's treatment of path dependence goes far beyond its use for understanding technological processes (something which we shall discuss in some detail later on) (David 1994, pp. 209ff.).

Bringing us back to technology matters, in a number of papers, Brian Arthur has attempted to demonstrate how the existence of path dependence (in technological matters) can be positively linked to the existence of increasing returns in the economy. Arthur argues that conventional theory builds mainly on the assumption of diminishing returns, 'negative feedback'. However, if we use the more realistic assumption (especially in knowledge-based industries in contrast to 'resource-based' industries where the law of diminishing returns still holds sway, according to Arthur) of increasing returns, this has several consequences for economic theory, Arthur argues. Most significantly, diminishing returns implies a single equilibrium point whereas increasing returns admits a number of equilibrium points. Hence, the choice the market makes might not be the best. Moreover, in the latter case the economic environment is much more unstable than in the first (Arthur 1994, p. 1). Furthermore, in order to illustrate his argument on the path-dependence effects of 'positive feedback', Arthur uses the history of the videocassette recorder as an example. At first, VHS and Beta existed side by side. Each of these could certainly have realized increasing returns as their market share increased. However, although it was not at all foreseeable in advance which equilibria would be selected, 'external circumstances', 'luck' and 'corporate manoeuvring' led to VHS eventually winning the competition race. Hence, regardless of technological competence 'whatever firm that first gets a good start' is in many cases able to corner the market. Consequently, 'once random economic events select a particular path, the choice may become locked in regardless of the advantages of the alternative' (ibid., p. 1). The reason why such lock-in and path dependence occur can largely be explained by such factors as large initial investments in research and development, positive learning effects ('learning by using'), regional external economies ('the industrial districts' which Alfred Marshall spoke of), economies of scope as well as by the observation that 'when one brand gains a significant market share, people have a strong incentive to buy more of the same product so as to be able to exchange information with those using it already' (ibid., p. 4). Perhaps most pertinently, in a number of articles Arthur has pointed to the stark historical importance of industrial location patterns. Small and even accidental events are in many cases responsible for any choice of location at the outset. However, as there are obvious net benefits to be gained in being located together with other firms, Marshallian positive external economies might in many cases lead to industrial 'agglomeration' over time. A famous case in point here is certainly Silicon Valley whose emergence, according to Arthur, must largely be regarded as the outcome of chance (ibid., p. 51).

PATH DEPENDENCE AND HISTORY

Hence, it is clear that the concept of 'path dependence' is useful in order to understand the process of technological change. Without doubt, technological processes over time are characterized by lock-in effects by 'historical accidents' (David) or 'small events' (Arthur). However, as both David and Arthur make clear, the alleged existence of path dependence also has consequences for standard economic theory. Thus, it is obvious, for example, that the existence of path dependency upsets any standard neo-classical theory which does not admit the existence of positive transaction costs. In a world of zero transaction costs (and no increasing returns of scale) markets would be perfect and there would be no place for either path dependency or, for that matter, institutions (North 1990, pp. 93ff.). However, most economists today acknowledge the existence of transaction costs (for example, information costs). Hence, it is possible that path dependence to some extent can be taken care of within a neo-classical framework (for example, as more or less typical specifications of Marshall's external economics).

Notwithstanding, the path-dependence argument has been extended to cover a more general assault on standard neo-classical economics. Certainly, in a broad sense the notion of path dependency can be regarded as a challenge to the neo-classical paradigm through its very recognition of the importance of institutions and the role of history (Arthur 1994; David 1985, 1994). Thus, the notion of path dependency suggests that lock-in effects and suboptimal behaviour may persist and that history matters in explaining these deficiencies. Without doubt, in an (economic) world of path dependency, positive transaction costs and perhaps also a high degree of uncertainty, there is no guarantee that rational and maximizing behaviour will lead to efficient (economic) solutions. Hence, by adding the purposeful actors to the picture, Douglass North argues that '[t]he increasing returns characteristic of an initial set of institutions that provide disincentives to productive activity will create organizations and interest groups with a stake in the existing constraints'. Moreover, North points out that in this sense purposeful action may lead to the perserverance of both productive and unproductive paths (North 1990, p. 99).

In an even more radical fashion, Hodgson, for example, has stated that the existence of path dependency not only illustrates the possibility of a number of different equilibria outcomes, but that it also undermines the belief in the selection principle as a means to achieve efficient outcomes in the long run. This means that it is not possible to regard 'natural selection' – as it was presented by Milton Friedman and Armen Alchian – as a safety net to guarantee that the market, regardless of the existence of path dependency, will pick the most 'efficient' solution after a process of trial and error characterized by brute competition. In a paper in which the evolution of money is used as an example, Hodgson argues against Carl Menger's classical standpoint that evolutionary selection tends to favour and replicate the actions of 'the most perspicacious and ablest economic subjects' (a thought that has since served as a main pillar, particularly for Austrian economics) (Hodgson 1993, p. 113). This is especially the case if we argue that the selection or market process as such is also an institution which favours path-dependent solutions and in this sense rather resembles Lamarckian humanly and socially shaped 'artificial selection' than Darwin's spontaneous 'natural selection'(Ramstad 1994).

Hence, as we have seen, the argument that the admission of path dependence has a number of implications for standard economic theory is not unusual. This, however, raises a number of pertinent questions. Is it possible to be more specific regarding the consequences of the introduction of the concept 'path dependence' into economics? What exactly is path dependency and to what extent can it be regarded as a challenge to standard neo-classical economics?

ASPECTS OF PATH DEPENDENCE

Confronting the issue to what extent path dependency is a challenge to standard (neo-classical) economic theory, Liebowitz and Margolis in an important contribution have suggested that the phenomenon of path dependency is best handled within traditional (neo-classical) economic analysis (Liebowitz and Margolis 1995, pp. 206ff.). In order to amplify this argument they introduce three different forms – or 'degrees' – of path dependency, differing mainly in the level of available information. In the first two instances, the situation of path dependency (the first and second degrees of path dependence) is most easily understood within a neo-classical framework. In the first degree of path dependence, Liebowitz and Margolis introduce the existence of positive information and transaction costs. Given positive costs in order to search for an alternative (better) choice, a rational agent may well stay on the previous path as he or she will acknowledge that leaving the path will incur higher costs than the choice of another path will yield in income. Hence, given the behavioural assumptions of standard neo-classical economics, path dependence will be the most rational option and satisfy any definition we may choose of maximizing (or for that matter satisficing) behaviour. Even though our authors do not explicitly say so, rational behaviour in situations of a high degree of uncertainty could also be subsumed under this first degree of path dependence. Moreover, this first degree of path dependence is akin to Akerlof's discussion concerning under which circumstances rational behaviour can comply with social norm following. Hence, it can be perfectly rational to comply with an existing norm if the cost and benefit schedule of non-compliance in relation to compliance is negative (Akerlof 1976).

With regard to the second degree of path dependence, the reason for following a certain path might be the incomplete information occurring at the time of the decision. Because of this an agent might later find out that the initial choice was apparently not the ultimate one. According to Leibowitz and Margolis, this cannot 'in a meaningful way' be defined as an inefficient solution since the information was not at hand when the decision was taken. Hence, in this instance the behaviour of path followers would at least adhere to the principle of 'bounded rationality' launched by Herbert Simon and others. Using the concept of 'bounded rationality' it is certainly also possible to argue that the existence of biased information as such does not exclude maximizing or rational behaviour. Hence, it is possible not only to recognize 'incomplete' information, but also information which is biased by selective information provided by the path or the institution (Hodgson 1988, p. 133). This means that it is possible to acknowledge the cognitive limitations of human agents without abandoning the neo-classical formula. However, it is open to question whether such a formula has any practical relevance for a state which is characterized by path-determined information, increasing returns and perhaps also radical uncertainty.

Last, the third degree of path dependence depicts a situation when the actor may be well aware that better (more efficient) alternatives exist but still rejects them and instead chooses the path-dependent outcome. While the first two degrees of path dependency are consistent with neo-classical rational behaviour leading to predictable and (at least bounded) efficient solutions, the third degree is obviously not compatible with a neo-classical framework of interpretation. Although such behaviour may exist, Liebowitz and Margolis argue, it is highly unusual in real-life situations. Instead, in most cases path dependence can be explained against the background of either the first or the second degree of path dependence.

Moreover, this 'third-level' path dependence is closely related to what Viktor Vanberg has chosen to call 'genuine rule following' in contrast to 'rational case-by-case adjustment': 'a disposition to abide by the rules relatively independently of the specifics of the particular situational constraints' (Vanberg 1988, p. 2). Furthermore this means that the rule is followed 'without choosing in each and every situation anew whether or not to obey' (ibid., p. 7). In stark contrast to Liebowitz and Margolis, Vanberg believes that genuine rule following is very common: 'the present argument starts from the presumption that genuine rule-following is indeed a real phenomenon rather than a mere theoretical fiction'. Furthermore, Vanberg goes as far as stating that 'a viable social order seems not even conceivable if the rules on which it rests would only be obeyed in those instances where the particular situational constraints render rule-compliance in fact the utility-maximizing choice' (ibid., p. 13; see also Vanberg 1994, ch. 2).

With reference to Nelson and Winter's discussion of routines, we must furthermore acknowledge that such rule following mechanisms can be long-lasting (Nelson and Winter 1982). Moreover, they are most certainly introduced when actors make their choices facing a high degree of uncertainty and imperfect information. In order to illustrate the validity of the claim that third-degree path dependency is also common, Rutherford presents a number of examples such as: many firms follow rules in this sense; many consumers tend to stick to a certain consumption pattern despite changes in relative prices; voters take time to vote in elections although they know that their vote makes no difference; non-voting carries no or very little social disapproval; and many persons follow 'a rule of honesty or of proper behaviour despite opportunities to violate the rule to his or her own advantage and remain undetected' (Rutherford 1994, p. 54). To this we can also add what Douglass North has especially emphasized: the fact that many people tend to stubbornly hold on to ideologies, often without better reason than that they have always done so (North 1990). Certainly, as Rutherford points out, it would theoretically be possible to make such genuine rule following consistent with rationalist behaviour if only we adjust the individual's utility function (for example, the desire for honesty or for that matter of rule following). To what extent this would also supply a rationalist explanation of the adherence to the rule is, to say the least, an open question (Rutherford 1994, p. 54).

Indeed, Liebowitz and Margolis are right in that if 'path dependency' is to serve as anything more than a catchword for a sweeping criticism of neo-classical economics, it is important that we try to be more specific regarding its theoretical status. Hence, it seems clear that path dependency in its third aspect – path dependency as 'genuine rule following' – cannot be said to be handled satisfactorily within a neo-classical framework. This is especially the case as 'genuine rule following' is more common than Liebowitz and Margolis are willing to admit. Hence, we might agree with Rutherford's judgement '[t]hat such genuine rule following behaviour exists is now widely accepted' (Rutherford 1994). Furthermore as Jon Elster has argued, social norm behaviour – in the sense of genuine rule following or path dependence of the third degree – must, along with altruism, envy and self-interest, be acknowledged as the basic 'cement of society' (1989, p. 287): 'Norms, in turn, are partly shaped by self-interest, because people often adhere to the norms that favour them. But norms are not fully reducible to self-interest, at least not by this particular mechanism. The unknown residual is a brute fact, at least for the time being' (ibid., p. 150).

PATH DEPENDENCE AND CHANGE

While there is certainly much to be gained by introducing path dependency/genuine rule following into economics there are certainly also some problems which should not be taken lightly. One question already dealt with is to what extent path-dependent behaviour or choice replaces rational behaviour. As Liebowitz and Margolis have argued, it is fruitful in this context to distinguish between different forms of path dependency while at the same time argue, in contrast to them, that genuine path dependence and rule following are quite common features in social society. Second, it might seem natural to think of path-dependent situations in a world of uncertainty and when information is socially selected; but how then does change occur? When is the path abandoned, and for what reasons?

Several scholars have recently argued that one way to start might be to acknowledge the existence of punctuated equilibrium situations (Gersick 1991; Andersen 1994; Nelson 1994). However, a problem with this approach is its focus on merely external factors ('shocks') in starting the rapid process of change (Thelen and Steinmo 1992). The question is, of course, whether such change can occur from internal causes, for example, by some kind of adaptive rationality model as suggested by Rutherford (Rutherford 1994, p. 80; Heiner 1983). According to such thinking, adaptation and learning occur over time. Adaptive behaviour and learning will in turn ensure change and can even lead to the abandonment of a certain path. An advantage of this approach is that it emphasizes small and gradual changes over time – and not merely external shocks.

The role of adaptation and learning in economic life has of course been discussed intensively during recent years and is inherent in much evolutionary theory – including the Nelson and Winter approach. However, there are at least two questions that might be put in this context. First, to what extent is adaptive learning really possible, given biased and path-determined information? In its strongest version this doubt would come close to deterministic approaches such as structuralism or social constructivism. Hence a number of epistemological questions could be raised in this context, for example, to what extent knowledge is cumulative, how determinate social codes are and so on. Most certainly, it is impossible to give a definite answer to such questions, which for a long time have contributed to a seemingly endless controversy between economics and sociology (Vanberg 1994, pp. 11ff.). Second, as, for example, Groenewegen and Vromen have argued, it is crucial to understand whether and to what extent adaptive learning (they use the firm as an example) should be seen as a parallel to a Darwinian selection mechanism, that is, that inferior ideas, strategies or paths will be abandoned and the better ones adopted by selection. They argue that learning on the whole is contextual and that path dependencies exist in human learning. Thus there is no a priori reason to believe that any evolutionary mechanism exists which will hinder positive feedback. However, even though the role of history and the feedback mechanism itself might prevent the search for better rules as well as lead to the adaptation of new rules occuring too slowly in relation to a changing environment, they argue that learning might lead to change, that is, to the adoption of a better solution and a change of path. There are two reasons for their somewhat eclectic standpoint. First, they point to the fact that there are a number of learning theories which differ widely on the determinacy of contextual and path-dependent learning. Second, they argue that individuals may employ 'different learning rules in different situations'. Hence the motivation of agents may differ regarding the 'appetite for exploring fresh alternatives'. They do not discuss under what circumstances such motivations differ, but instead propose 'further process analysis' (Groenewegen and Vromen 1997, pp. 54ff.).

Perhaps a general way of dealing with the problem of path dependency and change could take its point of departure from social science discussions during recent years regarding the relation between structure and agency. Within this discussion – which includes partakers such as Anthony Giddens, Alasdair Macintyre and Roy Bhaskar – an attempt has been made to replace structuralism by a more praxis-oriented view of the interrelationship between structure and agent.[2] Moreover, political institutionalists have also in recent years moderated the discussion by emphasizing interaction processes between actors and structures, and discussing the role of internal and external factors as well as gradual and abrupt patterns of change related to processes of historical evolution (Thelen and Steinmo 1992).

There may be different solutions to this dilemma but it is certainly a first-order issue if path dependence is to become really useful as a tool for understanding economic reality then the role of change should be further elaborated. As we know from historical experience, paths are followed but also abandoned. Hence, besides (punctuated) accidents we must acknowledge both the role of purposeful actors as well as the existence of strong positive feedback mechanisms. We still know too little to give each factor its proper weight or to understand how they interact in real economies.

CONCLUSION

We have so far seen that path dependence can be a useful tool for understanding technological development as well as serve as a challenge to standard economic theory. Lastly here the question will be put whether this concept can also be of use in understanding the trajectories of policy regulation. In an important contribution to the study of regulation, Dixit has emphasized the role of transaction costs when introducing and implementing new regulations. His point of departure is that the political process in principle should be looked upon as a principal–agent problem which takes place in real time: 'What we can do is to understand how the whole system consisting of markets and governments copes with the whole set of problems of conflicting information, incentives and actions that preclude a fully ideal outcome' (Dixit 1996, p. 3). Hence, any introduction as well as replacement of governance or governance regimes will lead to costs as well as gains. Whether there will be a net gain or a net loss is to a large extent an empirical question. Without doubt, a substantial part of the costs involved are of the kind which we commonly recognize as transaction costs. Moreover, as politicking – which, for example, Ronald Johnson and Gary Libecap remind us of in their contribution to this volume – is strongly characterized by contracting in a world of uncertainty where (political) actors often prefer to put forward incomplete contracts to pursue their own or others' (special) interests, it is likely that high transaction costs will lead to people observing some form of rule following, including 'genuine rule following'. Without any doubt, this will tend to enforce behaviour which we might want to call 'path dependent'. Hence, it seems very fruitful to study the role of rule following as well as path dependence in political processes, for example, when new governance rules are introduced and perhaps most pertinently during the process when they are implemented.

Rational choice theory has so far been the main challenger to sociological organization theory in order to understand how politics is made and implemented. Also, some institutionalists among political scientists have tried to disentangle how (political) institutions, rules and so on shape the outcome of such things as the political process and governance.[3] However, there seems to be a gap here between more crude 'rent-seeking' theories and institutional approaches which might be combined to some extent if we introduce an understanding of the political process as a process in which governmental and other governance bodies operate in a situation of uncertainty and incomplete contracting.

How can we then make use of the concept 'path dependence'? Political and institutional historians such as Theda Skocpol (1979) and others have long emphasized the role of history in understanding how governments and administrative bodies operate; their basic conclusion is that here as elsewhere 'history matters'. Others have spoken of 'national' traditions of governance in which the past plays an important role for the subsequent development of regulation – much in the same manner as when historians of technology talk about 'national innovation systems' and so on. For example, Arne Kaijser, has detected a special 'Swedish' regime of governance, an 'infrasystem', for railways, electricity and telecommunications. More specifically, he argues that in Sweden there existed 'a relatively stable' institutional regime for infrasystems from the 1850s to the 1970s which was 'changed considerably' during the 1980s and 1990s (Kaijser 1999, p. 224). Change, he argues, can come both from within the system as a consequence of different forms of friction as well as from the outside in the form of great technological leaps, political change and so on.

Hence, path dependence, 'history', undoubtedly plays an important role in understanding political processes as well as governance over time. However, when uncertainty and incomplete contracting are also added to the picture we are able to understand better why different forms of rule following (path dependence) are pursued in certain cases and not in others. In accordance with what was said earlier, such rule following occurs in cases when there is a 'radical' or even 'structural' uncertainty (ignorance?) (Langlois 1989, p. 228) and the process of contracting is very complicated. Moreover, by using these different theoretical tools we might also be better equipped to grasp why and for what reasons rules are abandoned. In this case we must certainly acknowledge the role of new technologies and so on, in arriving at a situation of 'punctuated equilibrium'. However, there are also 'internal' factors of great importance in this case. For example, as Douglass North has emphasized, different incentive structures are closely connected to the formal and informal 'rules of the game' (that is, institutions) (North 1990). As the historical record seem to suggest, the competition of economic entitlements seems to have been especially severe in cases where property rights were less developed and when incomplete contracting occured. [4] Moreover, in such cases we can be assured that conflicts between different interest groups appear in an acute and open form. Such conflicts in turn instigate change and might lead to changes in governance and regimes of regulation. Without doubt, this seems to be one way in which the paths of governance and policy regulation are determined.

In any case it is fruitful to use the concept of path dependence in order to understand the history of regulation. At the same time, however, we argue that it is vital that we develop a better understanding of how such paths are abandoned and changed. Perhaps a further development of the transaction cost analysis of politics is a fruitful road to pursue in the future.

NOTES

1. Clark and Juma (1987), p. 171. For other examples, see Hodgson (1993), pp. 205ff. and Mokyr (1990).
2. For Giddens' still very relevant discussion on these issues, see especially Giddens (1984), chs 1 and 2.
3. A brief overview of different modern theories of regulation is given in Baldwin and Cave (1999).
4. See, for example, Goldin and Libecap (1994), pp. 1–11.

PART II

Sweden as a Role Model of a Regulated Economy

7. Introduction

Lars Magnusson and Jan Ottosson

The main theme of this volume is that it is important to apply a longer historical perspective, both in identifying formative moments of regulatory settings and when discussing the forces which bring about changes of institutional change. The small export-oriented Swedish economy will be used as a role model to illustrate this theme. Until the 1990s, the much discussed Swedish model combined a remarkable economic growth with strong regulation of various important sectors.[1] One way of describing this model is to look at it as a compromise between labour, capital and the state. Hence the Swedish model implied state regulation of specific markets (finance, housing, transportation) and during some decades after the Second World War, there were ambitions to plan the economy at the macro level. To some extent, also, state-owned enterprises were part of the picture. However, the number of state-owned enterprises remained small in Sweden compared to, for instance, in France. Sweden has long been one of the most corporatist countries in Western Europe, together with countries such as Austria, mainly due to its strong and influential trade unions. The structure of political decision making made the 'Swedish model' synonymous with a corporatist state.

The chapters in this part of the book will discuss more closely various aspects of the model by examining the Swedish transport and communication sector. Until the early 1990s, this policy area was considered to be one of the most regulated in the Swedish economy. Above all, the relations between the government, politicians, different agencies and private interests, as well as the way in which decisions have been made in this sector, are central to the contributions.

Going back to the late nineteenth century, the role of the state was important in several respects when Sweden became a successful and export-oriented latecomer during the first Industrial Revolution. First, the state was a crucial actor in financing and initiating several infrastructure projects, such as canals and railways. Second, during this initial phase of the modern Swedish economy, close connections between private interests and the state were formed. During the second Industrial Revolution the division of labour between the state and the private actors in Sweden became even more pronounced, especially after the formative agreement between the labour unions and the national employers'

123

organization in 1938, the so-called 'Saltsjöbaden agreement'. This agreement implied that the state distributed economic growth created in the private sector (Magnusson 2000).

Also, in several network industries the state became more dominant during the interwar years, for instance, as guardian of various aspects of economic activities. This role of the state in the transport and communication sector was, however, not self-evident. On the contrary, from the introduction of modern infrastructure systems during the late nineteenth and early twentieth centuries a dual model, permitting both private and state ownership, was developed (Kaijser 1994). This model gave the state a central but not dominant role in regulating and owning such industries. In several cases, private actors were allowed to enter the market. The state acted as owner and as a regulator. Hence the invisible hand of the market was allowed to work in parts of each industry but was strictly regulated. Moreover, the Swedish model of dual infrastructure systems, where both private actors and the state coexisted in several network industries, was also partly found in the other Scandinavian countries (Thue 1995). However, during the first decades of the twentieth century several of these systems were nationalized but in some sectors a quite different development took place, permitting both private and public ownership.

After the Second World War, macroeconomic planning together with ambitions of regulating several areas of the economy evolved. Several economists have argued that the large amount of regulations implemented contributed to a slower economic growth, due to less competitive markets in Sweden (Lindbeck 1997; Fölster and Peltzman 1995; Krantz 2000). The development of various heavily regulated sectors of the economy was a fact until the late 1980s and 1990s when a new era of the Swedish economy began, with a number of industries being deregulated. Also, the role of the state was now crucial since new regulations and new institutional settings were formulated by public actors.

Of course, the ambition of the state regarding economic activities was not limited only to regulating various industries. It also included investment activities as well as distribution of subsidies. One of the most interesting aspects in this respect concerns how such measures were initiated, or changed, by public actors. Was the process of growing ambitions regarding what the state could – or should – do a reflection of market failures? Or was it a reflection of interest groups interacting with the state in a process where the actors' primary concern was rent seeking?

These empirical chapters on the Swedish model, deal with the question how institutions and regulations were formed in the transport and communications sector in Sweden during the twentieth century. The period embraces both the first and the second industrial revolutions, and includes structural changes in all transport and communications markets. This period also covers the emergence of regulations in several network industries. We would therefore suggest that the Swedish cases show a rather nuanced picture of a complex historical process.

Also, these stylized cases illustrate various policy implementations chosen with marked 'policy styles' (to paraphrase Hughes 1983). Differences between policy decisions and their implementation suggest that taking account of different institutional settings, a complex network of actors, as well as specific historical factors, give us more explanatory power in analysing the development of policy actions. Indeed, policy decisions are often the result of a dynamic process where such decisions often reflect a complex change in the relationship between formal and informal institutions and the actors themselves. These decisions were the result of a process ranging over a long period of time with several shifts in arguments, policies chosen and implementation. In almost all cases, the processes reflected neither broad public interest nor narrow self-interest. Comparing the development of policy actions in the sectors studied, the main difference is the marked policy patterns as well as the policy shifts. The paths chosen towards public ownership and massive regulatory policies included several steps, as well as various mixes of regulatory regimes.

Our main argument is that the Swedish experience shows, first, that the role of the state was not limited to reacting against private interests, that is, responding to market failures. Rather, the state and various public actors on different levels were active in the very formation of various regulations. Second, Anne Krueger's (1996) argument that programmes might be self-perpetuating after a while, seems to be supported by the Swedish experience. Third, in some instances interest groups are not represented only by private interests. Instead, public actors were important in forming groups, or clubs, with the aim of promoting the distribution of state investments.[2]

NOTES

1. The Swedish model has often been used as follows: first, as a metaphor for a growing market economy, where the unions and the employers' organizations have reached centrally co-ordinated agreements; second, it has been described as a middle way between socialism and capitalism; and a third interpretation suggests that a general welfare model might be a good description of the Swedish model (Magnusson 2000; Murhem and Ottosson 2000).
2. See also Vietor (2000) for a review of the factors behind the American regulatory patterns.

8. Compensating the periphery. Railway policy and regional interest groups in northern Sweden

Lena Andersson-Skog

INTRODUCTION

In the winter of 1997, the Swedish parliament decided to build a new railway, the Bothnia railway, along the coast of northern Sweden. The investment cost was calculated at SEK 8.2 billion (approximately US$1 billion).[1] This decision put an end to 70 years of regional struggle trying to realize this project. In official reports and investigations in 1923, 1949, 1987 and even as late as 1996, various public committees and special investigators made recommendations to the government that the project should be rejected because of the expected losses, and these recommedations were followed each time.[2] Why then, did the government approve the railway in 1997? How do we explain why the state changed its mind?

Here, interest group theory may be of help. Interest groups are often said to have a negative impact on economic growth and income distribution. However, Swedish development since 1950 to some extent seems to contradict this description. With strong interest groups, a high standard of living, and a still respectable growth until the 1970s, Swedish development needs explaining. Mancur Olson (1982, p. 90) has stressed that the Swedish interest groups, primarily the unions, encompass organizations or inclusive interest groups. Such groups have an incentive to redistribute income among themselves at the least possible social cost, and also to give some weight to economic growth and to the interests of society as a whole (ibid., p. 90). Thereby they seek consensus rather than confrontation since it is vital that a wide range of actors and other interest groups accept the legitimacy of their claims. In an attempt to explain why the decrease in Swedish growth rate has not become as severe as could be expected since the 1970s, Olson also highlights the importance of the Swedish state acting as a counterweight against the demands of the interest groups during the period of decline. The 'Northern Lights' show that a strong state can balance different special interests, thus keeping the economy away from institutional sclerosis for a long period of time (Olson 1990, pp. 87–91).[3]

However, even if the importance of 'bringing the state in' is recognized, there are still other, more complex perspectives that need to be considered to fully interpret the characteristics of the 'Northern Lights'. Focusing on the traditionally strong interest groups in Sweden – the unions – has blurred the activity of other important interest groups. For instance regional interest groups have had great success in shaping both economic policy and national regulation in Sweden. Most notable since the 1950s is perhaps the allocation of resources to some regions through economic policy and regional planning. There is also, however, another example, where regional considerations and regional interest groups have had a large impact on the extension and performance of a sector, namely in railway building and railway policy. In the Swedish context, with a geographically diversified multisectoral regional economic structure emerging from the middle of the nineteenth century, the political mobilization at a regional level, such as the personal networks and clubs established with regional businessmen and political officials acting in the national system, are worth exploring.

This opens up an alternative angle in studying the importance of interest-group behaviour and the state: to focus on the importance of regional action in the national political structure. In this chapter I shall discuss the relation between regional interest groups and the institutional structure in shaping railway policy over the century. The study will be concentrated on the railway interests in northern Sweden, in particular the struggle for the Bothnia railway, from the birth of the idea in the 1920s until the parliamentary decision in 1997 to approve the project. Here, I shall argue that two perspectives are vital in comprehending the outcome. First, the incentives created by the national railway policy for regional interest groups, and second, the strategies chosen by the regional interests in achieving legitimacy for their demands in the allocation process. But first, some words have to be said about railway policy and regional interest groups.

NATIONAL AND REGIONAL PERSPECTIVES ON THE RAILWAY INTERESTS

Throughout the industrialized world, the regional perspective has often been disregarded in studies of how national railway systems were regulated and institutionalized. There are exceptions, though. Competition between private railway companies often meant regional competition on markets for goods and services using the political arena as a battlefield. This, for instance, was the case in Denmark, where regional railway companies competed to get access to the German and British markets for agriculture (Ousaager 1988). State-owned systems were more directly dependent on political decisions. In the case of Norway, Frits Hodne has shown how regional interests in parliament played a major role in deciding how the income from customs and foreign trade should be used for investments in infrastructure (Hodne 1988).[4] In Finland, annual obligations to build a predetermined length of railway from the mid-1920s onwards were imposed upon the state railways. These railways were built in the interior of northern Finland, until then lacking modern transportation. In the Swedish case, Sverker Oredsson discusses the importance of regional interest groups in parliament when deciding the location of national railways as well as the question of private versus state ownership. Here, he points to the railway interest in northern Sweden as being especially important for actually creating a national railway system from the 1890s (Oredsson 1969, pp. 122, 144, 282–4). Lena Andersson-Skog has also suggested that a regional bias, compensating disadvantaged regions for the lack of transport infrastructure, has been present in Swedish railway policy from the late nineteenth century until the late 1970s (Andersson-Skog 1993). The regional interest was also important during the 1980s, when it was decided to construct the new *Mälardalsbanan*. Here, as Magnus Carlsson has shown, the interest group argued successfully that a new functional region would emerge as a result of the investment (Carlsson 1999).

There are two important reasons for regional interest groups to act in matters of infrastructure in general. First, there are the strong links between improved infrastructure and regional economic development and growth during industrialization (Tipton 1976). Second, the spatial and network dimensions make it possible both to maximize the benefits of an investment to a certain region and to provide some marginal benefits to other regions. At the same time, the entire network shares the costs.

It is easy to understand that the incentive for regional action in the national political system is strong. However, to be successful in competing for resources, it is important to gain national acceptance for the regional demands. The bargaining power of various interest groups differs when it comes to the allocation of investments in infrastructure since there are differences in entrepreneurial skills and political representation in the national political system, and also the economic and spatial conditions vary from region to region. Here, two important aspects have to be considered. First, the correspondence between the intentions of the national railway policy and the legitimacy of a certain interest group is crucial for the success in the allocation of national resources in the political system. Conflicting goals can coexist on different levels in the political system. Frank B. Tipton has emphasized the importance of how the cadres of state officials in Germany and Japan conceptualized their role in achieving a certain policy goal. The ideological forces they identified with, helped explain how the state acted in different railway matters (Tipton 1999, pp. 14ff.). Second, the actual structure of the state and the democratic system, that is, how state authority is distributed among different bodies, affects the access of different groups to the decision-making process. Dunlavy has shown that the different political structures in the US and Prussia also had an impact on the way the railroad sectors were organized. In the US, with a differentiated political structure whereby the policy-making process is located at different levels, there were opportunities for state interests (as opposed to federal interest) as well as other groups, to oppose or support railroad construction through the political process (Dunlavy 1994a, pp. 45ff., 131ff.).

In contrast, the homogeneous structure of the state agencies in Prussia created a uniform pattern, with less access for interest groups into the decision-making processes (ibid., p. 148). However, a too diversified and open organizational structure can also create lock-in situations. Avinash K. Dixit argues that the common agency structure is vulnerable due to contradictory goals and vague incentive structures where different interests compete (Dixit 1996, p. 95). A general conclusion is that a homogeneous, hierarchical political structure probably makes it more difficult for different interests to be heard compared to a more diversified and splintered structure, where a number of access possibilities are open to interest groups. It is also important to take into account the actions taken by various state officials. The way they interpret their mandate influences the ways in which different interest groups interact with the state at different levels.

Regional Mobilization, Regional Identity and National Legitimacy

The regional issue has experienced a renaissance during the last ten years, partly due to a major structural shift in the international economy, affecting various functional and administrative networks. The emergence of new relationships is driven by mutual interdependencies between infrastructure, the localization of economic activities and the political systems of various collectives. This involves new patterns of co-operation among existing and newly created political and economic units. The question of regional mobilization is, however, not new. For instance, Robert Putnam has highlighted the importance of regional social structures in explaining long-term economic development. In his study of regional development in Italy during the last seven centuries, Putnam states that a civic culture, manifested as horizontal organizations and political, social or economic networks, goes hand in hand with a strong democratic government. Together, this helps create conditions for economic prosperity, whereas weak government and few civic organizations coexist with inferior growth (Putnam 1993, pp. 175–6). From this perspective, regional interest groups could be seen as advocates of regional growth and welfare. An important question Putnam does not explore, however, is the question of regional mobilization on the national arena; how the civic culture or regional identity shared by a group, or a network of groups, is transformed into political action.

Regional mobilization reflects the competition for private and public investments. A vital question is what characterizes a regional interest group? The first and most obvious feature, that of a common geographical base, is as evident as it is insufficient, since all human activities can be related to a geographical location. Instead, it is the arguments from a regional stand in achieving a specific goal that can be said to constitute the very essence in a regional interest group. Here, I should like to suggest that three important aspects must be considered: the relation between regional identity and the economic structure, the way regional interests organise, and access to the political system.

The construction and characteristics of the regional identity is crucial for the existence of interest groups. In the industrialization process, Tipton has argued that the creation of a modern national identity related to the nation-state made the local elite react by creating a regional identity as a response to the intrusion of national administration into local affairs (Tipton 1976). That is to say, in a way the industrial state brought with it a competition between regions concerning the ability to attract relatively mobile resources such as skilled labour and to establish fixed infrastructural resources. Here, investments in internal and external cultural, political and economic networks were crucial to the further development of a particular region (Westin and Östhol 1992).

Lee J. Alston and Joseph P. Ferrie have discussed the relationship between the economic rationale and the social and political action in their work on southern paternalism and its impact on the formation of welfare policy in the US from 1890 to 1965. They point at three interdependent processes. First, the specific problems the plantation economy faced after 1865, which made paternalism a reasonable strategy for the plantation owners' continued economic wealth. Second, how the economic strategy transformed into the social arena as a social code and ideology, where the self-images and identity among this social, economic and political elite also reinforced the paternalistic behaviour in the political arena. Third, the access this elite had to decision making in the national political system and their ability to unite their interests to the general opinion helped keep the southern economic and social system intact for a long time and also helped to shape the ideologies underlying the federal welfare policy (Alston and Ferrie 1999).

Thus, it would seem that the existence and success of regional interest groups is closely related to the structure of the state and the way the political system is organized. At the same time, the logic of regional mobilization and organization may be found in the conditions of the regional economy and its political and social framework.

The Logic of Regional Railway Interests in Northern Sweden

The same three aspects can serve as a starting-point for a discussion of the mobilization of railway interest groups from northern Sweden. First, the relationship between economic structure and regional strategy has to be outlined. Northern Sweden has for centuries been considered as a poverty-stricken but still potentially prosperous region due to its plentiful natural resources, primarily iron ore. During industrialization, from the middle of the nineteenth century, timber, and a few decades later, hydropower and minerals other than iron ore, were added to the list. A pattern of a dual regional economy was early established. The export-oriented raw material industries interacted with self-subsistence farming in a sparsely populated sub-arctic climate where the urban areas were few and small and far away from the centres of the world market and the economic and political centre of the Swedish nation-state.[5] From 1945 to 1970, the economic structure rapidly transformed into a new duality with export industry and the domestic service production as the dominating sectors. From the late 1970s on, higher education has become an increasingly more important sector of the regional economy. Here the university cities and university college cities became local and subregional centres of growth. However, the distance between regional centres and national and international markets is still considered a major obstacle to economic development. While the demand of the transport systems earlier was focused on the transport of raw materials, the question of a fast and reliable passenger traffic was added to the needs from the mid-twentieth century.

   The economic structure that emerged during the industrializing period shaped the preconditions of the regional identity and strategy. While the local identity differs according to the life-style and economic conditions, often defined by the degree of economic and social integration along the river valleys, there is also an identity commonly accepted and used on the national scene.[6] Apparently, collective decisionmakers at the regional level must act outside their region *vis-à-vis* both private and other collective actors. They also have to act inside their own region in search of a regional identity. The creation of identity serves the interest of reaching fundamental consensus and legitimacy for the goals of development. It also defines who belongs and does not belong to a region and an interest group. In the case of northern Sweden, the regional identity was, and to a large extent still is, related to long distances, the dependency of raw-material industries and a non-urban life-style in a periphery far away from the national centres (Sörlin 1988). This identity is further enforced by the differences in climatic conditions, since a great part of northern Sweden has a sub-arctic climate, while the southern parts of Sweden are milder. Industrialization did not basically alter the character of the economy in northern Sweden, but rather reinforced the earlier structure. This contributed to the preservation of what constituted the regional image of this part of Sweden on the national level. This homogeneous identity veiled the distinctive subregional economic differences existing in northern Sweden. For instance, for the most northern county, Norrbotten, the iron-ore export and steelworks dominated the economic structure. In the county of Jämtland on the other hand, agriculture, commerce and forestry were the major industries. In the national arena, however, the similarities of the basic conditions were emphasized. As a consequence, the question of improved transportation became a common vital strategic matter for various regional interests from northern Sweden.

The mobilization of railway interests was carried out by the regional political and social elite in northern Sweden. Three major groups dominated the scene for a long time. The first group consisted of ministers and members of parliament from the region. The second group comprised regional state officials such as governors and officials in regional administrative bodies such as the county councils, but also the clergy.[7] These two groups had their major arena in the political system. The local and regional industrialists and major owners of natural resources established the third group. It did not act in parliament, but rather through other lobby organizations and by co-ordinating meetings between industrialists and politicians. A commonly shared vision in all three groups was that of the enlightened colonizers. They were modern men and women acting in the best interests of the region, the nation and their own prosperity. This does not exclude a strong social pathos. Many of the governors and industrialists were known as great beneficiaries and philanthropists in improving social and economic conditions in the region (Sörlin 1988).

The regional mobilization was concentrated in two different kinds of organization. First, a number of more formal organizations, often with a specific goal to achieve, were established. An example is the Botniabanegruppen, with the explicit task of promoting the building of the Bothnia railway. A second kind of association was organized like clubs, where anyone could enrol and participate in promoting a broad spectrum of topics related to strengthening the region. One example is Norrlandsförbundet (Norrland League or League of northern Sweden) established to promote the regional spirit through cultural events, public information and lobbying. While the interest groups had few members and were the important political actors, the clubs had considerably more members and functioned as a sounding board for regional issues.

A final aspect concerns how these interests succeeded in gaining access to the political decision-making process and in allocating investments to the region. It will be important to analyse the institutional structure shaping the decision-making process in the railway sector and the railway policy during different periods. Another question to explore is to what extent the regional arguments coincided with the goals embraced by the railway policy over time. In answering

this, the story of the Bothnia railway will be outlined in the context of the institutional structure in the railway sector since the late nineteenth century.

COMPENSATING THE PERIPHERY IN THE DUAL RAILWAY SYSTEM, 1875–1939

Until 1939 the Swedish railway sector consisted of a state-owned national railway network in the hands of a state agency, SJ, co-operating with a vast private network of private railways, divided among, at the most, a couple of hundred railway companies.

From 1853–54, the state had assumed responsibility for the national railway system, leaving the regional and local transport system to be constructed by private entrepreneurs.[8] This policy was strengthened in 1871, when a special railway loan fund was established for private railway enterprises. Of the 16 000 kilometres of railway constructed in Sweden, the private network accounted for almost three-quarters. There was also another distinct feature, namely the almost total absence of state-owned or private railways in northern Sweden until the 1890s. From the 1870s, the export industries in northern Sweden started to boom as a result of international demand. At the same time the first railway construction period ended, leaving northern Sweden without railways. In the light of the potentially prosperous economy, a parliamentary decision was made in 1886 to continue the construction of state-owned railways. It was not an easy decision, however, to extend the trunk-line system. Some groups in parliament, especially the Conservative Party and the Farmers' Party, argued that from now on the state should stop constructing railways.

To proceed with the constructions further north, the state demanded that the landowners, unlike in other parts of the country would, without compensation, provide the state with the land needed for the railway. The state did not expect any returns on the railway capital invested here. The different county councils in the provinces also agreed to this, which confirmed the picture of the region as backward, with few vital economic areas.[9] The railway was considered a lever of growth, compensating the region for its less-advanced economic development. From the late nineteenth century, a dominating feature in railway policy was the increasing responsibility taken by the state to compensate for 'unfair' transport preconditions by providing state railways in regions lacking private enterprise or capital (Andersson-Skog 1993, pp. 39–43). The national consensus in parliament in these matters from time to time helped different regional interest groups to allocate investments, subsidies and other support to their specific region. Thus, the regional bias was closely related to compen-sating regions for economic disadvantages. In the case of northern Sweden, this also led to free-riding behaviour from other regions. This was the case in the period from 1895 to 1930, when agricultural freight from southern to northern Sweden was subsidized. The main actors behind this subsidy were the farmers and politicians from southern Sweden, using the regional images of northern Sweden to expand their markets (Pettersson 1999b, pp. 284–9).

Regional Railways and the National Industrialization Policy

Hence, when the parliament in 1886 took the decision to extend the railway network to the northern parts of the country, the members of parliament from northern Sweden played a crucial part in the outcome (Oredsson 1969, pp. 122, 141, 282–4). Regional mobilization, however, had begun much earlier. Already from 1866 regional and local railway interests had emerged in northern Sweden. Local railway committees were set up and railway rallies were organized in almost every town. Here, both local municipalities and regional political bodies, such as the county council in the province of Västernorrland, provided capital to investigate alternative railway investments (Godlund 1962, pp. 384–5). In 1872 a regional interest group including businessmen and politicians was established in Stockholm under the name 'Norrlands väl', (Benevolence for northern Sweden), to promote regional questions – especially investment in state railways. For a couple of years, they also published a journal, *Norrlands framtid* (The future of northern Sweden), in which the extension of the state railways was the main issue.[10] But even if the interest groups were active and had support from their home regions, the outcome would probably not have been so successful if they had not had an important ally: the section in the state railway agency responsible for the construction. At this time, the railway agency was a dual organization, with one body for operations and traffic, and one for tracks and construction. Since the latter had fulfilled the original railway plan, the organization was looking for a new task and here the extension of railways to northern Sweden was the primary objective. The evaluations of the future of the new lines, made by the two agency bodies, showed clear differences (Oredsson 1969, pp. 285–6).

As a result, from the mid-1880s to 1915, the national system of trunk lines was extended to northern Sweden. Here, the lack of private capital was an obstacle to local railway plans. Already in the 1820s, private foreign entrepreneurs had tried to exploit the rich iron-ore deposits in this part of northern Sweden, but failed because of the lack of sufficient transport facilities. New attempts were made in the 1850s and later on in the 1860s, when Norwegian entrepreneurs with English and Dutch capital tried to build a railway from the Gulf of Bothnia to the ore fields in Gällivare (Andersson 1988, pp. 99–101). In the 1880s, a new company, the Gellivare Railway Company Ltd, gained control over the ore fields and also obtained a concession for a railway to the Gulf of

Bothnia from the ore fields. In 1888 the construction was completed with British and Dutch capital. In all these ventures, local businessmen had played an important role in raising capital and take out mining concessions for the ore deposits. They were co-operating both with foreign capital interests and with mine owners from southern Sweden in the endeavour to create a new industry.[11] But at the same time this development had become of prime importance for Swedish industrialization. From a national horizon, it seemed probable that foreign interests would be able to exploit the Swedish ore deposits, and control an economically and militarily important part of the nation. At this time, the Swedish state intervened in the interest of the Swedish mining industry and regional competitors owning other ore deposits. On behalf of the state, a leading Swedish industrialist, K.A. Wallenberg, negotiated with the railway company to sell the railway to the state in 1890 (Jonsson 1969). In the hands of the state, railway investments continued, and in 1903 the Atlantic coast was reached. The lack of local and regional capital, and the fear of German or American ownership, made it important for the state to act in order to secure natural resources of national importance.[12] Here, as in the case of the northern trunk line, regional interests prevailed in parliament by supporting both the political and military arguments to construct the railway. The iron-ore railway soon became one of the most profitable lines in the state railway network.[13]

Yet, many of the railways built in northern Sweden would have been financed by private means had they been constructed in southern Sweden. Their importance in the national transport system was minor, and some of them were motivated by cultural and social reasons. During the interwar period, the state was engaged in constructing secondary and tertiary lines of regional and local importance only. This period ended in 1937 with the completion of 2000 kilometres of what was to be known as the 'culture railway'. It was an inland railway, parallel to the trunk line, intended to 'civilize the wilderness' – to integrate the self-subsistence economy in the sparsely populated interior of northern Sweden with the national market economy. The project had already started in 1912, as the governor in the province of Jämtland ordered the work to begin before the parliamentary decision was made.[14] During the 25 years of construction, the project was questioned several times by the government but not by parliament. The ideology of regional development here outran the economic motives as the basis for decision making. The statement made by the minister of finance in a parliamentary debate in 1924 can illustrate this. The minister claimed, and rightly so judging from the balance sheets, that: 'the income from the traffic on this line will hardly even pay for the oil needed for the locomotive'.[15] Therefore, he asked parliament to postpone the building process. At this time, as usual, parliament decided to continue the construction.[16]

One can say that the regional development motive was an accepted motive on the national scene. Generally, the railways were considered as a lever of growth, compensating northern Sweden for the less-advanced economic development. At the same time, the regional interests were fighting to get what they really wanted: secondary railway lines connecting the coastal cities with their economic hinterlands along the river valleys and the inland railway. Also at this time, the different county councils promoted regional railway investigations in an attempt to convince the railway agency to choose their area. During this period of subregional struggle, members of parliament for northern Sweden voted in favour of a continuation of the inland railway but they fought against one another in the case of the connecting lines.[17]

There was only one large private railway in northern Sweden during this period, the east coast railway. In 1876, the Governor of Västernorrland, Curry Treffenberg, argued that it was of great regional interest for the state to construct a railway between the flourishing industrial city of Sundsvall and its regional administrative centre 50 kilometres to the north, Härnösand.[18] The state railway agency investigated the issue, and turned it down in 1890 due to the construction work on the northern trunk line (Godlund 1962, p. 408). Only a few years later, one of the major private railways, Bergslagernas järnvägar, together with business partners in the Sundsvall area, opened a discussion concerning the possibilities of extending the private railway network to Sundsvall but the project was not realized.[19] In 1898, however, other regional actors obtained concessions to construct a railway between the industrial city and port of Gävle and Härnösand.

During the construction period, actors in the provinces north of Härnösand tried to take advantage of this private enterprise. In 1918, the county councils of the two most northern provinces conducted a full technical and economic investigation for an electrified coastal railway further north to the Finnish border. The plan was to persuade the state railway agency to connect a new line to the private east coast railway, creating a new regional transport system, linking saw mills and pulp plants along the coast closer together, and thereby increasing the production capacity and creating the advantages of scale. The plans were given to an official state committee, but the government rejected them. In the meantime, construction work at the east coast railway was not completed until 1927 due to difficulties in raising capital, the increasing labour costs, and scarcity of material during the First World War.[20] In 1933 the company also sought to be nationalized.

The owners had overestimated the demand for railway transport in the area. During the 1920s, a structural crisis hit both the saw mill and forest industries at large, forcing them to reorganize production. This reduced demand for railway transport considerably. Parallel to this, lorries and buses had taken over most of the expected passenger traffic and the small consignment of goods. The nationalization of the proud private enterprise seemed to herald the end of railway construction in northern Sweden and an early indication of the structural and institutional changes to come in the railway sector.

SUBSIDIZING THE COMPETITION-VULNERABLE MONOPOLY, 1939–1988

When the private network was nationalized between 1939 and 1952, a new institutional structure with a transport monopoly in the hands of the state was created. However, this was a monopoly under pressure from lorry and bus competition, and the changing demand for transport. The railway system itself was also polarized between heavily used and electrified trunk lines and the formerly private network, consisting of mostly lightly used, unprofitable lines with obsolete technology. The former body responsible for construction and tracks was also dissolved as a result of the completion of state railway construction in 1937.

Some of the support in parliament in favour of nationalization had to a large extent stemmed from regional concerns – this time from interest groups in central and southern Sweden (Alvfors 1977). The changing conditions in the transport market from 1920 on, had ruined large parts of the vast private network of railways. Nationalization was considered the only option to save the regional transport system and the economic viability of the municipalities in southern Sweden (Andersson-Skog 1993, p. 136).

Following nationalization, there was a change in railway policy. The poor profitability of the private railways became the problem of the railway agency in the postwar period. However, parliament decided to close down several nationalized railway lines in southern Sweden. A total of 25 per cent of the network was closed down. Since competition increased, this did not solve the problem. At the same time, the state started to modernize the railway administration, and imposed more businesslike reforms, such as market calculation on business lines, a new book-keeping system and a more rigorous interest obligation. The result was an increasing deficit in railway operations from 1950 (Andersson-Skog 1993).

From 1937 to the late 1980s, no new railways were built. This does not imply that the regional bias in the policy was abandoned. However, its objectives had changed. This was in accordance with the new Traffic Policy Act passed by parliament in 1963, giving the state explicit social, economic and political responsibility for maintaining transport facilities in general at a comparable standard all over Sweden (ibid. 1993, pp. 138ff.). The regional efforts in parliament during the 1960s and 1970s were aimed at upholding this policy. For the first time ever, railway operation was now being subsidized. Between

1958 and 1988, railway operation became a social responsibility, and all political parties in parliament were unanimous in voting to maintain railway subsidies.

During this period the railways in northern Sweden had little success. But in contrast to the rest of Sweden, no lines were closed down and traffic services were maintained in this region, despite the severe economic losses. The idea of a coastal railway in northern Sweden was not abandoned by the regional interest groups. New railways were still considered to be of great importance for the economic development in the region. A number of official state investigations were also made which indicate that regional interests had succeeded in highlighting the issue even through the dark ages of the railway system. In 1944 the governors in Umeå and Härnösand met to discuss a railway link between Örnsköldsvik and Umeå (Godlund 1962, p. 409). Both in 1944 and 1945, bills were presented in parliament requesting an investigation into the possibilities of extending the nationalized coastal railway to the Finnish border.[21] The issue was passed on to an official state committee, whose mandate was to find solutions to a number of 'northern Swedish issues'. This committee in its turn handed the question to yet another committee, who were investigating the need for better transport in northern Sweden, and they calculated that the cost of a railway from Sundsvall to the Finnish boarder would be extremely expensive. Hence, their conclusion was that there were no strong economic arguments for a new coastal railway, running parallel to the already existing trunk line, and the subject lapsed until the 1980s.[22].

Regional Mobilization and a Changing Economy after 1940

In the 1940s a new regional movement was making itself heard. It had its beginnings in 1941, in an annual convention, the so-called *Härnömässan*, renamed the *Norrlandsmässan* from 1949. From then on, the convention was held in turn in different cities in the region. The initiators were regional businessmen and industrialists, together with regional state officials and engineering organizations all over northern Sweden.[23] The importance that the state accorded the conventions may be evidenced by the presence of a minister, often as keynote speaker, at each one. The most frequent attendees were the minister of transport and communication, and the minister of industry.[24]

The purpose of the conventions was to discuss the future of the region following the structural changes in most raw material industries in the region. However, the regional elite also shared the fear that the state would lose interest in supporting the economic development in the region.[25] They still considered the regional problems to be the long distances, the few urban areas, and the lack of good transportation.

In 1946, the author Albert Wiksten and Mrs Ingeborg Hedberg, married to one of the leading merchants in the Örnsköldsvik area, started to organize a more formal league to promote culture, economy and 'the regional spirit' in northern Sweden.[26] As a result, in 1952, Norrlandsförbundet (Norrland League), was established in Luleå. The League acquired a regional periodical from 1928, now renamed *Norrländsk tidskrift*, (Journal of northern Sweden).[27] Members included individuals, local political entities, such as the municipality administrations, and regional state officials. At its height, in the late 1950s and early 1960, the organization had almost 20 000 members.[28]

From the start the League was intended to function as a lobby organization towards the state. In 1950, the county councils in the four most northern provinces had joined together in a delegation of co-operation to further common regional views and issues in parliament. The most important part of the work was to create meetings on a regular basis between the governors, other regional state officials and members of parliament from northern Sweden. There were also obvious personal connections between the League and the delegation. The Chairman of the League, Chief Executive Officer Harry Ramqvist, served as secretary in the meetings. At these meetings, they discussed different important topics and agreed on strategies to be used in parliament as well as in other public arenas. [29]

Two major issues dominated the actions of these interrelated regional interest groups during the 1950s and 1960s: the need for better transport facilities in general and the importance of establishing a university in northern Sweden. In both cases, the arguments were similar to those earlier proved useful in railway matters: the conditions in northern Sweden have been unfavourable to the development of the regional economy. The problems were the long distances, high unemployment and a low proportion of the workforce with university education, the general lack of capital and a century-long exploitation of natural resources with only a fraction of the profits reinvested.[30] Better transportation facilities and access to higher education in the region were vital in order to alter the path of development. At the same time, the struggle for the location of the university strained the relations between the cities in the delegation. Nevertheless, the arguments towards the state did not change: the regional future depended on better transport facilities and other infrastructural investments.

THE RENAISSANCE OF REGIONAL RAILWAY INTEREST AFTER 1988

Two major changes occurred in the railway sector during the 1980s. First, railway technology improved. High-speed trains made railways competitive with cars on distances between 50 and 500 kilometres. At the same time a new institutional framework was established in the railway sector. It was fundamentally changed in two important respects. First, the former centralized state railway agency was divided into two separate organizations: the old state agency was now restricted to operating the network in competition with other operators; and a new agency, Banverket, was founded. Banverket was given the overall responsibility for railways in Sweden. The overriding objective was to provide a safe infrastructure for railway operators with due consideration to the environment and regional balance.

The organization was decentralized in five track regions, each responsible in its geographical area for playing an active role in community planning, maintaining track and investigating, proposing and constructing new railways. At the same time, the extension of the traffic and timetable outside the most profitable, national trunk lines was to be decided upon and paid for by regional and provincial political and administrative bodies.[31] An exception from the national system was made for the inland and the iron ore railways, where the operation and track responsibility was given to regional organizations. The inland railway consisted of the municipalities along the line, and the line was leased to regional private entrepreneurs. Even here, additional investments were made by the state to raise the technical standard to the requirements of good transports. A special subsidy was also given.[32] In the case of the iron-ore railway, the mining company formed a railway organization together with the railway agency, and acquired operational responsibility for the line.

This meant that a new dual system, similar to that in the period up to 1939, was created. The difference was that this time the dividing line was horizontal, not vertical: after 1988 the state owned all the track, but traffic was divided among state and private operators, in contrast to the pre-1939 period, when the various operators owned their own track and managed the operation on the lines. To some extent, this also made the prerequisites for interest group actions more similar to those before 1939.

During the classical railway period, the national industrialization policy in itself helped transform the content of railway policy into a pattern whereby railways were to compensate for regional economic shortcomings. Regional claims could thereby gain legitimacy by applying to an overall accepted ideology of economic growth and regional equality. Here the possibility of regional cross-subsidization over time is obvious and was also used. In the period between 1939 and 1988, it was harder for regional interests to make themselves heard. The changing economic structure made investments in roads more desirable, and railway investments decreased abruptly. Together with the stricter economic obligations for the railway agency, this made it difficult to promote new investments.

From 1989, however, the regional bias was reinforced once again, this time helped by the decentralized institutional structure in the railway sector and the new national growth-oriented policy. This helped create a new era of regional railway mania in Sweden. During the 1980s, the question of an extended coastal railway in northern Sweden was raised from time to time in parliament. As a result, in 1987, a special state report concerning the state of the transport system in northern Sweden was initiated. The question of the coastal railway was discussed but again rejected.[33] This once more drew attention to the railway interest groups from northern Sweden and it is against this backdrop that the case of the Bothnia railway is to be explored further.

Interest Groups and the Quest for the Bothnia Railway, 1989–1999

In order to comprehend the growing regional mobilization, some economic structural changes need to be emphasized. As mentioned earlier, the dominating export industry was from the 1960s paralleled by a growing public sector in administration, health care and education (Andersson-Skog and Bäcklund 1992, pp. 95–8). Of major importance was that a university was allocated to Umeå in the middle of the 1960s.[34] One of the major arguments behind its establishment was regional development. Simultaneously, the university hospital became a teaching hospital with extensive research funds. As a consequence, local expansion was rapid, and Umeå grew with it. In 30 years, the population more than trebled from 32 000 to roughly 105 000 inhabitants.[35] This remarkable growth made Umeå the largest city in northern Sweden. This expansion of an 'intellectual Klondike', together with a growing number of highly educated employees at the hospital and the university, brought with it the emergence of new regional interest groups centred around the idea of a new high-speed railway in the 1980s.

However, the former regional identity related to long distances and an economic structure lagging behind that of the rest of Sweden prevailed. This was caused by the rapidly declining population in the interior of northern Sweden from the 1960s on. Now, though, regional mobilization grew apace, and gathered around the slogan: 'We won't migrate'. The Norrland League was an important actor during this period, enlightening different political bodies about the severe problems faced by northern Sweden. One result of this process, however, was a concentration of the population in the coastal cities. This increased the economic differences between the inland and the coastal areas and reinforced the disadvantages of long distances at a subregional level.

In 1991, a new regional interest group was founded, the Botniaakademin (Bothnia Academy). The purpose of the Bothnia Academy was to increase knowledge and information about the so-called Bothnia region. This was a 'virtual' subregion created by the Academy, crossing administrative borders, and consisting of the two most northern provinces and Örnsköldsvik. The formation of the region derived from an old administrative principle of division from the sixteenth century, and at its heart were the cities of Örnsköldsvik and Umeå.

The Academy consisted of university people, regional state officials and businesspeople. Here the old elite joined forces with the new, such as professors, deans, chief administrators, doctors and so on. It is worth noting that the first chairman was Carl Kempe, the fourth generation of an old family of industrial capitalists in the forest industry whose company had most enthusiastically promoted the question of a new railway since the 1950s.

The Academy's fields of action were all related to scientific knowledge. One of the main objectives was to create a subregional consciousness or identity. A first achievement was to publish a newly written history textbook about the Bothnia region. The authors were all distinguished members of different departments of the university, and one of the editors was formerly the president of the university. In this book, the specific character of the economy, history and ethnic features in this part of northern Sweden was highlighted (Edlund and Beckman (eds) 1994). The group behind the Academy were also the prime movers behind the production of a regional encyclopaedia in four volumes, published in the early 1990s. One of the entries in the first volume was for the Bothnia railway, even though the railway itself did not in fact exist (*Norrländsk uppslagsbok* 1993).

An important motive behind the creation of the new region and the Academy, was to promote the construction of a coastal railway to Umeå. In this quest, the Academy co-operated with another regional interest group established in 1989, the Botniabanegruppen (Bothnia railway group). The organization consisted of businesspeople, politicians and industrialists from the Bothnia area. The idea of a high-speed Bothnia railway was first presented to the state in 1989. The Botniabanegruppen presented a cost–benefit analyses, showing what positive effects on regional development the railway would have. The main regional argument was that labour markets in the cities along the coast were considered complementary; whereas the labour markets in Örnsköldsvik and Sundsvall were dominated by manufacturing and processing industries, Umeå was dominated by teaching, research, service production, health services and administration. They also constituted gendered labour markets. A high-speed railway could increase integration by cutting travel time and thus making it possible for female workers to travel to Umeå and for male workers to travel from Umeå to the other cities to get jobs.[36]

However, during the autumn of 1990, the Banverket central headquarters decided in consultation with the regions concerned, to make a cost–benefit analysis of the railway line for the national planning period, 1994–2003. The material used was from the Botniabanegruppen's analysis of a year earlier.[37] The result showed that the railway line should be considered as one of a number of possible projects listed in the investment plan for the period in question. A national railway lobby organization, Rail Forum, initiated by ASEA/ABB, had also made investigations. In their plan for a new, national system of high-speed railways in 1992, the Bothnia railway was considered to be the least profitable. If an area of 30 sq km around each station was considered to be the catchment area for passenger traffic, then the most populated lines had figures of 2000 to 2500 inhabitants per sq km. The corresponding number for the Bothnia railway was only 900. The recommendation from Rail Forum was that other aspects had to be considered here, such as regional integration (Andersson 1992, p. 29). However, no such measures were yet taken by the state.

In order to strengthen the argument, and to show the importance of the Bothnia railway in promoting the economic and cultural development in the area, two professors (in political science and the history of ideas and both members of the Bothnia Academy), edited a book which focused on the need to create regional integration in northern Sweden in general but especially in the Bothnia region (Gidlund and Sörlin 1992). The different chapters in the book were presented at an international conference on European peripheries, held during the World Exhibition in Seville, in July 1992. To make the regional elite in the Bothnia area aware of the new, more scientific approach, the conference was scheduled at the same time as a major regional exhibition presenting various aspects of business life, education and research in northern Sweden. The minister of labour, also responsible for regional policy, was a keynote speaker at the conference.

At university level, the consultant who made the first cost–benefit analysis in 1989 was appointed to the university board. The influence from the Bothnia Academy was strong, since Carl Kempe at the same time presided as chairman for the board. The president of the university also made several statements indicating that the role of the university as a regional growth pole was intimately related to the success or failure of the Bothnia railway. Representatives from the Bothnia region acted forcefully in parliament to further the issue. One of the members of the Botniabanegruppen was also a member of parliament and of the special committee for traffic and transport questions.

In 1992/93, the government presented a proposition of planned infrastructure investments during the decade to come – 'the decade of infrastructure'.[38] The importance of an extended coastal railway in northern Sweden for the regional economy was mentioned explicitly. The government especially emphasized the most southern part, just outside of Sundsvall, and connecting to the already existing high-speed line.[39] Parliament discussed the proposition and gave high priority to the Bothnia railway. However, the final decision of how to proceed was left to the discretion of Banverket. Already the decision to include the Bothnia railway as one of many in the long-term investment plan had spurred the subregional race for investment allocation. In a report from the Governor of Jämtland in 1993, it was stated that if the Bothnia railway was built, the interior of northern Sweden would need considerable investment in order to maintain the regional balance between the coast and the inland areas.[40] The

Norrland League contradicted this view. The League was of the opinion that a railway along the coast would be of benefit even for the inland areas.[41] Parliament also stated that a special investigation was to be made about the economic and societal effects of the investment. [42] The report came in 1996, and showed that the expected revenues and the estimated regional effects on the economy were highly overvalued or at best uncertain. The conclusion was that there were insufficient grounds to start the project.[43] The same year, however, a new traffic policy act was passed, emphasizing a broad variety of regional, social and environmental goals that the transport system should fulfil. Here it was stated that the Bothnia railway was vital in the national railway system.[44]

The government presented a bill, which was accepted in parliament in winter 1996/97.[45] A railway company, Botniabanan AB, jointly owned by the municipalities and the state, was established to undertake the construction project. The decision in parliament in 1997, to grant funds for the investment between Örnsköldsvik and Umeå, the most northern part of the line, was taken in an era of increasing growth expectations. In parliament, regional actors dominated the debate. Between 1988 and 1998, 47 motions for the Bothnia railway were submitted. Of them, almost 75 per cent came from regional actors from all parties. A common theme was once more the conviction that the railway would create growth in the region.[46]

But another strong regional actor has also emerged since the late 1980s. With the decentralized agency structure, the regional administration in Banverket also became an important self-governed agent furthering the railway interests of northern Sweden. Banverket made several cost–benefit analyses and co-operated closely with the Botniabanegruppen.[47] As in the 1880s, the structure of the railway administration proved fruitful for a successful community of interest between the regional groups from northern Sweden and parts of the railway organization.

CONCLUDING REMARKS

In a time span of more than one hundred years, railway interests from northern Sweden have been very successful in their attempts to allocate resources to the region. A major explanation is the successful vindication of the regional identity in the context of the national political system, where the railway policy was based on a consensus of the importance of regional equity and the responsibility of the state to construct and operate the needed railways. Even at times when local competition over resources has been present, regional actors have often been able to join forces in parliament.

Of major importance has been the way regional interests have succeeded in adjusting to the railway policy and the degree of regional mobilization for a certain strategy. The Bothnia railway can illustrate this. From the 1940s to the late 1980s, investments in the railway sector as a whole decreased radically, and no new railways were built. References to the regional identity proved fruitful in other areas, and also helped to mobilize different actors in the region. During the late 1980s and 1990s, the arguments were conspicuously similar to those at the beginning of the twentieth century: the railway would further the economic integration in the local economy. This time it was a feasible argument. The success was related to with the regional activity all over Europe during the early 1990s, making it generally easier to gain regional investments. A powerful political regional mobilization together with visions of a new, national railway technology, rather than the contents of the railway policy, are the major factors behind the success of the project.

One vital regional interest was this time to be found in the railway administration in northern Sweden. The decentralization of the railway agency in 1988 created strong incentives as well as opportunities for the regional administration to co-operate with regional interest groups. It is also obvious that the Bothnia Academy was of importance. The Academy tried (and to some extent succeeded), to create a new subregional identity that was used to mobilize the local elite in the quest for a new railway. Yet, the new identity did not differ in any significant aspects from the traditional one: the same obstacles had to be overcome: distance, the natural environment and so on. But some distinctive features can be highlighted. First, with the co-operation and personal liaisons between the Bothnia Academy and the Bothnia railway group, a new alliance was established between old industrial capital mainly from Örnsköldsvik and new 'human capital' from Umeå. This opens the way for future projects, different from the traditional defence of the region. Other subregional actors noticed the innovation. Second, for the first time an outspoken distinction was made in the arguments concerning the future of the inland and the coastal areas. Here, the growth of the coastal areas was expressly stated as a precondition for the survival of the non-urban areas with a more traditional economic structure. This could be the first sign of a geographical division of the old strategy. In the future perhaps the coastal areas will not need to refer to archaic regional features to reallocate resources, while this will be even more important for the interior of northern Sweden. However, established attitudes and values are hard to abandon. In a recent survey, mapping out the preferences of the elite in the Bothnia area, 78 per cent considered the extension of the Bothnia railway to the Finnish border as the most vital project for the future regional development (Gidlund et al. 2000, p. 15).

Here it may be emphasized that the impact of regional interest groups is not an issue that is specific to Swedish development, but rather a delicate political matter in most European countries where regional planning has become an important element of economic policy. The magnitude of the regional influence on political and economic behaviour is indicated by the size of the European Union's regional funds. This implies that regional mobilization and the actions of regional interest groups in the political system will continue to be of vital interest in the further development of the European economy as well as for the research agenda in economic history.

NOTES

1. Value added tax is excluded from this sum. If included, the investment cost will be about SEK 10.7 billion.
2. *Ostkustbanekommitténs betänkande* (1922); SOU (1946:84); Ds K 1987:14, *Norrlandstrafiken*; SOU (1996:95). This opinion was shared by, for instance, the geographer Sven Godlund (1962).
3. For an alternative interpretation of the nature of Swedish interest organizations, see the comparison of Swedish and British unions made by Douglas (1992).
4. Hodne does not discuss regional consciousness since he focuses on voting behaviour *per se*. The outcome, however, indicates another regional dividing ground, namely pre-modern and modern characteristics.
5. At the beginning of the twentieth century there were only ten towns with more than 1000 inhabitants (Andersson-Skog and Bäcklund 1992, p. 77).
6. For a more detailed description of the local conditions, see Andersson-Skog and Bäcklund (1992). This picture can be modified, though. The most striking example of an alternative identity is that of the Sami people, the original inhabitants of Sweden. Since their interests have been suppressed and ignored in the formation of the industrialized Swedish economy, this complication can be ignored in this chapter.
7. In 1860 the regional administrative structure was radically altered. Locally, new municipalities were created and on the regional level county councils were given the responsibility for promoting regional development. The most important task was to handle the increasing poverty in rural areas, but health services, education and public transportation were also major tasks. Between 1862 and 1887, an average of 16–20 per cent of the county councils' budgets in all of Sweden was dedicated to traffic investigations for railways (Wikstrand 1987, p. 27).
8. This paragraph builds mainly on Andersson-Skog (1993).
9. *Statens Järnvägar 50 år. 1856–1906* (1906).
10. The organization also established a journal, *The Future of Norrland*, but it survived only a few years. Most of the articles advocated railways for northern Sweden. Documents from the archive of the Norrland League (Norrlands förbundets arkiv).
11. For a discussion, see Axelsson (1964).
12. See Jonsson (1969) for a discussion of the foreign threat.
13. The importance for regional development had already been recognized by Heckscher (1907) in his thesis. There he pointed out that the railway had led to an 'American development', creating a whole new society out of nothing within a couple of years (Heckscher 1907, p. 93).
14. *Statens Järnvägar 75 år. 1906–1931* (1931, pp. 90ff.).
15. *Statens Järnvägar 75 år. 1906–1931* (1931, p. 306).
16. Of the railway motions concerning the inland railway until 1930, 75 per cent of the motions were approved of. This should be compared with the average approval rate of 25 per cent of railway motions during the same period. See SOU (1924:30, p. 355), and Andersson-Skog (1993, pp. 186–7).
17. *Statens Järnvägar 75 år, 1906–1931* (1931, pp. 300–312).
18. BiSOS Landshövdingeberättelser. Västernorrlands län 1876–1880.
19. Ibid. This was also partly due to the fact that a private railway of that magnitude would create a national railway in private hands, which the state opposed (Andersson-Skog 1993).
20. SOU (1933:13).

21. Motion AK 1944:126, given by Skoglund and Mähler (1994).
22. SOU (1946:84). In 1957, however, a part of the attempted railway was realized when the industries in the Örnsköldviks area built an industrial railway, Örnsköldsvik-Gullänget, between two local industrial plants (Granqvist 1971, pp. 8–9).
23. Documents from Norrlandsförbundets arkiv, Sundsvall.
24. Correspondence from Norrlandsförbundets arkiv, Sundsvall.
25. Härnömässan 1941, Norrlandsförbundets arkiv, Sundsvall.
26. Correspondence and protocols from Norrlandsförbundets arkiv, Sundsvall.
27. The first edition had already been printed before the meeting in Luleå. See *Norrländsk tidskrift*, no. 1, 1952.
28. Annual report from Norrlandsförbundet, Norrlandsförbundets arkiv, Sundsvall.
29. Protocol from Landstingens samarbetsdelegation, Norrlandsförbundets akiv, Sundsvall.
30. Tekniska föreningens årsredogörelse, Härnösand 1947, Norrlandsförbundets arkiv, Sundsvall.
31. Since 1999, these bodies have co-operated under the control of a new national authority, Rikstrafiken.
32. See *Riksdagens revisorers förslag angående Inlandsbanan, Förslag till riksdagen 1995/96:RR4*, pp. 34, 68, 73.
33. *Ds:K 1987:14 Norrlandstrafiken.*
34. The importance of one man can hardly be overestimated for this outcome: Minister of Transport Gösta Skoglund, born in northern Sweden.
35. *SOS Folkräkningen 1960, Umeå kommuns årsstatistik* 1998.
36. This idea is developed most explicitly in a text by Stellan Lundberg (1992). Lundberg was also the consultant who made the first cost–benefit analysis.
37. *Botniabanan – en samhällsekonomisk bedömning*, Förstudie, December 1991. Banverket, p. 1.
38. Proposition 1992/1993:176, Riksdagstryck.
39. Proposition 1992/1993:176, Riksdagstryck.
40. *Framtida järnvägsinvesteringar ur ett inlandsperspektiv* (1993, p. 3). See also the arguments for another new railway in northern Sweden in Westlund (1993).
41. *Kommunikationerna i Norrland måste bli bättre*, Norrlandsförbundet, no printing year available, Norrlandsförbundets archive.
42. Betänkande 92/93:TU635, Riksdagstryck.
43. SOU (1996:95, pp. 10–11).
44. SOU (1996:26).
45. Proposition 1996/1997:53 *Infrastrukturinriktning för framtida transporter.*
46. Bills 1987/1988–1997/98, Riksdagstryck.
47. Except the first one from 1991, Banverket have made 15 different investigations of various sections of the line.

9. The state and regulatory orders in early European civil aviation

Jan Ottosson

INTRODUCTION

Recently, there has been growing interest concerning the interaction between the state and regulation of the new technologies. Economic theory in the neo-classical sense has, however, not been especially helpful in providing answers to important questions regarding why the state initiates or changes its policy towards new technology. Two main analytical traditions concerning the role and function of the state in the shaping of regulatory orders have dominated the discussion. The positive school emphasizes the state as the guardian of public interest, while the older versions of the normative school saw the state as captured by interest groups (Dixit 1996). However, the interrelation between the state and interest groups has lately been a matter for some discussion by social scientists, critical to the older static analysis of interest groups introduced by Olson (1965, 1982). In the recent discussion regarding the function of interest groups, the importance of 'defining moments' or 'windows of opportunity' has been emphasized (Johnson and Libecap 1998). The possibility of interest groups acting in political situations characterized by uncertainty and crises has been of special interest. In this respect, the learning behavior of politicians facing a new situation has recently attracted the attention of political economists (Jonung 1999).

In this chapter I shall address the question why European states choose to regulate, intervene, and subsidize new technology and new industries in different ways. I shall concentrate mainly on two forms of state involvement in this respect: subsidies and the question of state ownership (Millward and Singleton 1995; Foreman-Peck and Millward 1994; Goldin and Libecap 1994). By doing so, it will be possible to further interpret the windows of opportunity and the role of interest groups versus politicians in these respects. By using the example of early civil aviation in Europe, with special emphasis on the Swedish case, I shall first argue that the various patterns of state involvement can be considered neither as a case of market failure only, nor as an example of interest group actions only.[1]

Second, the different ways actors created and acted upon ideas of the role of the state in a new means of transport show that the initial position of state involvement was not a clear-cut matter. The Swedish case of early civil aviation shows a complex web of actors and entrepreneurs interacting with the state in the process of building new institutional settings. Also, the subsequent changes of state involvement require more discussion of the learning processes involved in the interaction between politicians and private actors.[2] I suggest that patterns of state intervention in one country can be traced to institutional arrangements in other sectors. Also, such state intervention patterns were inspired by the development in other countries. Both these issues suggest that a more dynamic approach will be beneficial for explaining various responses among politicians and private actors towards the art of commercial flying.

EARLY CIVIL AVIATION IN EUROPE

The comparatively young civil aviation industry had passed through several stages of regulation and state ownership before the recent deregulatory development. As aviation historian Peter Lyth remarks, one of the most advanced technologies in commercial use has also been one of the most regulated industries.

After the First World War, commercial civil aviation started in several countries in Western Europe and in the US. As in other network industries, with the most important example given by the railroads, the state took a variety of positions regarding its function (Dobbin 1994, chapter 4, this volume; Dunlavy 1994a; chapter 3, this volume).

The early 1920s is a somewhat neglected period of civil aviation. In several countries there was a short era of 'freedom in the air' directly after the First World War. This raises several important topics regarding the nature and the development of regulatory orders. Since the industry started within a few years in several countries, it makes an especially interesting case study to explore differences in policies chosen by the different governments in Western Europe. The period during the first part of the 1920s also opens up a discussion of why different states chose various strategies towards this new means of transportation, and the subsequent change in these policies.

Since the birth of the new technology, the relationships between the state and the early aviators was quite complex. In most countries, various sections of the state bureaucracy showed an active interest in the new means of transportation, for example, the Post Office and the military. The connections between the military and the forerunners of the aeroplane were close, since airships and balloons were used by the military early on. Aviation enthusiasts were not only military men. Engineers and mechanics were also thrilled by the new opportunities of transport. Also, businessmen not afraid of high-risk investments could be found among the pioneers. Politicians showed various degrees of interest, ranging from a hesitancy to fanaticism.

Aviation developed rapidly after the Wright brothers challenged the old 'lighter than air' principle. In the early 1910s, a number of daring flyers performed flying shows, breaking new records in flying time, speed and altitude. In Germany, the first civil aviation company, DELAG, Deutsche Luftschiffahrt A.G. ran regular, scheduled airship services between 1911 and 1913. The final outcome between the two technologies, manifested in airplanes and airships, was still an open question in the 1910s.

Innovative efforts by aviators such as Henri Farman, the Wright brothers, and others showed some similarities. In most cases, the early aviation industry was closely connected with flying schools, private entrepreneurs, and aviators. In Europe, associations such as the Aero Club de France were important in forming informal institutions (rules of the game) regarding certificates and demands on the pilot as well as rudimentary security rules. These associations played an important role in early aviation before 1914 in creating norms and rules. They also served as a platform in the early formation of civil air law and initiated conferences regarding multilateral and bilateral agreements in air law.

The outbreak of the First World War changed the scene completely. The new technology of flying was soon used in the war theatres and technological development boomed. After the armistice in November 1918 a new generation of military pilots became unemployed. Also, the aviation industry soon showed serious structural problems. As a result of overcapacity, military suppliers became bankrupt throughout Europe. In several countries new strategies to stay in business were developed by the aviation industry. One business opportunity was the emerging interest in civil aviation, thus creating a demand both for pilots and airplanes. Consequently, in a number of European countries the first phase of civil aviation took off.[3]

The experiences gained during the First World War were crucial in several respects in the development of the interwar civil aviation airlines. Technology and engineering skills had improved dramatically during the war, as well as the political insights of the importance and the potential of aviation, both for military purposes and for civil purposes in peacetime.

During the interwar period, several commercial airlines in Europe were national, mostly state-owned air carriers, operating under the principles of national air sovereignty.[4] In the mid-1920s, the largest companies were found in England (Imperial Airways), the Netherlands (KLM), Germany (Deutsche Lufthansa, which was restricted in its operations by the terms of the Versailles Treaty) and France.[5] For England, the Netherlands and France, improved and faster transport routes to their respective colonies was an important factor in promoting financial support from their states (Germany was an exception).[6]

Among the smaller European states, the Nordic countries faced somewhat diverging experiences regarding the development of the first airlines. Denmark, together with Sweden, had an early tradition in flying. Denmark's Det Danske Luftfartselskab (DDL) started in October 1918, and was one of the first airlines in Europe (Buraas 1972, p. 20). Norway, on the other hand, did not have a national regular airline service until 1935, run by Det Norske Luftfartsselskap (DNL), founded in 1927. Earlier attempts had soon floundered (Buraas 1972, p. 20). One such example, the company Det Norske Luftfartrederi which was founded in 1918, survived only a few years and was originally backed by Norwegian shipowners.[7] *Aero OY*, Finland's first regular airline service of some significance, started in 1923 as part of the strategy of the German aviation industry empire of Hugo Junkers to create seemingly nationally controlled airline companies around Europe. Instead, the discreetly German-controlled civil aviation companies were founded in order to create a civil market after the war (Böhme 1982, p. 92).

One of the most pertinent problems of the civilian air transport after 1918 was to ensure sufficient revenues. Since the planes could carry only a small number of passengers, air mail became a strategic question. Therefore, relations between national post offices, governments, the aviation industry and the military were important in determining the policies towards the new industry. One of the most important questions raised early on concerned subsidies, for example, the amount of the subsidy, how many companies could benefit from it, and according to what principles it should be granted to the companies. Another one was related to ownership: should the new companies be private, partly state owned, or fully state owned? From the start, the position of the state towards this new means of transportation was already quite complex.

In contrast to the later development in civil aviation, the early period was characterized more by liberal solutions. Later on, state involvement became much more pronounced, in terms of the amount of regulation, the degree of state ownership, and the subsidies given.

BRITAIN

In Britain, the first companies began operating in 1919, after a government decision in April the same year to allow civil air transport companies to apply for concessions. Several private airlines were established, for example, AV Roe & Company, Aircraft Transport and Travel (1919), Handley Page Transport Ltd, Instone Airlines, Daimler Airways (1922), British Aerial Transport

Company, and British Marine Air Navigation (BMAN). The pioneer companies often began regular flight services using slightly modified bombers. Therefore, passenger comfort and safety was rather rudimentary, a fact which, together with relatively high prices, resulted in low passenger density during the first years of regular services. The route over the channel to Paris was especially popular and the most competitive among the new companies.

The British government was initially hesitant about air transportation, despite the Weir Committee's recommendation to support the new companies through subsidies (Lyth 1993; Birkhead 1958). The first reaction to giving subsidies to the first airline companies was indeed hostile, perhaps best formulated by Winston Churchill in 1920, when he stated that the new companies should 'fly by themselves'. Several of the newly started private companies became bankrupt in 1921 as a result of the harsh economic conditions in the economy after the war, and the problematic situation with insufficient revenues relative to the cost structure of the companies.

On 19 March 1921, the British government suddenly reversed its earlier policy and gave subsidies to three companies after a report from the Cross-channel Subsidies Committee. The reason behind this change seems to have been the rapid developments in France and the Netherlands, where the governments contributed large subsidies. National interests were at stake, since the British government decided that it was also important to allow British companies to fly over the Channel to the continent. At this stage, several competing firms were given subsidies. The three companies, together with the newly founded Daimler Airways (1922), were the subject of discussion in 1923. The Hambling Committee argued that the four companies would benefit from a merger.[8] The resulting large company was still privately owned. The government owned deferred shares and the right to appoint two directors on the board. The new company, Imperial Airways, became a privately owned monopoly which was granted state subsidies, starting its operations in 1924. The British government thus had its own 'chosen instrument' in civil aviation.

FRANCE

The French government showed a more direct interest in the civil aviation industry. This interest manifested itself in large subsidies to a number of privately owned companies. In January 1920, the French government created an Under-secretariat of State for Aeronautics and Aerial Transportation. During the first years after the First World War, eight private companies set up in business.[9] Some of the largest of these companies during the 1920s were Aéropostale, Air Union, and S.G.T.A.

The decade saw a rapidly developing advancing industry, due to determined state support. The subsidies in France were among the highest in Europe at the time.[10] The situation with several competing privately owned airlines receiving subsidies ended in 1932, with new contracts and a 25 percent state ownership in subsidized companies. The following year, Air France started its operations after a merger process initiated by the state. The French state owned 25 percent of the shares up to 1939 (Lissitzyn 1942, p. 116).

GERMANY

Despite the chaotic political and economic situation in late 1918, the German state was actively promoting civil aviation. However, the 1920 Treaty of Versailles raised several obstacles for the German aviation industry by limiting the capacity of aeroplane production as well as limiting the opportunities for flying. On a central level, the German policy was liberal in the sense that it permitted several private or semi-private aviation firms to fly to various destinations. The first German aviation company given permission to fly in January 1919 was Deutsche Luftredeeri. The company began operating between Berlin and Weimar in February the same year. The three main owners of the Luftredeeri represented various interests in the syndicate: AEG, Zeppelin, and the Hamburg-Amerika-Line (HAPAG).[11]

Another important company in this period was Lloyd Luftdienst, consisting of six companies, one of its principal owners was a shipping line. Another serious competitor was Aero-Union. In 1924, Lloyd Luftdienst and Aero-Union merged into a new company, Deutscher Aero-Lloyd. A further group of aviation companies was formed around the German firm Junkers, which had been made vulnerable at the end of the war, with large unsold stocks, and by the treaty of Versailles. The strategy chosen by Junkers was international expansion. Through various methods Junkers was able to start manufacturing and exporting aeroplanes, for example, the Junkers F-13, while not formally breaking the treaty. The Junker Company concentrated its efforts towards Scandinavia, Eastern Europe and the Baltic states.

Germany's positive interest in flying and civil aviation was shown in the subsidy program given to the first flying companies. Both regional and local governments also supported the aviation companies with various subsidies.

However, the liberal attitude towards the early aviation companies changed drastically in 1925. That year the German government took over 80 percent of the shares in Junkers, due to a severe economic crisis in the company. The year after, in 1926, the German state merged Junkers and Aero-Lloyd, resulting in Deutsche Lufthansa. In this company, the German state owned a substantial part of the shares. Together, the state, regions and private interests owned the bulk of the shares. However, public ownership was substantial, due to the fact that a number of regional companies with shares in Lufthansa were owned by the regional states in Germany. Also, several of the private companies owning shares were state owned. In reality, therefore, the German state had considerable influence in the new company. Lufthansa now became the 'chosen instrument' of the Weimar Republic.

THE SWEDISH CASE

In the case of Swedish civil aviation, the state adopted several different positions towards state ownership, from a liberal phase towards direct state ownership, but finally sharing ownership with the other Scandinavian states as well as private owners through the formation of the airline company SAS (Scandinavian Airlines System) in 1946. In early civil aviation both airports as well as civil aviation companies were private, a situation that would soon be changed since several airports became publicly owned, either by the state or by the local municipality. The Swedish parliament and government were fairly passive during the first decade of the emerging technology, which appeared in Sweden for the first time in 1909. The Swedish Aeronautical Association (Svenska Aeronautiska Sällskapet), which was founded in the year 1900, promoted early airships and balloons. This society was the most important body in advancing the interest in the art of aviation, and later on, the regulation of its technology.[12]

The Aeronautical Association was also important in promoting and initiating the first legislation regarding air traffic in Sweden, as well as in initiating Scandinavian co-operation regarding air traffic regulations in 1918. The small group of key people in this association were also appointed to sit on various state committees, which initiated the first legislation. Important actors in this respect were those behind the first airplane industries: engineers, entrepreneurs, and military officers trying to start regular airline companies.[13] It was not until the early 1920s that Sweden approved the first civil aviation legislation. The model of maritime transportation influenced key parts of the governance structure. In maritime transport, harbors were owned by the state, and the shipping companies run by private entrepreneurs, in the Swedish case with significant subsidies. Another important part of this new legislation was the creation of the first forerunner of a state agency, dedicated to the regulation and monitoring of Swedish civil aviation. As discussed above, these duties were performed for well over a century by a private association. This association was also deeply involved in the design of the new agency.

Another important aspect concerns the active role of other state agencies in the development of the new means of transportion. Two state agencies, the Swedish Post Office and the National Board of Water Power, were crucial in promoting early Swedish aviation. The Swedish Post Master General was interested in flying, and knew the leading Swedish pioneers of the period; he early became a keen ambassador of aviation, by subsidizing civil aviation companies through generous airmail rates. The national Swedish Post Office became one of the key players in the development of this new technology since it saw several reasons for promoting flying activities: it would, for instance, be possible to speed up the mail service, by adopting the new means of transportation. The National Board of Water Power started its own civil aviation service in the early 1920s in northern Sweden, after the failure of a private company to promote the necessary service. The Board first tried to find the best flying company among several competitors. However, flying conditions in northern Sweden were worse than the relatively small private company expected, and this private failure led to the conclusion that the Board themselves should start a regular airline service for a limited period.

Directly after the First World War, the first commercial air traffic companies started in Sweden. Due both to financial and technological difficulties, all of the early forerunners among civil air traffic companies ran into serious financial problems and went bankrupt in the aftermath of the crisis following the war. These companies were, however, important in one respect – they were all granted concessions from the Swedish state to run airlines. They were also privately owned, without direct subsidies. In Sweden, the first airline company of any significance, Svenska Lufttrafikaktiebolaget (SLA), was founded in 1919.[14] The founders of SLA were a group of Swedish bankers and businessmen, representing Swedish export industry, the largest commercial banks, and shipowners.[15]

Several other companies were granted concessions for commercial air traffic in the late 1910s, including Enoch Thulin (Thulinverken also flew on a regular basis in southern Sweden to Denmark for a short period) and P.O:s Flygkompani, others were AB Göteborgs flygdroskor, Malmö Flygkompani (1920), Karlslunds flygskola, Kommanditbolaget Örebro Flygkompani and Sveriges Luftpostlinjeaktiebolag.

However, these were all comparatively small and lacked sufficient funds. Another early example of a regular air service was, as mentioned above, the flights in northern Sweden. They were administered by the National Board of Water Power, as part of the construction of a large plant for electrical energy.

However, the company SLA operated for only two years on a fairly limited number of routes.[16] The state did in fact give subsidies to the company by granting generous loans, but the capital was never used. One of the most important prerequisites for the company to start up, though, was the support of the Swedish Post Office. The positive attitude from Julius Juhlin, at this time Post Master General of the Swedish Post Office, towards the new means of transport was crucial. This company had been especially designed to be of an experimental nature; one of its significant contributions was the building of Lindarängen airport in the Stockholm area.

In 1918, a bill introduced the first parliamentary interest in civil aviation, regarding the role of the state in supporting this new industry.[17] This resulted in a parliamentary investigation, published in 1921, recommending that the state should support airports, weather forecasting, lighthouse signaling systems and so on, and give subsidies to private and state-owned airlines.[18] At this point, however, there were no suggestions that only one company should be supported through charters. On the contrary, the report did not support either both private or state monopolies, and instead, the committee suggested a market structure consisting of several private air companies. Several members of the committee, selected by the government, were active in various aviation projects, and were members of the Swedish aviation club. One striking aspect is the common military background shared by many of those engaged in early civil aviation.[19] However, parliament's response to the committee's recommendations was not enthusiastic at that time, due to the unstable public financial circumstances, as well as the unclear market situation. The bankrupt Svenska Lufttrafikaktiebolaget, SLA, was hard hit by the severe crises of the early 1920s, with the result that Sweden did not have any operating flying company of any significance in 1922–23. Such was the dismal end of Swedish civil aviation, *Gründerzeit*.

To sum up, this first period of an emerging airline industry was characterized by the absence of legislation up to the early 1920s. The state allowed several private competing firms to enter the market, while the new form of transport benefitted by various subsidies from two state agencies. However, the largest private enterprise, surviving the first shakeout, could not recover from the insufficient revenues without direct public subsidies, as well as unclear leadership.[20]

During the second period of Swedish civil aviation policy, the foundation of the private company AB Aerotransport (ABA) marked the beginning of a new, more active, state strategy towards Swedish civil aviation. For the first time, a Swedish company was granted a de facto monopoly concession, together with a substantial subsidy.

ABA was founded on 27 March 1924 by brothers Carl and Adrian Florman, both with a military background as flying officers. After the failure of the first Swedish aviation companies, the Florman brothers initiated a discussion on the possibilities of setting up a new airline company. One observation from the earlier adventures and financial breakdowns was the urgent need for subsidies. Without subsidies it would be impossible to continue. One important aspect of the strategy was the possibility of acquiring the right to start airmail services for the Swedish Post Office, which was also a crucial aspect in the early development of the company. The Post Office agreed to co-operation with ABA and, with a contract to deliver mail by air, Florman contacted British manufacturers in order to obtain airplanes. When the British company failed to fulfill the contract, Carl Florman made contact with Junkers. The result was that Junkers became a majority owner by acquiring 58 percent of the capital stock of SEK 356 000 and they also agreed to deliver airplanes.[21] However, since foreign owners were allowed to own only 20 percent of the capital stock of a company according to Swedish legislation of 1916, the situation became problematic. The crucial question of obtaining state subsidies and interest-free state loans depended on total Swedish ownership of the company. From the beginning of 1925 the shares were thus transferred to Swedish owners. But it was a phoney transaction: in reality, Junkers owned the company until the early 1930s (Böhme 1982).

As early as November 1923, Carl Florman had started to apply for subsidies when he met the Minister of Transport, Sven Lübeck (Conservative). Florman argued that the subsidy would be of great importance to the building of a Swedish aircraft industry. The creation of ABA was thus an important part of that process, according to Florman. The negotiations were successful and in October 1924, the company asked for government subsidies for the flights, arguing that it had already obtained the airmail contract, thereby showing their willingness to prove that they had already started services. They also asked Viktor Larsson, a Social Democrat and newly appointed Minister of Transport, for loans to buy airplanes. The company was given these subsidies in mid-1925 after recommendations by a fast-track parliamentary committee consisting of a small group of aviation experts.[22] The parliamentary commission argued in particular that the airlines in other European countries were heavily subsidized, which could result in foreign companies operating on the Swedish market. This possible threat to Swedish interests was a powerful argument. There were five other reasons for providing the subsidies, according to the minister: the promise of faster passenger transport; the military aspects; the possibilities for faster postal services; the promotion of the Swedish aircraft industry; and lastly, the provision of better health care through ambulance flights.[23] Opponents argued that the subsidies would be more beneficial for Swedish industry if they instead were given to the Swedish Air Force. Nevertheless, despite this criticism, the vast majority of other interests, ranging from commercial trade associations to various state agencies and the military, were positive to the proposal. After being initially worked out by ABA it was accepted by parliament, including guarantees for losses.[24]

Ironically, the 'Swedish' airline company was a subsidiary to Junkers, using flying equipment from Junkers as well as technical assistance and German pilots. Junkers in fact operated in Finland, the Baltic states, Denmark (Dansk Lufttransport) and Sweden. Therefore, Junkers were able both to get national subsidies and to export machines.

However, the Florman brothers soon discovered that they were threatened by another new company, Nordiska Flygrederiet, which was set up during the summer of 1925. It was owned by Deutscher Aero-Lloyd, a competitor to Junkers in Germany. The strategy was to obtain subsidies for routes from Sweden to Germany. The first proposal from the government was to divide the total sum of SEK 500 000 between the two companies. After a fierce struggle, the Florman brothers managed to obtain the whole subsidy and Nordiska Fly-grederiet was denied any. Subsequently, the merger process in Germany between the former competitors, Nordiska Flygrederiet and Junkers, resulted in Lufthansa, as mentioned earlier. The new company's preference was that Nordiska Flygrederiet should act as a representative and subsidiary in Sweden, rather than ABA. After turbulent discussions, however, Lufthansa finally decided to support ABA. Having survived these two conflicts, the Florman brothers managed to balance between German interests and the Swedish state, while receiving public support.

During the second part of the 1920s, the company received larger and larger subsidies from the state every year, but despite this support, the company ran into great financial difficulties. For several years in the late 1920s, the losses were larger than the subsidies.

AB Flygindustri (ABF), the aircraft company and ABA subsidiary, owned by Junkers, which operated closely with the Florman brothers, also ran into financial problems, and went bankrupt in the early 1930s. An important factor was the decision to create a Swedish air force, which resulted in the need for a Swedish manufacturer. Both ABF and ABA were important partners for the German owner and the Swedish management of the Florman brothers.

Summing up the second period, we can conclude that there was one important difference compared with the earlier period: the extension of state measures and regulations. The earlier subsidies had been relatively limited in scale. The new contract with ABA was indeed grander. Another important factor was the granting of monopoly rights to one single private company.

The third phase in the development of Swedish commercial air traffic was characterized by the nationalization of ABA, the private monopoly company. The growing number of subsidies required by the ABA company eventually led to a new ownership structure. In the early 1930s, the state demanded rep-resentation on the board of directors. In 1935, the Swedish parliament accepted a proposal from the government regarding the ownership structure of ABA. The new structure gave the state 50 percent of the shares in the company. The old management with Carl Florman maintained its position, but the board of directors had already been extended to include two representatives of the state. From now on, the company was state owned, but the management basically remained the same, except for the new members on the board.

CONCLUSION

The role of the state in regulating, intervening and subsidizing the infant European civil aviation industry gives us insights into the processes of the emerging technology and the positions taken by the state. It is also a good example of the complex learning processes when politicians try to cope with uncertainty and incomplete information, and it sheds light on the formation of interest groups as well as the role of entrepreneurs entering the political arena. The European examples of early civil aviation also suggest that the political options were not clear-cut. The natural monopoly argument was one of several options available, but was not chosen immediately. Instead, there was a short period of relatively low entries and several competing private companies. The question of state ownership entered the political scene at different stages in different countries. The role of subsidies was debated, and it was not uncontroversial, as the British example shows. However, all countries very soon adopted a generous policy towards the new companies.

When comparing the development of some early European civil aviation companies, the first conclusion is that the first six to seven years after the First World War were characterized by a rather liberal policy, especially with respect to subsidies and the question of private ownership. Indeed, in the cases discussed above, private initiatives and also semi-private regulations were at hand. During the formative 1920s, the policy changed in a number of countries regarding subsidies to the new aviation companies. In some countries a number of private airlines received subsidies, while in others only one company was the 'chosen instrument'. After merger processes, the newly formed monopolies could be both private, as in Britain and Sweden, or state owned, as in Germany. It seems that the politicians were influenced by the actions of other states regarding both the amount and the principles of giving subsidies to aviation companies.

I have argued that the evolution of the airline industry in Sweden up to the 1930s could be described in three phases, with a view to the relationship between the state and the new industry. The close interaction between public and private interests was an important characteristic of the emergence of the Swedish airline industry, but the role of the state was not one of total dominance of the industry from the beginning. Instead, the process proved to be more complex. In the first phase, from the end of the First World War until 1925, the Swedish state regulated the business, while private interests initiated new companies (with minor exceptions). The Swedish Society of Aeronautics was, however, the most important interest group both in initiating and investigating new regulations.

The responsibilities of the state were considered to cover matters to do with airports (together with local authorities), radio signaling, weather forecasting, and other utilities. The second phase involved further responsibilities; the state started to give subsidies, and to grant exclusive monopoly rights to one single private company. In this case, ABA, which was secretly owned by the Germans, had a marked national profile in order to obtain subsidies. In the third phase, the state nationalized the private monopoly.

The case of the growing civil aviation industry in Sweden could of course be analysed using interest group theories to some extent. However, perhaps the most vital point in such a discussion concerns the formation of interest groups and the composition of the parliamentary investigation committees. For a number of years, a few individuals with expert knowledge, often with a military background, were key members of such committees. As an organization, the KSAK, the aviation club of Sweden, experienced diminishing influence. Influential individuals, on the other hand, continued to be important in relation to the government. After the shakeout in the early 1920s, a new situation emerged, with no surviving Swedish aviation companies. In this window of opportunity, the Florman brothers entered the political scene, applying for subsidies.

The special case of the talented Florman brothers, using nationalistic arguments in order to get subsidies, while in fact being a German daughter company, gives another dimension to the classical interest group discussion. Carl Florman, in particular, showed talents as a political entrepreneur, persuading the ministers of transport, while having the support of important parts of the old flying establishment in Sweden. The process of nationalization might be understood to some extent by arguments regarding market failure. But in this case, also, the same key persons were still operating the company.

The differences between the making of policy decisions and their implementation suggest the fruitfulness of taking account of different institutional settings, a complex network of actors, as well as the specific historical factors. This gives us more explanatory power in analysing the development of policy actions chosen, compared with the two static models mentioned in the introduction. Indeed, policy decisions are often the result of a dynamic process, where the decisions reached frequently reflect a complex change in the relation between formal and informal institutions and the actors themselves.

These decisions were the result of processes ranging over a long period of time, with several shifts in arguments, policies chosen, and implementation. Generally, the processes reflected neither broad public interest nor narrow self-interest, although such factors were also important elements. It might be argued that the dynamic elements themselves in the interaction between market and politics as well as between private actors and public interests call for more sophisticated tools of analysis.[25]

Comparing the development of policy action in Britain, France, Germany and Sweden, the main difference is the marked policy patterns as well as the policy shifts. The paths chosen towards public ownership and massive regulatory policies included several steps, as well as various mixes of regulatory regimes. The transition process from a period of free flying towards a more regulated governance regime in early European civil aviation suggests that mechanisms behind governance changes might be better understood as a process of how politicians cope with new circumstances, new technology, and new private actors.

NOTES

1. Dobbin (1994) and Dunlavy (1994a) are good examples of comparative perspectives on the development of railway policies in various countries.
2. This discussion is inspired by Dixit's and Williamson's notions of the role of transaction costs in the political economy. See Dixit (1996) and Williamson (1996). In this context, actors are acting in uncertainty, with bounded rationality, and the political contract is complex and incomplete.
3. Lyth (1997b). See also Davies (1964) and Lissitzyn (1942).
4. This principle was the result of the Paris Air Convention of 1919, abandoning the pre-war discussion of freedom of the air (Lyth 1997bb, p. 155).
5. Regarding the German case, see Fritsche (1992).
6. The development of civil aviation in the United States can be considered more liberal in some dimensions compared with the later European experience. Lyth rightly suggests that the American policy could best be described as *regulated competition*, permitting several companies. After the creation of the Civil Aeronautics Board (CAB) in 1938, a oligopolistic market structure remained the same until the era of deregulation in the 1970s (see Lyth 1997b, p. 156).
7. Lufttrafikkommittén (1921), p. 94; Buraas (1972), p. 20.
8. Lyth (1993).
9. Seven of these companies were founded in 1919. Davies (1964), p. 28.
10. It is interesting to note that in the French aviation company CIDNA, the Czechoslovak government had a 20 percent minority of shareholding.
11. See also Feldman (1996).
12. The society was the forum and a club of military officers, engineers, financiers, early aviation industry entrepreneurs, as well as active pilots. Often, these early Swedish enthusiasts were industrialists, pilots, and military officers, all at the same time (for example, Carl Cederström and Enoch Thulin). One key person in this organization was Karl Amundsson, a Swedish officer, the First Chief of the Swedish Air Force in 1925. During the first decade of its existence, some of the influential members of the society were most interested in airships and the 'lighter than air' principle. This conservatism was of course much debated in the society.
13. Information regarding the Swedish Aeronautical Society (from 1921, the Royal Swedish Aeronautical Club), Swedish National Archives, KSAK:s Archive, vol. II, 1; Söderberg (1990), also Böhme (1995).
14. Lufttrafikkommittén (1921).
15. The founding of the company was the result of a study made by a committee initiated by this private consortium, chaired by Mr K.A. Wallenberg. The committee consisted of Hans Ericson (chairman, manager of Rederi AB Svea, a shipowning company), E. Lundqvist, Karl Amundsson, Ivar Kreuger, J.O. Roos af Hjelmsäter and Lenn Jacobsson (secretary). According to a contemporary Swedish business journal, financial companies that were closely affiliated with the banks, such as Emissionsinstitutet, Centralemission, and Svenska Emissions AB, and shipowning companies, such as Ångfartyg AB Tirfing, Svenska Lloyd, and Ostasiatiska Kompaniet, were among the investors of the new company. Also, firms from the engineering industry, such as Scania Vabis and SKF together with private persons such as Erik Brodin,

Axel Ax:son Johnson (shipowners) and the above-mentioned Ivar Kreuger. *Affärsvärlden* 7 (1919), p. 658.
16. *Svenskt flyg och dess män* (1940); Lufttrafikkommittén (1921), pp. 94ff.
17. Bill introduced by Eric Nylander in the Swedish parliament in 1918. Nylander was a member of the Conservative party in the Second Chamber of the Swedish parliament, with a commercial background, especially in exports, he also chaired Exportföreningen; *Svenska Män och Kvinnor* (1949), p. 574. The Swedish state had even earlier regulated other aspects of this new mean of transportation, regarding security issues and so on, during the early 1910s.
18. A formal air authority agency started in 1922.
19. Böhme (1995) clearly describes the relationship between the military, the military aircraft industry, and the fast-growing interest of civil aviation among military aviators. Private investors started to be seriously interested in late 1917, early 1918. I would like to thank Ulf Olsson for his comments on this relationship between the military and early aviation.
20. The first legislation was introduced in September 1914, prohibiting foreign aircrafts from flying over Swedish territory. This legislation was proposed by the Swedish Aeronautical Society in 1913; Swedish Aeronautical Society.
21. Another financier was Carl Cervin, a Swedish banker, and Florman's father-in-law (Böhme 1982, p. 92; Nordlund 1989, p. 176). Carl Florman was also involved in the creation of a military Swedish air force in 1924/25 (former subdivisions of the Swedish navy and army).
22. Several of these experts had been engaged in earlier parliamentary committees, for example, Amundsson.
23. SOU (1929:21), p. 5.
24. Böhme (1982), p. 68; *Bihang till riksdagens protokoll vid lagtima riksdagen i Stockholm 1925* (1925).
25. Here, I should like to draw attention to Kreuger's (1996) seminal work on American Sugar.

APPENDIX 1

Table 9A.1 Subsidies to some European civil aviation companies, 1925

Company	Share capital, SEK	Value of the planes, SEK	Depreciation, accounts for 1925, % of total value	Subsidies 1925, SEK	Other revenues from traffic 1925	Subsidies as % of total income	1925 losses, SEK	Number of passengers on subsidized lines	Subsidy in relation to passengers SEK
AB Aerotransport, Sweden	666 000	1 300 000	14	305 000	421 114	42	38 800	2 277	135
Imperial Airways, England	24 400 000	2 900 000	10	2 500 000			410 000	11 163	220
Air Union, France				1 450 000	850 000	63		7 700	198
Compagnie Général, France	3 400 000			2 400 000	780 000	76	550 000	5 960	595
Compagnie Internationale, France	1 402 500			1 850 000	240 000	88	47 500	2 478	1 300
Lignes Farman, France				440 000	150 000	74		3081	145
DDL, Denmark	250 000	308 000	27	350 000	148 828	71	91 864		

Source: Swedish National Archives, ABA archive, Huvudarkivet, FI:5, ABA AI 009, Historik, allmän 1926, Memo regarding ABA, p. 21.

Table 9A.2 Subsidies to civil aviation in various nations, 1927–1930

Country	No. of aircraft	Flying km	Passengers	Line subsidies, SEK	Total state subsidies, SEK	Line subsidies, SEK/flying km	Total state subsidies, SEK/flying km	Year
Italy	54	1 992 000	15 629	9 400 000	9 700 000	4.72	4.87	1928/29
England	19	1 816 000	27 659	6 300 000	8 100 000	3.47	4.46	1929/30
Sweden	4	212 400	2 250	500 000		2.35	0.00	1928
Poland		1 040 000	6 593	2 200 000	2 600 000	2.12	2.50	1927/28
Germany	170	10 217 000	111 000	17 900 000	49 300 000	1.75	4.83	1928
Denmark	5	148 000	1 602	150 000	250 000	1.01	1.69	1928
Netherlands	21	1 623 000	17 007	900 000		0.55	0.00	1928
France	342	60 440 000	15 857	25 000 000	46 000 000	0.41	0.76	1929
USA	294	16 838 000	52 934		28 900 000	0.00	1.72	1929/30
Soviet Union		1 352 000	3 700			0.00	0.00	1928
Austria		643 000	5 477			0.00	0.00	1928
Czechoslovakia		415 000	4 233			0.00	0.00	1928
Switzerland	35	183 000	2 090			0.00	0.00	1928
Belgium and Congo	23	643 000	9 854			0.00	0.00	1928
Finland	5	195 000	3 201			0.00	0.00	1928

Source: SOU (1929:21), p. 43.

Table 9A.3   AB Aerotransport (ABA), passengers, freight and postal services, 1924–1939

Year	Passengers	Freight (kg)	Post (number, millions)	Revenues, SEK	Subsidies, SEK	Cost, SEK	Profit/Loss, SEK	Subsidy/total revenues, SEK
1924	6 111	12 80	0.1					0.0
1925	9 687	11 633	0.5	421	306	766	−39	42.1
1926	10 176	14 185	1.0	423	471	1251	−357	52.7
1927	14 807	45 037	0.7	587	559	1206	−60	48.8
1928	14 948	52 199	1.6	745	487	1240	−8	39.5
1929	5 914	39 270	5.6	644	512	1535	−379	44.3
1930	17 326	33 430	4.1	769	537	1418	−112	41.1
1931	19 624	44 970	5.8	979	542	1488	33	35.6
1932	6 440	40 628	4.8	1069	637	1671	35	37.3
1933	10 056	65 758	7.2	1461	647	2024	84	30.7
1934	18 072	102 586	10.4					24.5
1935	22 960	127 830	13.5					22.0
1936	23 649	132 321	23.3					18.7
1937	56 531	386 251	53.6					18.2
1938	60 046	494 731	67.2					15.8
1939	59 835	510 867	52.8					12.7

Source: Flying safe. 20 years of air traffic 1924/1944, AB Aerotransport.

10. Liberalization and control: instruments and strategies in the regulatory reform of Swedish telecommunications

Carl Jeding

INTRODUCTION

In most of the industrialized world, technological, economic and ideological changes have led to pressures to liberalize the telecommunications markets.[1] The threat of international competition has led all major industrialized countries to introduce competition in their national telecommunications markets. In most cases this has implied privatizing the previously state-owned monopoly operators.

In general, four types of gains from liberalizing the telecommunications sector have been expected. First of all, liberalization is expected to lower telecommunications costs and stimulate the development of new products and services. This, in its turn, would then lead to higher productivity and efficiency throughout the whole economy. Second, it would stimulate growth of the telecommunications sector itself, an argument that becomes increasingly important as the 'digital revolution' seems to keep making telecommunications an ever expanding part of the international and national economies. Third, a liberalized telecommunications market with developed services and low prices would attract international companies that rely on good communications, such as most knowledge-intensive business corporations. Fourth and last, the liberalization would make domestic telecommunications operators more competitive, so that they can compete successfully on the developing international market.[2]

In this chapter it is argued that this liberalization process has not been one of deregulation. In choosing the case of the liberalization of the Swedish telecommunications market, we shall examine how the introduction of competition in that market was closely linked to a change in the regulatory system and a shift of emphasis in state regulatory activity, but not to the abandonment or decrease of regulation.

Steven K. Vogel (1996) argues regarding the nature of the wave of regulatory reform that has swept the industrialized world during the last 20 or so years, that what we have witnessed is reregulation, not deregulation. People commonly confuse the introduction of competition in monopoly markets (liberalization) with the reduction or elimination of government regulation (deregulation). Those two are not necessarily linked to each other (Vogel 1996, pp. 3–4). This semantic confusion has to do with a deeper one of logic, and that is the assumption that governments and markets have a zero-sum relationship. An increase in the power of one, the thinking goes, must mean a decrease in the power of the other. In the real world, however, there is no such contradiction between more competition and greater government control (ibid., p. 3; Samuels 1992).

The Swedish telecommunications market is in fact a striking example of this. After an initial build-up of the telephony in Sweden, where private local initiatives constructed telephone networks with limited geographic range, the state took control of the national telephone system through buying up these local operations and connecting them to the national trunk line system (Skårfors 1997). The resulting state monopoly was, however, a *de facto* rather than a legal one. There was no law forbidding other operators than the national administration to start telephone operations should they wish to do so. Thus in order to liberalize the market, that is, introduce competition, the state had to introduce new regulations to facilitate entry into the market and to hinder abuse of the dominant position by the administration.

WHAT DO WE MEAN BY REGULATION?

In order to discuss fruitfully whether the observed liberalization has been accompanied by deregulation as well, we must begin by defining what we mean by regulation. Regulation can be defined in a whole range of ways. A narrow definition regards it as a specific set of commands, where a binding set of rules is applied by a body specifically devoted to this purpose. The other end of the scale regards it as all forms of social control or influence, thus including all mechanisms shaping individual or organizational behaviour in the term 'regulation' (Baldwin and Cave 1999, p. 2).

A middle position between those two defines regulation as deliberate state influence. This could cover all state actions designed to influence industrial or social behaviour, and thus range all the way from legislation to actions based on economic incentives (such as taxation or subsidization), to the supply of information (ibid., p. 2). John Francis restricts this slightly by giving the following definition of regulation: 'regulation occurs when the state constrains private activity in order to promote the public interest' (Francis 1993, pp. 1–2).

A very specific definition is offered by Clifford Winston, who defines economic deregulation as 'the state's withdrawal of its legal powers to direct the economic conduct (pricing, entry, and exit) of nongovernmental bodies' (Winston 1993, p. 1263). By inversion that would mean that regulation is defined as the state having those powers. Although the definition is perhaps overly narrow in that only the directing of pricing, entry and exit are included, the specification that regulation has to do with legal powers is important.

It is an important point of departure in this chapter that state or government control over an industry or a company is not the same as regulation. State actions are not regulations simply because they are carried out by the state (Majone 1990a, pp. 1–2). The state can exert influence or control in a whole range of ways, but in order to analyse this state influence more precisely we need to set up a number of defining criteria which separate regulation from other forms of state control.

First of all, economic regulation concerns economic sectors and markets. This may sound tautological, but that definition excludes a substantial part of all political initiatives and legislation.

Second, we regard regulation as actions of a legalistic character. This implies a number of things: on the one hand it means that regulation involves the issuing of a binding set of rules. This separates regulation as something of a commanding nature from other types of incentive-based regimes such as tax breaks, subsidies and so on. This further means that regulation requires some sort of control that it is followed, and enforcement. On the other hand the legalistic character implies that regulation is fairly stable over time.

The legalistic nature of regulations further means that they need to be general in regard to actors. Regulation of the telecommunications sector needs to apply to the sector as a whole, and its rules should not be actor-specific. Yet primarily we see regulation as something aimed at specific sectors of the economy, which excludes more general forms of legislation, such as, for instance, competition law in general, from the term regulation.

One further feature of regulation is that it should constitute deliberate actions as opposed to unintended side-effects of other forms of state action. This means, for instance, that unintended effects of regulation of some other sector of the economy, which also happens to have an influence over the telecommunications market, should not be regarded as telecommunications regulation. Thus we hold that regulation is something which is specifically aimed at expressed goals. This does not imply an overidealistic assumption that all regulation is introduced out of public interest for some collective greater good.[3] But policy initiatives such as regulation (or deregulation) are bound to be motivated by the actors taking those initiatives. Why regulate, at this time, and in this way? Even if such justifications are not taken at face value, they are nevertheless important for understanding regulations and their objectives.

With the above qualifications and explanations, we can now summarize that for the purposes of this chapter we shall regard regulation as deliberate state actions, legally based, and aimed specifically at achieving expressed goals in some sector of the economy.

WHY REGULATE?

Regulation theory has developed as an important field of research in its own right within a wide range of academic disciplines, from economics, through political studies and sociology, to anthropology. The explanations to how regulations arise, develop, and decline vary greatly among the writers. A common way of grouping these different approaches is, however, to focus on the motives for and driving forces behind regulation. With that classification scheme, three broad categories emerge: those that focus on public interest, private interest and institutions (Francis 1993, pp. 1–8; Peltzman 1989; Stigler 1971; Steinmo et al. 1992; North 1990; Dixit 1996).

Historically telecommunications have been among the most strictly regulated areas of national economies. The regulation and/or public control over the telecommunications sector has taken various forms in different countries, ranging from strict and elaborate systems of regulation for private operators to full-blown legal and commercial state monopoly.

The motivations for this heavy involvement of the state in the telecommunications sector have varied through different countries and periods of time. A number of common features in most of those motivations can, however, be identified.[4]

First of all, and perhaps the reason why the state has become involved in the sector in the first place, is that telecommunications have been regarded as a vital national resource for economic and technological development. When the telephone was introduced in Europe during the last decades of the nineteenth century, it would perhaps have been a logical choice for the telegraph administrations to take an active part in building up the new medium as well. This, however, did not happen since the telephone was not regarded by the administrations as having any significant interest to them. Not until the use of telephony started to pose a threat to the revenues from their telegraph monopolies did the administrations start taking an active interest (Jeding 1998; Skårfors 1997). The motivations for the present wave of liberalizing the telecommunications sector also stress this importance of the sector to the whole economy of states, although the policy implications are different this time.

Infrastructural resources in general have often been considered key resources of this kind, but the relative importance of telecommunications has increased throughout the twentieth century. Matters of national security and the importance of having access to a stable system of communications in times of war or other types of crisis also fall into this category (Headrick 1981, ch. 11). Furthermore, the sector has held a symbolic value in the sense that a well-developed telecommunications system has been regarded as a sign of being an economically and technologically advanced nation.[5]

Second, the telecommunications sector has long been regarded as a natural monopoly. This argument is based on the idea that the economies of scale involved in producing telecommunications services mean that one producer could do it more cheaply than if several operators were to share the market. Another argument in this strand is that competition in telephony would lead to wasteful duplication of network resources. Much has been written on the alleged natural monopoly of telecommunications.[6] One recent study argued convincingly that the natural monopoly of Swedish telecommunications was actually socially constructed by the actors involved in building up the Swedish telephone network during its initial phase (Helgesson 1999). At any rate, if telephony at any stage has been a natural monopoly, most people seem to agree that it is not so any longer.

The third class of arguments relates to the necessity of technological compatibility within the telecommunications systems. These systems are characterized by a strong 'technical linkage'; that is, they require an extensive amount of co-ordination in order to function as a whole.[7] Such co-ordination is of course more easily achieved if the number of interested and involved parties is minimized.[8]

Fourth and last are the various public service objectives that most governments apply to the telecommunications sector. Access to at least basic telephony services at affordable and unitary rates is in most industrialized countries regarded as a basic right of their citizens. There is, of course, considerable national variation as to what should be included in these 'basic rights' and what constitutes 'affordable prices'. The point here, however, is that governments regard the provision of services to sparsely populated areas and to less well-off consumers as something the market forces will not take care of without some amount of regulation or state involvement.

REGULATORY CHANGE

Against the background of the above, we see two powerful forces at play in the set of rules for the telecommunications market. On the one hand is the strong tradition of rigorous regulation in almost all aspects of the industry. On the other is the strong will and pressure to liberalize the market. As we shall see, these two forces are not necessarily opposed. The crucial question seems to be: how should the regulatory system be reformed in order to achieve the desired liberalization? The simplest and most straightforward way to deal with that question is to argue that regulations are inherently inefficient, create inefficiencies, and obstruct the market signals. The reduction of regulation will therefore bring about more liberal and efficient markets.[9]

Other writers instead argue that some form of reregulation is needed to liberalize the telecommunications market, and that this initially may lead to an increase in regulatory activity.[10] According to this view, liberalization of a network industry can be seen as a three-stage process. In the first phase the industry is characterized by monopoly. Since the national monopolists typically are very powerful in this phase, European countries in general have chosen state ownership for them, in order to have more direct control over their actions. As markets are gradually opened up to competition the industry enters phase two. Here the monopoly situation is replaced by a dual system where monopolies in some markets or segments of markets coexist with competition in others. This situation with large asymmetries between competitors, where the large ex-monopolists typically have a great advantage from their vertical integration, calls for an increased amount and intensity of regulations. This 'hump' of regulation is, however, of a transitory nature, and once the industry has reached a more mature stage of competition the amount of regulation and regulatory activity will shrink away to some minimum of competition law, assisted by self-regulation and co-ordination from the market actors themselves (Bergman et al. 1998).

Yet others claim that the specific nature of the telecommunications sector extends the needs for regulation beyond any transitional period of liberalization (Preissl 1998), or even that the liberalization movement actually calls for more regulation. The argument departs from the fact that in industries such as public utilities in Western Europe, the issue has usually not been one of deregulation in the sense of removing administrative 'red tape'. Rather the aim has been to open the markets to competition, or even to create competition in markets where none has existed for a very long time. In doing this, the first step has been to reshape the old state monopoly into something which more closely resembles a private operator. But this also implies a risk of creating an actor with powers to behave as a classic profit-maximizing monopolist, with all the welfare losses that come with that.

In order to deal with that risk, the new corporatized or privatized operators have been given commercial freedom in a number of respects, while the core activities of these industries have become subject to formal legislative regulation.

> [F]rom the lawyer's point of view, it may be suggested that the process of privatiz-
> ation (and the so far rather limited opening-up of markets) has led to a growth rather
> than a diminution of formal legislative regulation. ... Indeed, it might be suggested

that with regard to former nationalized monopolies, competition is only possible through the creation of artificial legal structures rather than through the operation of market forces. (Usher 1994, p. 1).

Steven Vogel suggests that the liberalization of telecommunications markets has produced a gap between governmental goals and capabilities. While governments have divested themselves of their traditional instruments of influencing the telecommunications sector, their goals have remained the same. This 'capability gap' has formed a primary impetus for regulatory changes, that is, for introducing new forms of regulation rather than reducing it (Vogel 1996, pp. 25–31).

One problem with this discussion about the effects on the regulatory system of liberalization is of course the difficulty of finding measures. Clearly measures of the number of people employed in supervising and enforcing the regulations, or the budget devoted to it, are inadequate. What is of interest in this context is the extent and intensity of regulations, that is, how much the various parts and/or functions of the market are affected, and to what extent. Thus the strategy adopted here will be to look at the changes in the regulatory system in a functional way, in other words to study the desired functions of the regulatory system, and compare whether or not the liberalized system is coupled to more or less of formal regulation.

THE SWEDISH CASE: TWO DIFFERENT REGULATORY SYSTEMS

The liberalization process of the Swedish telecommunications market meant radical changes to the principles for state regulation or intervention as the regulatory system for the telecommunications sector changed. The term 'regulatory system' is here meant to include the legal system relating to the telecommunications sector, and the organizational set-up through which the state has tried to influence it.[11] From having had one state-owned operator with a monopoly on equipment and service provision, Sweden's telecommunications market became one of the most liberalized in the world by the mid-1990s (Karlsson 1998, p. 303).

Regulation Under State-owned Monopoly

When the Swedish telecommunications administration Televerket (or its predecessor Telegrafverket) was established in 1853 it was in the shape of a state-owned public enterprise.[12] This kind of enterprise has traditionally been used in Swedish administration in the communications sector and in some other industries regarded as nationally vital and/or strategic. Organizationally it takes a middle ground in the administrative system. On the one hand it is more independent from the state than a regular civil service authority, both relating to the goals it should achieve and how these are executed. On the other hand its actions are considerably more restricted than those of a state-owned limited liability company (ibid., p. 79).

In a number of important respects, Televerket's status as a state-owned public enterprise restricted its independence in operational and policy matters, and made it an instrument of the government for pursuing telecommunications policy. For instance, Televerket was not an independent legal subject. It had to follow administrative laws and regulations like civil service authorities, and its decisions could be appealed against to the government.

Although Televerket had some freedom to decide on its own internal economic matters, all its major and strategically far-reaching decisions had to be taken by the government or Riksdag. The Riksdag also decided on the annual budgets and investment plans of Televerket, in addition to having influence on the prices of its products and services. This meant that in reality, the Director-General of Televerket was primarily responsible to the government rather than to the board of Televerket. Moreover, Televerket did not have its own assets, which instead were part of state property (ibid., pp. 79–80). What gave Televerket some real influence over telecommunications policy was the asymmetric relationship between the administration and the Ministry for Communications, where the latter was very small and almost all the staff and expertise was with Televerket (Ioannidis 1998, ch. 7).

A Liberalized Regulatory System

During the 1960s and 1970s, telecommunications was almost a non-issue on the Swedish political agenda. Some minor steps towards corporatising parts of Televerket's equipment industry were taken, albeit in a hesitant and non-systematic way. Political concerns were mainly focused on whether or not employment figures in the industry would decrease as a result of changing technology towards more electronic equipment (Karlsson 1998, ch. 3).

The process of liberalizing the Swedish telecommunications market gathered pace in the second half of the 1980s, and in 1993 it resulted in a new telecommunications legislation bill. The bill included a new telecommunications act, a revised radiocommunications act, and a proposal to corporatize Televerket. In the bill, the state's policy objectives for the telecommunications sector were revised. First of all a new policy objective was to create opportunities for efficient competition in the telecommunications markets. Competition should be the instrument with which consumers should get lower prices, higher quality, and a wider choice of services.[13] Also, the state's responsibility for providing universal service to all citizens was expanded. Technological development in the sector had created new opportunities for communication, so that telefax and low-speed modem data communications should now be included in the basic telecommunications services available to all regardless of geographical location.

The corporatization of Televerket into Telia AB implied a number of structural and administrative changes. The state kept a 100 per cent ownership of Telia, but the new policy objective of introducing competition meant that Telia should act as an independent operator and that regulation should be neutral towards operators. That in turn implied that many of Televerket's responsibilities as the state's policy instrument had to be transferred to an independent regulator, the National Post and Telecom Agency (PTS).

PTS was installed as the government's 'watchdog' with an overall responsibility for the national telecommunications system. The agency took over from Televerket a number of competences, such as responsibility for the national numbering plan, frequency administration, standardization issues, and representing Sweden in international co-operation.[14]

A new feature of the telecommunications act was to introduce a licensing procedure for operators who wanted to offer telephony services to customers. The principle was that all operators who applied for a licence should get one. The licences could, however, be linked to certain conditions, such as to connect all other subscribers and operators, as well as allowing third party traffic. Interconnection tariffs should be cost based and 'reasonable', and PTS was given powers to mediate or even make decisions in the case of interconnection tariff conflicts between operators.[15] Other licensing conditions included obligations to convey messages to emergency services, recognize the needs of persons with disabilities, and the needs of the Swedish total defence and so on.[16]

To summarize this section, the new regulatory system based on the telecommunications act of 1993 meant that the state lost its most powerful regulatory tool – control over the market through direct control over the monopoly operator. Instead a new system was introduced, based on new legislation with a new independent regulator, PTS, to oversee the market. At the same time the motives for state control persisted, or even expanded as efficient competition in the telecommunications market was introduced as a new policy objective on top of the already existing such as an efficient telecommunications system, sustainable and accessible during crises and wartime, and accessible to all citizens at affordable prices.

This change of the regulatory structure of Swedish telecommunications implied two things. First, the pledge by the state not to use its ownership of Telia as a means of implementing telecommunications policy, coupled with the stable, or even increased ambition of policy goals formed a capability gap. In other words, if the government divested itself of one important tool to control the telecommunications sector but still wanted to influence it, it would have to find some other, new means of doing so. Hence reregulation. The new regulatory structure with an independent watchdog (PTS) and a new set of legislation was created to fill the gap between the government's goals and capabilities.

Second, this new regulatory structure did not necessarily imply less state control over the telecommunications sector. Theoretically there is no reason why control through an intermediary, such as an independent supervisory agency, should be less effective than direct control over the operators, allowing for agency costs. Indeed, the main motivation for initiating the regulatory change was that it would allow a more efficient fulfilment of the policy goals for the sector. But the regulatory reform meant that the government would have to use different tools for its control: formal regulation, bearing in mind the definition in the previous section, rather than direct control.

REGULATION UNDER THE TWO DIFFERENT SYSTEMS

As a next step in the analysis of the two regulatory systems, this section deals with how the state tries to achieve its policy objectives under the two different systems. The analysis will start from the policy objectives declared in the telecommunications act of 1993, and compare the means through which those objectives were achieved under the state-owned monopoly system and the liberalized system, respectively.

The list of regulatory activities discussed in this chapter is by no means complete. A number of tasks connected to public goals for the telecommunication have remained stable throughout the liberalization process. In a number of cases the only change has been that a particular task has been transferred from Televerket to PTS, where in practice the same employees perform the same job as before. Among such tasks are, for instance, administrating the national numbering plan, or allocating radio frequencies. Since the purpose of this chapter is to compare the differences in carrying out the political objectives for the telecommunications sector under the two different systems, such aspects of state intervention will be left out of the discussion. Worth noting also is that the overview deals primarily with the instruments for involvement or regulation, rather than the effects of it. Whether the objectives are more fully achieved through one set of institutions or another is left out of the discussion.

The policy objectives of the telecommunications act of 1993 are expressed in its section 2, and are stated as follows:

> The provisions of the act aim at ensuring that private individuals, legal entities and public authorities shall have access to efficient telecommunications at the lowest possible cost to the national economy. This implies, *inter alia*

1. that anyone shall be able to use, at his/her permanent place of residence or regular business location and at an affordable price, telephony services within a public telecommunications network,
2. that everybody shall have access to telecommunications services on equivalent terms, and
3. that telecommunications shall be sustainable and accessible during crises and wartime.

The government or the public authority appointed by the government may decide that private individuals, legal entities and public authorities shall be ensured access to telecommunications services or network capacity through public procurement.[17]

Ensure Efficient Telecommunications

This objective is of course a complex task and difficult to achieve. It has in part to do with stimulating investments into telecommunications, and to make sure that improvements and technological advances are realized in the national system. It has also to do with ensuring that the national telecommunications resources are compatible and working as a coherent system, given the positive network externalities of telecommunications.

Under the state-owned monopoly system, investment into the national telecommunications system was highly politically controlled. Televerket was the only main operator to invest in the Swedish network, and the Riksdag had to approve of its investment plans (Karlsson 1998, p. 80). The unity of the system of course stemmed from the fact that there was only one player operating. The monopoly in terminal equipment was supported by a very rigorous set of regulations. The rule was that all parts of the telephone network, as well as all equipment connected to it, should be owned and maintained by Televerket. It was thus forbidden for subscribers to attach any piece of equipment to the network, or to the equipment provided.[18]

The equipment market was the first segment of the sector to be opened to competition in 1980. Under the liberalized system, equipment has to be type approved by PTS before being put on the market, and increasingly the control is reduced to finding unapproved equipment that causes disturbances in the network in some way.[19] This, then, is clearly a case where liberalization has brought about a decreased amount of regulatory activity while the policy objective has remained the same.

Another issue related to ensuring that the telecommunications network functions satisfactorily as a whole is that of interconnection between operators. The telecommunications act states that:

A party supplying telecommunications services ... is liable on request to facilitate interconnection with any other party providing telecommunications services ...

The compensation for the provision of interconnection of telephony services delivered to a fixed termination point shall be fair and reasonable in relation to the performance costs.[20]

The problem is that Telia owns and operates the largest part of the Swedish telephone network, most importantly the access network, while at the same time operating as a service provider. This vertical integration of the infrastructure with the 'downstream' service sector gives Telia an incentive to charge their competitors a higher price for access to the network than their own service branch. At the same time it is in the interest of the entrant operators to overemphasize the advantages and underestimate the costs of the incumbent for providing access, in the hope that PTS will give them favourable treatment as new entrants. Finding the 'right' price for these access and interconnection fees is important for keeping both investment in new infrastructure and the utilization of the existing infrastructure at an optimal level.[21]

In terms of regulation, this means that PTS have to make sure that the operators fulfil the requirement to facilitate interconnection. Most importantly it means that whenever conflict occurs over interconnection tariffs, PTS will have to mediate between the parties, and ultimately decide at which level the tariffs are 'fair and reasonable in relation to the performance costs'. This arguably represents one of the most important tasks of the regulatory authority, and one that has come into existence only with the new regulatory system.

The effect of liberalization on the extent and intensity of regulation aiming at ensuring efficient telecommunications is thus somewhat mixed. On the one hand the detailed and rigorous regulatory apparatus concerning equipment that can be connected to the network has been removed. Instead, the technical coherence of the system is largely upheld by self-regulation, where the regulatory task of PTS consists mainly of issuing type approval of equipment that is put on the European market.

On the other hand a substantial amount of regulation and regulatory activity is dedicated to ensuring that operators facilitate interconnection with other operators in their networks. This is a regulatory task which is of great importance for the allocation of resources to and within the system, and therefore has significant consequences for the operators as well as for the telecommunications system as a whole. It is also a regulatory task which, of course, did not exist before liberalization.

Ensure Sustainable and Accessible Telecommunications During Crises and Wartime

The level of the total defence needs for telecommunications is ultimately decided by the Riksdag. The state's activity in this respect typically involves constructing protected sites for key elements of the telecommunications system, and carrying out tests of how the system works during manoeuvre exercises. These activities are funded through the defence budget. Under the old system Televerket performed all those functions, whereas under the liberalized system PTS follows a procurement procedure whereby different operators can bid for the contracts under competition. The activities to ensure national needs for telecommunications during crises in peacetime follow the same procedure, but are financed through fees from licence holders.

Here, too, the policy objectives have remained constant. What is new is that PTS procures the actual work from operators, rather than having Televerket do it as under the monopoly system. The carrying out of the procured tasks, such as constructing protected sites for important nodes in the telecommunications system, is a question of operation rather than regulation, regardless of who performs it. This means that the fact that other operators carry out some of these tasks instead of the state-owned operator, does not mean a decrease in regulation. The extent of regulation used to achieve the policy objective of ensuring sustainable and accessible telecommunications is thus rather the same under the two different systems, or has increased slightly with the addition of liberalization as a new procurement procedure.

Ensure Universal Service

As expressed in the telecommunications act, the objective is that anyone should be able to use, at his/her permanent place of residence or regular business location and at an affordable price, telephony services within a public telecommunications network; and that everybody shall have access to telecommunications services on equivalent terms.[22]

Here the definition as to what should be included in the universal service has changed over time with technological development. The instrument for ensuring that it is fulfilled has, however, remained about the same. Under the state-owned monopoly system it was the responsibility of Televerket to fulfil the universal service requirements, and their decisions could be appealed against to the government. Under the liberalized system, such responsibilities can be included in the licence conditions of any operator. In fact, and as a pro-competitive measure, Telia is the only operator whose licence at this time[23] includes an obligation to provide telephony services to anyone requesting it.

As the market becomes more mature and there is less justification for unilaterally putting the whole burden of supplying services to unprofitable areas, it might be reasonable to devise some system whereby the operators share the costs of this. That will then require some further regulatory activity from PTS to allocate those costs between the operators.

Included in the notion of universal service is that it should be provided at 'an affordable price'. This is a long-standing political objective, which under the monopoly system led to strong political control over Televerket's tariffs. According to one study, the politicians on Televerket's board were rarely interested in major strategic decisions. They did take a strong interest, however, when tariffs were discussed (Ioannidis 1998, p. 297).

Under the liberalized system price controls are less of a political issue. Subscribers' prices are set independently by the operators. Given the homogeneity of services, at least for standard telephone calls over the fixed network, price competition is by far the most important means of competing for the operators. The government naturally has no power (and no expressed ambition) to use its ownership of Telia to set any specific prices for the subscribers.

The main regulatory task in that respect is to supervise the tariff bases of Telia, and above all their interconnection rates. Here PTS spends some considerable effort in supervising Telia's records to ensure that no cross-subsidies or other abuses of their dominant position is taking place. Also the competition authority is involved here, in controlling that the market is characterized by sound competition, and that no cartel agreements are set up.

The relevant section of the telecommunications act further states that everybody shall have access to telecommunications services on equivalent terms. That passage is intended to cover the needs of people with disabilities, and implies services such as text telephony, speaking directory enquiries and so on. As in the case with defence needs, those services are financed over the state budget, and are procured by PTS under competition.

Ensure Competition

Introducing competition in the telecommunications sector is the most important change with the new regulatory system, and the very base for it. Section 3 of the telecommunications act states that: '[W]hen implementing the act the endeavour shall be to create scope for and maintain efficient competition within all parts of the telecommunications sector as a means of achieving the objectives specified in Section 2'.[24] A significant part of the act is devoted to ensuring that an efficient competition is established and upheld in the various segments of the telecommunications sector. For this purpose PTS is given far-reaching powers for supervising the licence holders, and matters related to promoting competition takes up a large part of the work of the agency. Naturally much of this work is related to alleged abuse of dominant power by the incumbent Telia. This is one area where the amount of regulation has clearly increased due to the liberalization of the telecommunications markets and the introduction of a new policy objective.

In summing up this section it might be useful to present the regulatory activities prompted by each policy objective under the two different regulatory systems (see Table 10.1).

Table 10.1   Regulatory activities under two regulatory systems

Objective	Monopoly system	Liberalized system
Control of terminal equipment	Strictly regulated monopoly	Self-regulation. Type approval and market control by PTS
Interconnection	–	PTS supervises and mediates/decides in conflicts
Price control	Strong political influence by the Riksdag/government	PTS controls that the tariffs are cost based
Defence needs	Riksdag decides level, Televerket carries out work	Riksdag decides level, PTS procures work
Universal service	Televerket obliged to provide universal service	Obligation included in licensing conditions
Competition	–	PTS supervision of operators Competition authority supervises general competition features

CONCLUSIONS

The case of the Swedish telecommunications sector seems to justify Vogel's notion of a gap between political goals and capabilities. The liberalization of the system meant that the state divested itself of its most powerful regulatory instrument – the direct control of the monopoly operator. At the same time all the existing political objectives remained constant and a new objective, the promotion of efficient competition, was added.

This capability gap opened for a change of regulatory systems. First of all it followed that the style of regulation would have to be different. The liberalized regulatory system called for neutral regulations and did not sit well with special relations between the state and Telia. Thus the direct political control of Telia had to be replaced by more general telecommunication legislation, and the regulatory and administrative functions held by Telia were transferred to an independent regulatory agency. In short, the regulatory influence had to shift from being specific and applying to specific issues, into being of a more general nature, applying to all the players on the market.

The instrument through which the state can primarily control operators under the liberalized system is by conditioning their licences. Since these licences, in order to stimulate investment and attract operators, must be transparent and stable over time, that also means that the regulatory influence over the telecommunications market has had to shift from *ex post* to *ex ante*. In an institutional context which is incorporated in a political system that provides safeguards against legislative and executive opportunism, the regulatory system is more likely to have credibility and attract long-term investments.[25]

Another result, paradoxical to some, is that the liberalization does not seem to have given any clear evidence of a reduction of regulations. Instead, we see a whole range of new regulatory measures introduced with the new system, most of these related to the promotion of competition.

If we thus accept Vogel's thesis that the new regulatory system has emerged to fill the gap between political ambition and ability, this leads to the conclusion that deregulation, that is, the abandonment of regulation, is not likely to occur as long as the policy objectives are constant. Arguably some of the regulation could take different forms. For instance, part of the promotion of competition could gradually become less sector specific and be handled by more general competition law. Part of the universal service obligation could also possibly be handled through more general regional policy. The total amount of regulatory activity and market intervention would, however, remain roughly constant.

NOTES

1. For an emphasis of technological developments as the driving force behind deregulation, see Koebel (1990); for an emphasis more on the issue of property rights related to deregulation in general, see De Alessi (1980). For an emphasis on economic factors, see, for instance, Jackson and Price (1994), pp. 1–4.
2. Vogel (1996), pp. 29–30; Ioannidis (1998) touches on the motivations behind liberalization in Sweden.
3. For an overview of some of the theories on why states regulate markets, see, for instance, the introduction to this volume, and Baldwin and Cave (1999).
4. Baldwin and Cave (1999) give another taxonomy of rationales for regulating in general. These four broad categories presented here seem better suited to the specific case of telecommunications.
5. Helgesson (1995); on 'technological nationalism', see Fridlund (1999), pp. 40–46, 219.
6. For instance, by Hultkrantz (1996), and Noam (1992), ch. 2; Helgesson (1999), pp. 331–40, gives an overview of the history of the concept 'natural monopoly' in relation to telephone services.
7. Foreman-Peck and Millward (1994), pp. 1–2; Kaijser (1994) discusses the issue of technical linkage.
8. This becomes even more apparent when the co-ordination has to take place on the international arena. See, for instance, Jeding (1998) and Genschel and Plümper (1997).
9. See, for instance, Niskanen (1993); Averch and Johnson (1962) do not explicate this in normative terms, but argue that economic regulation of telecommunications is likely to be ineffective.

10. See, for instance, Bergman et al. (1998).
11. This definition corresponds to those of Karlsson (1998) and Thue (1995).
12. The term in Swedish is *Affärsverk*. Karlsson (1998) translates this into state-owned public enterprise, whereas Noam (1992) suggests the term public service corporation.
13. Telecommunications Act 1993:597, p. 3.
14. SOU (1992:70), ch. 7.
15. Telecommunications Act 1993:597, §20, 20 c, 33.
16. Ibid., p. 17 a.
17. Ibid., p. 2.
18. This rule went so far as to include such equipment as note pads and stickers (Karlsson 1998, pp. 141–2).
19. As from April 2000, the type approval procedure will gradually be replaced by a system of market control. This system relies even more heavily on self-regulation by the industry, and the regulator's role will be to identify products that can cause disturbances in the network after they have been placed on the market.
20. Telecommunications Act 1993:597, s. 20.
21. See, for instance, Bergman et al. (1998), ch. 6.
22. Telecommunications Act 1993:597, p. 2.
23. January 2000.
24. Telecommunications Act 1993:597, p. 3.
25. Levy and Spiller (1994).

11. From informal practice to formal policy: path dependence and the case of Swedish transport aid

Thomas Pettersson

SOCIAL PRACTICE AS THE DRIVING FORCE BEHIND INSTITUTIONAL PATH DEPENDENCE

A common thought in institutional economic theory is that the economic rules, or the institutions, are deeply rooted in the culture and the history of society (North 1990; 1995). For that reason, differences in ideological preferences and cultural patterns can to some extent explain why institutional conditions differ between countries which are similar in other respects (Pettersson 1999a; Dixit 1996; North 1981; Harris et al. 1995; Magnusson and Ottosson 1996; Dunlavy 1994a; Dobbin 1994; Andersson-Skog 1993). This can, on the other hand, also be a reason why the expected economic development is sometimes absent when new economic regulations are introduced to promote growth. The attempt to reform the Russian economy after the Soviet breakdown in 1991 illustrates the complex relationships between new formal institutional conditions and their effect on established informal institutional economic conditions (Winiecki 1996). Institutional conditions may for that reason appear to be more difficult to change than other aspects of economic development. In New Institutional Economics (NIE), the concept 'institutional path dependency' is used for analysing why institutions that do not promote growth are developed, even when better solutions (from a growth perspective) are available.[1] In NIE the relations between culture, historical tradition and path dependence are not defined in a formal way and empirical research with the aim of testing the presence of institutional path dependence is so far very rare. The purpose of this chapter is first to define institutional path dependence in a way that allows empirical testing and then to investigate the existence of path dependence with Swedish transport aid as a case study.[2]

Institutional path dependence can be interpreted as institutional stability or rigidity, but not in this investigation. Instead, path dependence suggests change, but change that follows a certain direction; change that follows a path. Path dependence should therefore be defined in a way that incorporates both change and continuity in the analytical framework; a definition that holds both the analogy of a step along the path and the path itself. Therefore, the first question should be: what is the path? In this chapter, institutional path dependence is defined in relation to the social and economic practice in the regulated sector: 'Institutional path dependence is at hand when new institutional conditions develop in a way that maintains an economic and social practice within the sector of the economy that the institutional conditions regulate' (Pettersson 1999a, p. 9).

This way, social and economic practice represent continuity, or the institutional path, on which steps are taken in the form of new formal institutions. In this context, practice refers to the distribution of rights and duties, as well as to the distribution of economic and political resources in the regulated sector. Established practice shapes new formal institutions in a path-dependent way mainly through tacit knowledge, routines and ideological preferences. To analyse the driving forces that lead to institutional path dependency, a distinction is made between formal and informal institutional conditions, where formal institutions refer to codified rules and legislation, and informal institutions refer to ideological preferences, cultural patterns, routines and tacit knowledge (North 1990; Nelson and Winter 1982; David 1985). For the purpose of empirically testing the presence of specific informal institutions, informal institutions are divided into ideological preferences for either economic growth or economic equality.

Taking the previous definition of institutional path dependency as a starting-point, three criteria for path dependence can be defined. The first of these criteria is that new institutional conditions arise with a maintained social and economic practice within the regulated sector. The second criterion for path dependency is that the institutional condition subsists when there are alternatives which are better and well known from the point of view of public economy. A third criterion is that an institutional condition is given a stronger legitimacy when interest groups give it a new impetus by relating the condition closer to its practice. Taken all together these criteria imply that a model for analysing the driving forces behind institutional path dependency needs to include social structures and interest groups in the analytical framework. In Table 11.1, formal institutional conditions, interest groups and informal practices are defined and related to one another. Interest groups can act as agents of both change and continuity, dependent on their relationship to established practice in the regulated sector. Interest groups are forced to legitimize their demands by relating them to practice and in that way adapting them to generally accepted ideological preferences (North 1996).

Table 11.1   Path-dependent relationships between practice, interest groups and formal institutional conditions

Analytic level	Path dependent relations
Formal institution	Transport aid's organization and formal rules
Interest groups	Active interest groups among civil servants, firms and political parties
Practice	Social and economic practice in the regulated sector embedded in informal institutional conditions such as 'tacit knowledge' and general ideological preferences

INSTITUTIONAL PATHS IN SWEDISH REGIONAL POLICY

Both economic and ideological factors will be analysed as driving forces behind the design and the distribution of transport aid. If the presence of institutional path dependence is to be analysed, it is also necessary to investigate other possible explanations. For this reason this study first comprises an analysis of the distribution of transport aid between companies, and the distribution's relation to the regional economic structure and to the general goals of regional policy. This is done to determine to what extent economic conditions have been driving forces behind the development of the transportation grant. If economic conditions and economic change can account for the characteristics of transport aid, then it cannot at the same time be path dependent, according to the criteria mentioned earlier in the text.

Second, interest groups which have acted in the decision-making process are studied. This is done in order to determine the influence that interest groups have had on the development of transport aid. If the actions of well-organized interest groups can account for the characteristics of transport aid, then it cannot at the same time be path dependent, again according to the criteria mentioned earlier. All in all these two traditional perspectives (public interest and public choice) on the driving forces behind economic regulations, make it possible to assess to what extent institutional path dependency can contribute to an explanation of the development of transport aid, since these traditional explanations cannot be considered compatible with a path-dependent development.

Transport aid was introduced in 1971 as part of Swedish regional policy. It is allocated to certain goods-producing companies in northern Sweden to subsidize their transportation costs. The aim was to strengthen these companies' ability to compete in markets in southern Sweden and abroad. Transport aid is selectively designed and does not include all companies in the support area; only companies in some industrial trades are entitled to support, and only for goods which are considered to be processed.

The aim of the case study is to investigate the presence of and the driving forces behind institutional path dependency in the rise and development of Swedish transport aid.

The first step of this investigation is to compare transport aid with another form of governmental regional support, location aid. The purpose is to study the relationship of transport aid to general political goals in both traffic and regional

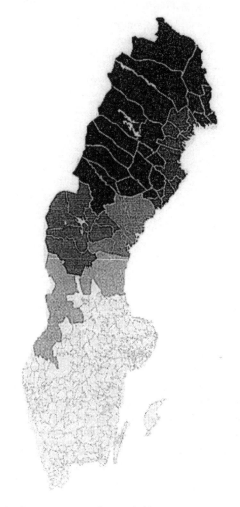

Note: Darker shade of grey represents a larger subsidy.

Source: Pettersson (1999a), p. 56.

Figure 11.1   Transport aid distribution area

policy and to the organizational conditions in each sector. Therefore, the comparison will in this stage of the investigation focus on the formal structure of the aid, that is, regulations and administrative routines.

Transport aid is basically an export subsidy. It compensates firms by refunding up to 50 percent of their transport costs. Frequent transport over long distances from locations in the northernmost area of Sweden will qualify for the largest subsidy (Figure 11.2).

Transport aid has thus retained its basic construction, in contrast to location aid and also in contrast to regional policy at large. This may indicate that transport aid has not followed the same path as regional policy at large. This opens up the possibility of analysing the presence of institutional path dependence by using a comparative method. There may be an explanation for transport aid's characteristic development in the mixture of traffic policy and regional policy, which have characterized transport aid's formal institutional condition (Table 11.2).

Table 11.2   The institutional condition related to goals in regional policy and traffic policy

Goals from traffic policy	Goals from regional policy
General construction of the subsidy	Demand for processed goods
Aimed at the transport	Aimed at the goods to be transported
General rules	Selective rules
Regional equality and national integration as main political goals	Growth and employment opportunities as main political goals

Source: Pettersson (1999a), p. 69.

To fit into the frame of Swedish regional policy, transport aid was given a contradictory set of regulations. Ideological preferences for both economic growth and economic equality were built into the formal institutional condition. As shown in Table 11.2, traffic policy has directed transport aid towards regional equality from a transport cost perspective, while regional policy has directed the regulations towards discrimination between companies, for example, with a demand for processing transported goods and discriminating against shipping. Can this mean that transport aid is path dependent? To explore the foundations of path dependence we need first to examine the general economic and political setting that surrounds transport aid. The analyses of the formal institutional condition in this part of the investigation give rise to interesting questions. Can specific economic conditions in the north of Sweden account for the characteristics of transport aid? Or, can the existence of active and well-organized interest groups account for transport aid's development? In the next step, explanations from a path-dependence viewpoint will be challenged by two alternative sets of explanations: public choice and public interest.

ECONOMIC AND POLITICAL FORCES BEHIND TRANSPORT AID

In order to find the reasons for the differences between transport aid and the general development of regional policy, economic driving forces behind the development of transport aid will first be investigated. For that purpose, economic development in the area designated for transport aid will be compared with the development in another area of Sweden. The aim of this comparison is to illustrate the impact that certain structural features in regional development may have had in order to legitimize the introduction of transport aid, and to what extent a public interest approach can explain the introduction of transport aid. The comparison focusses on population development, the development of the economic structure and certain features in the development of the transport sector.

The investigation shows that a relatively transport-intensive industry in the north of Sweden, based on raw materials, may have contributed to legitimizing transport aid, compared to other regional policy matters (Pettersson 1999a, pp. 90–94). This is reflected in the transport aid distribution as shown in Table 11.3, where quite a large amount of transport aid has been distributed to the forest industry, which has relatively unprocessed products. This distribution of transport aid is contrary to the general goals of the regional policy, which have been to promote regional processing and industrial development. In this context, transport aid has also been criticized in official reports for conserving the economic structure in the region (ibid., p. 137). This indicates that the distribution of transport aid differs from the formal goals of regional policy generally. This may also be an indication of institutional path dependence, since transport aid distribution appears to follow a path other than that of regional policy at large.

It appears that transport aid has been used in practice to stimulate regional equality from a transport cost perspective rather than stimulate growth and industrial development. The result of the study in this part of the investigation therefore indicates that a public interest approach can explain only parts of the development of transport aid. The weakness of this approach lies in explaining why transport aid, which was introduced to stimulate regional processing, was also used for transporting raw materials and relatively unprocessed goods, in spite of the criticism against transport aid for conserving the industrial structure.

Therefore, an interest group approach will be attempted, and contrasted with an approach based on institutional path dependency.

Table 11.3   *Transport aid distribution among industries, 1971, 1977, 1982, 1988 and 1995 (in percent)*

Industry	1971	1977	1982	1988	1995
Sawmills, carpentry shops, etc.	37	30	35	34	35
Mining and metal industry	17	26	42	37	37
Chemical industry	11	6	10	14	11
Paper mills	24	20	0	0	0
Foodstuffs industry	5	7	8	8	9
Earth and stone industry	6	6	5	5	4
Other industries	1	6	2	2	4
Total (rounded)	100	100	100	100	100

Source: Pettersson (1999a), p. 61.

The decision-making process will be studied with regard to a general (the goals and the organization of regional and traffic policy) and a specific (the development of transport aid) level, as well as to informal (economic growth or economic equality as an ideological base for legitimacy) and formal (the regulations of the transportation grant) institutional conditions (see Table 11.4). In this section, the starting-point for the analyses is first a basic public choice approach, where the question is to what extent strategies of interest groups can explain the distribution and development of transport aid, and second the three criteria for institutional path dependency that were defined earlier.

Three categories of actors are analysed in this interest group study: members of parliament, civil servants on different levels, and business organizations. This comparison is necessary in order to analyse which actors had been active in the decision-making process. For example, we would expect to find the forest industry to be an active interest group, since they occupied a favorable position in the analyses of transport aid distribution. The study showed, however, that the initiative for transport aid was taken by officials in the county administrative boards in northern Sweden, the Ministry of Transport and the Swedish state railway. Members of parliament became active at a later stage when transport aid was introduced in a government bill. Firms in the support area did not become active in the decision-making process until the parliamentary resolution in 1979, which from a public choice point of view must be considered unexpected. It is also apparent that transport aid, to a larger extent than location aid, was based on ideological preferences for equality. For example, in debates in parliament, transport aid was presented as a way of promoting regional equity and providing equal production conditions in the whole country.

Table 11.4   Central components in the transport aid decision-making process, 1970–1995

Informal conditions legitimizing the transport aid
• Growth or regional equality as ideological base for political legitimacy
General formal institutional conditions
• Regional policy at the EEC level
• Goals for Swedish regional policy at large
• The national economic development at large
Specific formal institutional condition
• The formal rules of transport aid
• The formal organization of transport aid
Established practice in traffic policy and regional policy
• Distribution of rights and resources, administrative routines and tacit knowledge

---

Source: Pettersson (1999a), p. 101.

Members of parliament and civil servants have in this case taken economic equality as a base for legitimizing transport aid, and at the same time subordinated its importance to the development of individual companies. This could also explain why transport aid, in spite of the criticism that it preserved the industrial structure, has been used to subsidize the production of relatively unprocessed goods. In this way the motivation for transport aid could be adjusted to a comprehensive equality–ideological framework; a connection that might have helped to raise support for transport aid even from members of parliament outside the support area. This ideological characteristic can also be a starting-point for analysing path dependency in the development of transport aid, since legitimacy from equality–ideological preferences can be traced back to earlier forms of government activity in the transport sector.

References to previous practice in traffic policy had an impact on the decision-making process, since the reorganization of the traffic policy in 1963 was considered to have decreased the scope for traditional forms of regional policy in this area (Sannerstedt 1979, pp. 115–18). When the conditions for competition changed in the transport market during the interwar and the postwar periods, traffic policy had to change. Traffic policy was adjusted to the new market conditions in accordance with the parliamentary resolution of 1963, which emphasized competition on equal terms between different types of transportation and emphasized the need for efficiency in order to promote economic growth. This implied that transport subsidies, which had been applied earlier in the area of traffic and railway policies, were forced out of the new institutional conditions of traffic policy. For this reason, the parliamentary resolution from 1970 to introduce transport aid made it possible for the traffic policy to survive, but within regional policy. The impact of a practice from traffic policy is also illustrated in the way people were selected for administrative duties. A person with a background in the transport sector was given priority when administrative posts in the area of transport aid were advertised. This is reflected in the fact that the staff have mainly been recruited from the Swedish state railway (Pettersson 1999a, pp. 146–52.

The weakness of the public choice approach lies in the fact that it cannot explain both the rise of transport aid within regional policy, and the winding up of similar transport subsidies within traffic policy. Interest group theory can, however, explain the mobilization of interest groups for transport aid at a later stage, when the new set of rules became known to the firms and the members of parliament in the support area. To proceed with the analyses of driving forces behind institutional path dependence we need to broaden the scope to find an analytical starting-point to study the impact of the historical development of institutional conditions.

PRACTICE AND TRADITION IN TRAFFIC POLICY BEFORE TRANSPORT AID WAS ESTABLISHED

The historical development of institutions in the transport sector before transport aid appears to have been an important aspect of the interest group actions behind the establishment of transport aid. Institutional path dependency can reproduce itself by giving interest groups the opportunity to gain strength in the decision-making process by adapting their demands to practices in earlier institutional settings. In this way, interest groups can legitimize demands for new institutional solutions and at the same time reproduce a path-dependent development of new institutional conditions. Path dependency can therefore explain the deviating development of transport aid compared to regional policy in general. Transport aid was motivated by interest groups which pointed to a previous practice in traffic policy. This makes transport aid unique among other forms of regional policy that lack a reference to traffic policy.

The pattern of active interest groups has been consistent in the rise of transport aid. The initiative was taken by a specific interest group which at an early stage defined the basis of legitimacy for transport aid and in this way related it to a practice in earlier traffic policy, through argumentation and presentation of facts. It remains, finally, to analyse how the formal institutional solution, interest group strategies and previous practices in traffic policy can be brought together in an explanation of how institutional path dependency has affected the development of transport aid. First we shall investigate the impact on transport aid of previous practice in traffic policy by turning back to the nineteenth century and the expansion of railways in Sweden, which also initiated a tradition of promoting regional equity from a transport cost perspective.

At the turn of the nineteenth century, the northernmost part of Sweden (Norrland), benefitted from an export-oriented growth, and the population was growing steadily. Small-scale farming was still the main source of employment, and the farms were mostly geared to subsistence agriculture. Forestry and mining industries developed rapidly and provided an opportunity for farmers to increase their income. In Norrland, this resulted in a dual economy as forestry and mining depended on exports, while agriculture still produced for local markets. In the south of Sweden, agriculture was facing a period of stiff competition from other European countries, as well as urgent demands for rationalization. The farms in southern Sweden developed into large-scale industries and needed to expand their markets, both nationally and internationally. During the latter half of the nineteenth century, railway transport increased in volume. From 1853 to 1854, the building of railways gained momentum in Sweden, as the Riksdag decided that a number of trunk lines should be built and operated by the state. There was no doubt among politicians that regional economic prosperity was more or less directly linked to the existence of a railway transport network (Pettersson 1999b, pp. 282ff.).

During the 1880s, when there was a downward economic trend, business and industry demanded that transport prices on state-owned railways should be reduced. In 1887, a committee was appointed to lay down the fundamental principles which were to determine the tariffs on the state-owned railway. It was suggested, among other things, that the tariffs for the transport of goods should be even more differentiated than before with regard to the value of the goods in relation to the freight costs and the distance. The longer the distance, the lower the freight charges per ton and kilometer. During the 1880s and 1890s, several members of the Riksdag submitted bills suggesting a reduction in freight costs, and the demand for transport subsidies had quite an impact on a number of areas in the 1890s. First, subsidies were given for the transportation of lime by railway, to encourage the use of calcium in agriculture.[3]

Furthermore, the 'Norrland Tariff' was introduced in 1895, which meant that the transportation of grain, root vegetables, and flour to Norrland was subsidized by a 25 percent discount on the standard freight rate, on condition that carriage was paid for a total transport distance of more than 800 kilometers and goods weighing not less than 8 tons per wagon, and all in all, not less than 125 tons per year. In the years 1901, 1902, and 1914, the Norrland Tariff was extended to include other farm products. Moreover, in 1900, the geographical area affected by the tariff regulations was extended to comprise all railway stations in Norrland. Common to all reductions in freight rates, not only the Norrland Tariff, was that privately owned railways also supported the system.

One factor behind the emergence of the Norrland Tariff was the victory of protectionism in the Riksdag in 1888. This change in policy brought into power the supporters of agricultural and industrial protectionism. The Second Chamber of Parliament was dominated by farmers, whose inclinations were clearly more protectionist than before. Several bills and committee reports had a ring of protectionism:

> During the last few years, bigger and bigger loads of potatoes have been imported from Stettin, whence they were first sent by railway from different parts of Pomerania and then shipped in sacks by steamers to Stockholm. Despite the gains of 2–3 middle men ... this business was profitable, whilst the high railway freight charges kept the farmers of Småland, and Västergötland, and even Östergötland, from sending their surplus quantities of potatoes to Stockholm. (Pettersson 1999b, 284ff.)

Swedish agriculture was affected by international competition at the end of the nineteenth century. This was due to the new means of transport and the modern infrastructure developed in many countries in Europe and in Russia during the preceding years. Thus, the railway had its pros and cons for the farmers in southern Sweden. It opened the door for stiff competition, but it could also extend markets. By introducing lower freight charges within the country, the farmers wanted to bar the competition from abroad.

Another argument in favor of the Norrland Tariff had its background in the supply problems of northern Sweden. Norrland was not self-sufficient in grain and root vegetables, but depended on supplies transported from the south. Grain and root vegetables had low market prices in relation to weight; that is, these goods did not quite buy their way with regard to freight costs, when transported by railway. Thus, business owners in Norrland were forced to store large quantities of grain, root vegetables, peas and so on, in the autumn, when the harbors were still open. This was an expensive and not very good solution. By subsidizing the railway freight for these goods, there would be a shift from shipping to railway transport, which could be effected all the year round. Furthermore, the bills often emphasized the advantages of effecting this transport by railway from the point of view of railway economy. Despite the subsidies, the revenues would contribute to the stability of the Swedish state railways (SJ).

In this way, an alliance was established between the interests of Norrland and those of the farmers in the south. The farmers had some problems in finding a market for their products; in Norrland, however, their products were in demand. The Norrland members of the Riksdag, for their part, were in favor of subsidies since such support would lower the prices of grain and root vegetables, particularly the price of potatoes. Moreover, the import of these products to Norrland did not compete with the regional production of such crops, since the production was small, or non-existent. The political alliance turned out to be long-lasting, founded as it was on protectionism, maintenance, and ideas of fairness; the state had built the railway with public means, therefore it should be useful to the whole country. This is the historical background of how special tariffs and other forms of transport subsidies became legitimate instruments for regional equity in the transport sector and in Swedish traffic policy.

ECONOMIC CHANGE AND INSTITUTIONAL PATH DEPENDENCE

To analyse the impact of path dependence on the development of the transport aid, we need to examine which of the three criteria for institutional path dependency have been satisfied in this case study. First, has a new institutional condition been established with an unchanged practice in the regulated sector? The study has shown that a practice from the previous traffic policy has lived on in the institutional condition of transport aid, through a continued subsidization of the cost of transportation similar to a historical tradition in early railway policy. The incentives in transport aid's formal institutional condition for processing transported goods cannot be directly linked to a previous practice in traffic policy. This formal goal was, however, set aside in practice, since a relatively large part of transport aid has been subsidizing the transport of relatively unprocessed goods, which was a reason for the criticism that transport aid has received in previous studies. This also illustrates the stability of an existing practice despite the incentives built into new formal institutions.

Discrimination of shipping constitutes another continuity of practice, since shipping was discriminated against both during the earlier Norrland Tariff and during the period of transport aid. In the case of transport aid this led to numerous debates in the Riksdag, since discrimination of shipping went against the traffic policy guidelines which had previously led to restrictions imposed by the Riksdag regarding the possibilities of subsidizing transport within railway policy. A tension between regional policy and traffic policy can be noted here, something which has probably had an impact on the institutional condition of transport aid. A practice from earlier traffic policy, which entailed a leveling of transport costs, has been difficult to combine in practice with goals from regional policy that have emphasized growth and industrial development. This indicates a path-dependent development of transport aid, since its practice seems to be related to a 'path' other than mainstream regional policy.

Second, has the institutional condition been able to live on despite the existence of well-known and more effective alternatives from the point of view of public economy (from a normative point of view)? In this connection, an alternative solution must, by contemporary actors, be considered to promote growth and regional development in a better way than transport aid. Since transport aid was continuously criticized in parliamentary reports and debates for conserving the economic structure in the support area and for distorting the competition on the transport market, there was probably a certain pressure to change transport aid or replace it with other measures that were more neutral with regard to competition. This pressure for change was brought to a head in the 1990 parliamentary resolution, when the government suggested radical changes in the design and organization of transport aid. However, the government bill was rejected by the Riksdag, and transport aid continued in the same form as before. One reason for this might be that transport aid's original ideological basis of legitimacy differs from the ideological basis of the criticism that transport aid received. In the 1980s the goals and the organization of regional policy changed due to growth-oriented ideological reasons, at the same time as ideological preferences for equality were played down. Transport aid, however, has not changed in this direction, with regard to neither organization nor form, in spite of the fact that both the government and the officials in the Transport Council (the administrative organization) have urged an adjustment of transport aid to fit the general direction of regional policy at large. If the general direction of regional policy in the 1980s and 1990s reflects a more growth-oriented economic policy, then transport aid has resisted institutional change, in spite of the existence of better and more well-known alternatives with regard to promoting growth. The second criterion for institutional path dependency, therefore, may be considered to be satisfied.

Third, has transport aid been legitimized in new ways when faced with an economic pressure for change? This criterion acts on the assumption that interest groups in an institutional path-dependent relationship would formulate new motives in defense of the institution when it is subject to economic pressure for change. These new arguments should be derived from the underlying basis of legitimacy, which in the case of transport aid has been an emphasis on ideological preferences for equality. That way, new motives for transport aid would tie it closer to the ideological path that legitimized transport aid at an earlier stage.

Interest groups have on several occasions expanded the basis of legitimacy of transport aid by presenting new arguments to support it. One example is that transport aid was directed towards small and medium-sized companies in the 1980s. Such arguments were not presented when the aid was introduced in 1970, but were later emphasized by members of the Center and Social Democratic Parties. An interesting aspect of this institutional change is that the new motives were also characterized by ideological preferences for equality,

196 Sweden as a role model of a regulated economy

since transport aid, helped by this change, would be able to support small firms in their competition with large firms in the same sector. This supports the assertion that the main legitimacy of transport aid has been derived from ideological preferences for equality rather than ideological preferences for growth. The conclusion is consequently that interest groups have managed to establish a stronger ideological legitimacy for transport aid. All three criteria for institutional path dependency can therefore be considered to be satisfied in the case of transport aid. Although other perspectives on driving forces behind institutional change (in this case study in the form of public interest and public choice theories) can explain parts of the development of transport aid, institutional path dependency helps to bridge the gap between these alternative approaches by emphasizing the need to study the historical setting in which new institutions are established and by emphasizing a long-run perspective on institutional change.

CONCLUSIONS

By demonstrating how institutional conditions in traffic and regional policy have gradually developed during the twentieth century, the deviating development of transport aid within regional policy is explained in a historical perspective where institutional path dependency may indicate how previous institutional conditions influence the establishment of new institutions. In this connection, the concept of institutional path dependency can add to a theory of the driving forces behind the historical development of institutions and also show that a rapid change of the institutional condition on one level is often balanced by stability on other levels. In the case of transport aid, stability was found in institutional practice and in the active interest groups at an early stage. Therefore, path dependency, in the case of Swedish transport aid, has shown that *a political compensation for long distances* has found different formal expressions with different formal motives, in spite of the fact that the distribution of economic and political resources remained the same. The stability of this distribution of resources, in spite of changing formal institutional conditions, would be the nucleus of institutional path dependency.

NOTES

1. North (1990) uses the term *institutional* path dependence to distinguish it from biological and technical path dependence. For an example of technical path dependence, see David (1985).
2. This chapter is based on my doctoral thesis *Compensating for distance? Transport aid, 1970–1995. Ideology, economy and path dependence* (Pettersson 1999a). If not explicitly stated otherwise, references in this text are to my thesis.
3. On the following analyses of the Norrland Tariff, see Pettersson (1999b), pp. 281–300.

Bibliography

Adams, Charles F. Jr. (1871), 'The government and the railroad corporations', *North American Review*, **62**: 31–61.

Adams, Charles F. Jr. (1893), *Railroads: Their Origins and Problems*, rev. edn, New York: Putnam.

Adams, Henry Carter (1954, [1886]), 'The relation of the state to industrial action'. Reprinted in Joseph Dorfman (ed.), *Two Essays by Henry Carter Adams*, New York: Columbia Press.

Adams, T.S. (1928), 'Ideals and idealism in taxation', *American Economic Review*, **18**: 1–8.

Adams, Walter and Brock, James W. (1991), *Antitrust Economics on Trial*, Princeton, NJ: Princeton University Press.

Adler, Jonathan H. (1992), 'Clean fuels, dirty air: how a (bad) bill became law', *Public Interest*, **108** (Summer): 116–31.

Adler, Jonathan H. (1994), 'Green pork in the corn barrel', Commentary, *The Washington Times*, January 14.

Agell, Jonas, Thomas Lindh and Henry Ohlsson (1995), 'Growth and the public sector: a critical review essay', Working paper Department of Economics, Uppsala: Uppsala University.

Akerlof, G. (1976), 'The economics of caste, and the rat race and other woeful tales', *Quarterly Journal of Economics*, **90**.

Alchian, Armen A. (1965), 'Some economics of property rights', *Il Politico*, **39** (4): 816–28.

Allison, Paul D. (1995), *Survival Analysis Using the SAS System*, Cary, NC: SAS Institute.

Almanac of American Politics (1998), Washington, DC: Gambit.

Alston, Lee J. and Joseph P. Ferrie (1999), *Southern Paternalism and the American Welfare State. Economics, Politics, and Institutions in the South, 1865–1965*, Cambridge: Cambridge University Press.

Alvfors, Karl-Gustav (1977), *Det svenska järnvägsförstatligandet. Svensk järnvägspolitik under 1930-talet*, Eksjö: Svenska järnvägsklubbens skrifter no. 21.

Andersen, E.S. (1994), *Evolutionary Economics. Post-Schumpeterian Contributions*, London and New York: Pinter.

Anderson, Larry G., Pamela Wolfe, Regina A Barrell and John A. Lanning (1995), 'The effects of oxygenated fuels on the atmospheric concentrations of carbon monoxide and aldehydes in Colorado', in Frances S. Sterrett (ed.), *Alternative Fuels and the Environment*, Boca Raton, FL: Lewis, pp. 75–101.

Andersson, Evert (1992), *Höghastighetståg i Sverige. En framtidsstudie inför 2000-talet*, Rail Forum Dialog nr 2/92: Stockholm.

Andersson, Lena (1988), 'Staten, malmbanan och malmbolagen. Kampen om de norrbottniska resurserna under 100 år', in *Malmbanan 100 år. 1888–1988*, Norrbottens museum: Luleå, pp. 99–101.

Andersson-Skog, Lena (1993), *Såsom allmäna inrättningar till gagnet, men affärsföretag till namnet. SJ, järnvägspolitiken och den ekonomiska omvandlingen sedan 1920*, Dissertation, Umeå: Umeå University, Sweden.

Andersson-Skog, Lena (1997), 'The making of national telephone networks in Scandinavia: the state and the emergence of national regulatory patterns', in Magnusson and Ottosson (eds), pp. 138–54.

Andersson-Skog, Lena and Dan Bäcklund (1992), 'Infrastruktur och regional integration', in Gidlund and Sörlin (eds), pp. 70–114.

Andersson-Skog, Lena and Olle Krantz (eds) (1999), *Institutions in the Transport and Communications Industries. State and Private Actors in the Making of Institutional Patterns, 1850–1990*, Canton, MA: Science History Publications, Watson Publ.

Andrussier, Sean E. (1991), 'The Freedom of Information Act in 1990: more freedom for the government; less information for the public', *Duke Law Journal*, pp. 753–801.

Aronsson, Thomas and Mårten Palme (1994), 'A decade of tax and benefit reforms in Sweden effects on labour supply, welfare and inequality', Working paper series in economics and finance (Online) 18, Stockholm: EFI, Stockholm School of Economics.

Arrow, K.J. (1974), *The Limits of Organization*, New York: W.W. Norton.

Arthur, Brian W. (1988), 'Self-reinforcing mechanisms in economics', in: P.W. Anderson, K.J. Arrow and D. Pines (eds), *The Economy as an Evolving Complex System*, Redwood City, CA: Addison-Wesley.

Arthur, Brian W. (1994), *Increasing Returns and Path Dependence in the Economy*, Ann Arbor, MI: University of Michigan Press.

Associated Press (1994), 'Energy Department may bury study criticizing EPA ethanol mandate', Clean Air Report, Thursday, March 10.

Atack, Jeremy and Peter Passell (1994), *A New Economic View of American History from Colonial Times to 1940*, 2nd edn, New York: W.W. Norton.

Atkinson, Anthony and Timothy Smeeding (1995), *Income Distribution in OECD Countries*, Paris: OECD.

Averch, H. and L.L. Johnson (1962), 'Behavior of the firm under regulatory constraint', *American Economic Review*, **52** (5), December: 1052–69. Reprinted in Bailey and Rothenberg Pack (eds), pp. 131–48.

Axelsson, Alf W. (1964), *Gällivareverken: investerings- och spekulationsob-jekt 1855–1882. En lokalhistorisk studie kring kampen om naturtillgångarna i Norrbotten*, Luleå.

Bailey, E.E. and J. Rothenberg Pack (eds) (1995), *The Political Economy of Privatization and Deregulation*, Cheltenham, UK and Lyme, NH, USA: Edward Elgar.

Bain, Joe S. (1956), *Barriers to New Competition*, Cambridge, MA: Harvard University Press.

Baldwin, Robert and Martin Cave (eds) (1999), *Understanding Regulation: Theory, Strategy, and Practice*, Oxford: Oxford University Press.

Bank for International Settlements (1998), *68th Annual Report, 1 April 1997–31 March 1998*, Basle: BIS.

Banks, Jeffrey S. (1991), 'The space shuttle', in Cohen and Noll (eds).

Banks, Jeffrey S., Linda R. Cohen and Roger G. Noll (1991), 'The politics of commercial R&D programs', in Cohen and Noll (eds).

Barnet, Richard J. and Ronald E. Müller (1974), *Global Reach: The Power of the Multinational Corporations*, New York: Simon & Schuster.

Barnett, William P. and Terry Amburgey (1990), 'Do larger organizations generate stronger competition?', in Jitendra Singh (ed.), *Organizational Evolution: New Directions*, Newbury Park, CA: Sage, pp. 78–102.

Barnett, William P. and Glenn R. Carroll (1987), 'Competition and mutualism among early telephone companies', *Administrative Science Quarterly*, **32**: 400–21.

Barnett, William P. and Glenn R. Carroll (1993), 'How institutional constraints affected the organization of early American telephony', *Journal of Law, Economics, and Organization*, **9**: 98–126.

Barro, Robert (1991), 'Economic growth in a cross section of countries', *Quarterly Journal of Economics*, **106**: 407–44.

Barron, David N. (1992), 'The analysis of count data', *Sociological Methodology*, **22**: 179–220.

Barzel Yoram and Christopher D. Hall (1977), *The Political Economy of the Oil Import Quota*, Stanford, CA: Hoover Institution Press.

Baum, Joel A.C. (1998), 'Organizational ecology', in Steward R. Clegg, Cynthia Hardy and Walter Nord (eds), *Handbook of Organization Studies*, London: Sage, pp. 77–114.

Becker, Gary (1983), 'A theory of competition among pressure groups for political influence', *Quarterly Journal of Economics*, **63**: 371–400.

Becketti, Sean (1986), 'Corporate mergers and the business cycle', *Economic Review*, **71**: 13–26.

Bergman, L., C. Doyle, G. Jordi, L. Hulkrantz, D. Neven, L. Röller and L. Waverman (1998), *Europe's Network Industries: Conflicting Priorities*, London: Centre for Economic Policy Research, SNS.

Bergström, Villy and Jan Södersten (1984), 'Do tax allowances stimulate investment?', Uppsala: Uppsala University, Department of Economics Working Paper Series.

Berk, Gerald (1994), *Alternative Tracks: The Constitution of American Industrial Order, 1865–1917*, Baltimore, MD and London: Johns Hopkins University Press.

Betänkande 92/93 (1993), TU 635, Riksdagstryck, Stockholm: Swedish Parliament.

Bihang till riksdagens protokoll vid lagtima riksdagen i Stockholm 1925 (1925), *Kungl Majt:s proposition nr 93*, 1 saml, åttonde bandet, no. 93, Stockholm: Swedish Parliament.

Bijker, W., T. Hughes and T. Pinck (eds) (1987), *The Social Contruction of Technological Systems*, Cambridge, MA: MIT Press.

Binder, John J. (1988), 'The Sherman Antitrust Act and the railroad cartels', *Journal of Law and Economics*, **31**: 443–68.

Birkhead, (1958), 'The Financial Failure of British Air Transport Companies, 1919–1924', *Journal of Transport History*, 1st series, Vol. IV, No. 3, pp. 133–45.

Bishop, Mathew (2000), 'The mystery of the vanishing taxpayer', *The Economist*.

BiSOS Landshövdingeberättelser, Västernorrlands län 1876–1880: Stockholm.

Bittlingmayer, George (1985), 'Did antitrust policy cause the great merger wave?', *Journal of Law and Economics*, **77**: 1–32.

Björklund, Anders, Mårten Palme and Ingemar Svensson (1995), 'Tax reforms and income distribution: an assessment using different income concepts', *Swedish Policy Review*, **2**: 229–66.

Blakeman Early, A. (1994), 'Regulation of fuels and fuel additives: renewable oxygenate required for reformulated gasoline', Sierra Club, Comments to the Environmental Protection Agency Notice of Proposed Rulemaking, Public Docket A-93–49, February 14.

Bohi, Douglas R. and Milton Russell (1978), *Limiting Oil Imports: An Economic History and Analysis*, Baltimore, MD: Johns Hopkins University Press and Resources for the Future.

Böhme, Klaus-Richard (1982), *Svenska vingar växer. Flygvapnet och flygindustrin 1918–1945*, Stockholm: Militärhistoriska Förlaget.

Böhme, Klaus-Richard (1995), 'Connections between commercial and military aviation in a neutralist country', in William F. Trimble (ed.), *From Airships to Airbus: The History of Civil and Commercial Aviation*, vol. II, *Pioneers and Operations*, Washington, DC and London: Smithsonian Institution Press.

Bolet, Adela, M. Kessler, Richard J. Murray, X. Frances and Jonathan B. Stein (1983), *A Report of the Energy and Strategic Resources Staff*, Washington, DC: Center for Strategic and International Studies, Georgetown University.

Bordo, M.D., C. Goldin and E.N. White (eds) (1998), *The Defining Moment.*
The Great Depression and the American Economy in the Twentieth Century,
Chicago: University of Chicago Press.
Boskin, Michael J. (1990), 'New directions in tax policy', in Boskin and McLure
Jr. (eds), pp. 3–7.
Boskin, Michael J. and Charles E. McLure Jr. (eds) (1990), *World Tax Reform*,
San Francisco, CA: ICS Press.
Botniabanan – en samhällsekonomisk bedömning (1991), Förstudie, December,
Borlänge: Banverket.
Bruchey, Stuart (1990), *Enterprise*, Cambridge, MA: Harvard University Press.
Buchanan, James M. and Gordon Tullock (1962), *The Calculus of Consent*,
Ann Arbor, MI: University of Michigan Press.
Buraas, Anders (1972), *Fly Over Fly: Historien om SAS*, Oslo: Gyldendal.
Burrows, James C. and Thomas A. Domencich (1970), *An Analysis of the
United States Oil Import Quota*, Lexington, MA: Heath.
Burt, Tim (1999), 'Raiding the Smorgasbord', *Financial Times* (US edition),
March 26, p. 20.
Busch, Andreas (2000), 'Unpacking globalization: approaches, evidence and
data', in Colin Hay and David Marsh (eds), *Demystifying Globalization*, New
York: St Martin's Press, pp. 21–48.
California Energy Commission, Fuel Resource Office (1999), 'Timetable for
the phaseout of MTBE from California's gasoline supply', Docket No. 99-
GEO-1, June.
Callender, G.S. (1902), 'The early transportation and banking enterprises of
the states in relation to the growth of corporations', *Quarterly Journal of
Economics*, **17**: 111–62.
Cameron, A. Colin and Pravin K. Trivedi (1986), 'Econometric models based
on count data', *Journal of Applied Econometrics*, **1**: 29–53.
Carlsson, Magnus (1999), *Särintresset och staten. En studie av beslutsprocessen
rörande Mälarbanans tillkomst*, Licentiate Thesis, Department of Economic
History, Uppsala, Sweden: Uppsala University.
Carroll, Glenn R. (1985), 'Organizational ecology', *Annual Review of
Sociology*, **10**: 71–93.
Carroll, Glenn R. and Michael T. Hannan (1995), 'Resource partitioning', in
Carroll and Hannan (eds), *Organizations in Industry*, Oxford and New York:
Oxford University Press, pp. 215–21.
Carroll, Glenn R. and Paul Huo Yangchung (1986), 'Organizational and insti-
tutional environments in ecological perspective', *American Journal of
Sociology*, **91**: 838–73.
Chandler, Alfred D. (comp.) (1965), *The Railroads, the Nation's First Big
Business; Sources and Readings*, New York: Harcourt, Brace & World.

Chandler, Alfred D., Jr. (1977), *The Visible Hand: The Managerial Revolution in American Business*, Cambridge, MA and London: Belknap Press/Harvard University Press.

Chandler, Alfred D., Jr. (1990), *Scale and Scope: The Dynamics of Industrial Capitalism*, Cambridge, MA: Harvard University Press.

Cheung, Steven N.S. (1974), 'A theory of price control', *Journal of Law and Economics*, **17** (April): 53–72.

Cheung, Steven N.S. (1982), *Will China Go 'Capitalist'?*, London: Institute of Economic Affairs.

Chicago Conference on Trusts: Speeches, Debates, Resolutions ... (1900), Chicago: Civic Federation of Chicago.

Clark, N.G. and C. Juma (1987), *Long-run Economics: An Evolutionary Approach to Economic Growth*, London: Pinter.

Cleveland, Frederick and Fred Powell (1909), *Railroad Promotion and Capitalization in the United States*, New York: Longmans, Green.

Coate, Stephen and Stephen Morris (1995), 'On the form of transfers to special interests', *Journal of Political Economy*, **103** (December): 1210–35.

Cochran, Thomas C. (1965), *Railroad Leaders 1845–1890: The Business Mind in Action*, New York: Russell & Russell.

Cohen Linda R. and Roger G. Noll (1991), *The Technology Pork Barrel*, Washington, DC: Brookings Institution.

Congressional Budget Office, United States Congress (1981), *An Analysis of President Reagan's Budget Revisions for Fiscal Year 1982*, March, Washington, DC: Government Printing Office.

Congressional Budget Office, United States Congress (1984a), *An Analysis of Congressional Budget Estimates for Fiscal Years 1980–82*, June, Washington, DC: Government Printing Office.

Congressional Budget Office, United States Congress (1984b), *Crop Price Support Programs: Policy Options for Contemporary Agriculture*, February, Washington, DC: Government Printing Office, pp. xiii, 1, 30–43.

Congressional Budget Office, United States Congress (1985a), *Reducing the Deficit: Spending and Revenue Options*, February, Washington, DC: Government Printing Office.

Congressional Budget Office, United States Congress (1985b), *Reducing the Deficit: Spending and Revenue Options: A Report to the Senate and House Committees on the Budget*, Part II, Washington, DC: Government Printing Office, p. 159; 1986, pp. 130–32; 1987, pp. 115–23; 1988, pp. 161–5; 1989, pp. 161–8; 1990, pp. 181–8.

Cowell, Alan (1999), 'Britain's truckers feel new pressures', *New York Times*, March 24, p. C4.

Cowie, Roger (1993), 'Using tax incentives to improve American competitiveness', *American Business Law Journal*, **31** (3): pp. 435–45.

Crocker, K.J. (1996), 'Regulatory issues with vertically disintegrated public utilities: a transaction cost analysis', in John Groenewegen (ed.), *Transaction Costs and Beyond*, Boston, MA and Dordrecht: Kluwer Academic Press, pp. 85–103.

David, P.A. (1985), 'Clio and the economics of QWERTY', *American Economic Review*, **75** (2): 332–7.

David, P.A. (1988), *Path Dependence: Putting the Past into the Future of Economics*, Economic Series: Institute for Mathematical Studies in The Social Sciences, Stanford, CA: Stanford University.

David, P.A. (1994), 'Why are institutions the "carriers of history"? Path dependence and the evolution of conventions, organizations and institutions', *Structural Change and Economic Dynamics*, **5** (2): 209ff.

Davies, R.E.G. (1964), *A History of the World's Airlines*, London and New York: Oxford University Press.

de Alessi, Louis (1980), 'The economics of property rights: a review of the evidence', *Research in Law and Economics*, **2**: 1–47. Reprinted in Bailey and Rothenberg Pack (eds).

de Alessi, Louis (1983), 'Property rights, transaction costs, and X-efficiency: an essay in economic theory', *American Economic Review*, **73** (1) March: 64–81.

Del Valle, Christina (1995), 'Meet Bud Schuster, Prince of Pork', *Business Week*, May 15, pp. 86–7.

Delacroix, Jacques and Glenn R. Carroll (1983), 'Organizational foundings', *Administrative Science Quarterly*, **28**: 274–91.

Delacroix, Jacques and Michael E. Solt (1988), 'Niche formation and foundings in the California wine industry', in Glenn R. Carroll (ed.), *Ecological Models of Organizations*, Cambridge, MA: Ballinger.

Demsetz, Harold (1967), 'Towards a theory of property rights', *American Economic Review*, **57**: 347–59.

Demsetz, Harold (1969), 'Information and efficiency: another viewpoint', *Journal of Law and Economics*, **12** (April): 1–22.

Dillenbäck J. and T. Ångström (1950), 'AB Aerotransports Linjetrafik', in G. Edlund et al. (eds), *Handbok i samfärdselteknik, Avd. sjöfart och luftfart*, Stockholm: Natur och Kultur.

Dixit, A.K. (1996), *The Making of Economic Policy: A Transaction-cost Perspective*, Cambridge, MA and London, UK: MIT Press.

Dobbin, Frank (1992), 'Metaphors for industrial rationality', in Robert Wuthnow (ed.), *Vocabularies of Public Life*, London: Routledge, pp. 185–206.

Dobbin, F. (1994), *Forging Industrial Policy. The United States, Britain, and France in the Railway Age*, Cambridge: Cambridge University Press.

Domberger, S. and J. Piggot (1994), 'Privatization policies and public enterprise: a survey', in Matthew Bishop, John Kay and Colin Mayer (eds), *Privatization and Economic Performance*, Oxford: Oxford University Press, pp. 32–61.

Douglas, Mary (1992), *Risk and Blame. Essays in Cultural Theory*, London: Routledge.

Dowrick, Steve (1996), 'Swedish economic performance and Swedish economic debate: a view from outside', *Economic Journal*, **106**: 1772–9.

Dugger, W.M. (1993), 'Transaction cost economics and the state', in Christos Pitelis (ed.), *Transaction Costs, Market and Hierarchies*, Oxford, UK, and Cambridge, MA, USA: Blackwell, pp. 188–216.

Dunlavy, C.A. (1991), 'Political structure and early railroad policy in the United States and Prussia', *Studies in American Political Development*, **5**: 1–35.

Dunlavy, C.A. (1992), 'Political structure, state policy, and industrial change: early railroad policy in the United States and Prussia', in Steinmo et al. (eds), pp. 114–54.

Dunlavy, C.A. (1994a), *Politics and Industrialization. Early Railroads in the United States and Prussia*, Princeton, NJ: Princeton University Press.

Dunlavy, C.A. (1994b), 'How did American business get so big?', *Audacity, The Magazine of Business Experience*, Spring 41–9.

Dunlavy, C.A. (1999), 'When business outgrows the law: lessons from the American experience', *Northwestern Journal of International Affairs*, **1** (Spring): 19–27.

Edelman, Lauren (1990), 'Legal environments and organizational governance', *American Journal of Sociology*, **95**: 1401–40.

Edelman, Lauren (1992), 'Legal ambiguity and symbolic structures', *American Journal of Sociology*, **97**: 1531–76.

Edlund, Lars-Erik and Lars Beckman (eds) (1994), *Botnia: En nordsvensk region*. Umeå.

Eisner, Marc Allen (1991), *Antitrust and the Triumph of Economics*, Chapel Hill, NC: University of North Carolina Press.

Elster, J. (1989), *The Cement of Society: A Study of Social Order*, Cambridge: Cambridge University Press.

Ely, Richard T. (1887), 'III. The Future of Corporations', *Harper's Monthly Magazine* (July): 259–66.

Ely, Richard T. (1900), *Monopolies and Trusts*, New York: Macmillan & Company.

Feldman, Gerald D. (1996), *The Great Disorder: Politics, Inflation and Society in the German Inflation, 1914–1924*, New York and Oxford: Oxford University Press.

Fink, Albert (1979, [1880]), 'Argument before the Committee of Commerce of the House of Representatives of the United States on the Reagan bill for the regulation of interstate commerce', in Alfred D. Chandler (ed.), *The Railroads: Pioneers in Modern Management*, New York: Arno, pp. 3–55.

Fink, Albert (1979, [1876]), 'Report of the Vice President and General Superintendent, Louisville & Nashville Railroad Co., 1873–4', in Alfred D. Chandler (ed.), *The Railroads: Pioneers in Modern Management*, New York: Arno, pp. 21–67.

Fligstein, Neil (1990), *The Transformation of Corporate Control*, Cambridge, MA: Harvard University Press.

Fligstein, Neil (1996), 'Markets as politics', *American Sociological Review*, **61**: 656–74.

Florence, P. Sargent (1953), *The Logic of British and American Industry*, London: Routledge & Kegan Paul.

Fölster, Stefan and Sam Peltzman (1995), 'The social cost of regulation and lack of competition in Sweden', working paper, Industrial Institute for Economic and Social Research, 438, Stockholm: IUI.

Foreman-Peck, J. and R. Millward (1994), *Public and Private Ownership of British Industry 1820–1990*, Oxford: Clarendon Press.

Förslag till riksdagen 1995/96 (1996), RR4, pp. 34, 68, 73, Stockholm: Swedish Parliament.

Framtida järnvägsinvesteringar ur ett inlandsperspektiv (1993), Östersund, Sweden: Länsstyrelsen, Jämtlands län.

Francis, J. (1993), *The Politics of Regulation: A Comparative Perspective*, Oxford, Blackwell.

Fridlund, M. (1999), *Den gemensamma utvecklingen: Staten, storföretaget och samarbetet kring den svenska elkrafttekniken*, Stockholm: Brutus Östlings Bokförlag, Symposion.

Fritsche, Peter (1992), *A Nation of Fliers: German Aviation and the Popular Imagination*, Cambridge, MA, and London: Harvard University Press.

Furubotn, Eirik G. and Rudolf Richter (1997), *Institutions and Economic Theory: The Contribution of the New Institutional Economics*, Ann Arbor, MI: University of Michigan Press.

Gardner, Bruce L. (1987), *The Economics of Agricultural Policies*, New York: Macmillan.

Gardner, Bruce L. (1995), 'Fuel ethanol subsidies and farm price support: boon or boondoggle?', University of Maryland, unpublished manuscript.

Garrett, Geoffrey (1995), 'Capital mobility, trade and the domestic politics of economic policy', *International Organization*, **49**: 657–87.

Garret, Geoffrey and Peter Lange (1995), 'Internationalization, institutions and political change', *International Organization*, **49**: 627–55.

Gavett, Earle E. (1988), 'The economics of fuel ethanol: a comparison of three major studies', speech presented at the Energy from Biomass and Wastes, 12th Conference, New Orleans, February.

Gavett, Earle E., Gerald E. Grinnell and Nancy L. Smith (1986), 'Fuel ethanol and agriculture: an economic assessment', US Department of Agriculture, Office of Energy, Agricultural Economic Report 562, Washington, DC: Government Printing Office.

Genschel, P. and T. Plümper (1997), 'Regulatory competition and international cooperation', MPIfG Working Paper 97/4, Cologne: Max-Planck-Institut für Gesellschaftsforschung.

Gersick, C.J.G. (1991), 'Revolutionary change theories: a multilevel exploration of the punctuated equilibrium paradigm', *Academy of Management Review*, **16** (1).

Giddens, A. (1984), *The Constitution of Society*, Cambridge: Polity.

Gidlund, J.E. and S. Sörlin (eds) (1992), *Botniaregionen. Modernisering och livskvalitet i en nordeuropeisk region*, Umeå: CERUM Perspektiv.

Gidlund, J.E., S. Sörlin and S. Gidlund (2000), 'Ensan hemma. Den norrländska elitens syn på regional utveckling', CERUM working paper, No. 17, Umeå.

Giovannini, Alberto (1990), 'International capital mobility and capital-income taxation', *European Economic Review*, **34**: 480–88.

Gisser, Micha (1993), 'Price support, acreage controls, and efficient redistribution', *Journal of Political Economy*, **101** (August): 584–611.

Godlund, Sven (1962), 'Vägar, järnvägar och flygplatser: Några drag i kommunikationsväsendets utveckling i Västernorrland de senaste hundra åren', in Harald Wiik (ed.), *Västernorrland – ett sekel, 1862–1962*, vol. 1, Stockholm: P.A. Norstedts and Söner, pp. 348–438.

Goldin, C. and G. Libecap (eds) (1994), *The Regulated Economy. A Historical Approach to Political Economy*, Chicago: University of Chicago Press.

Goodrich, Carter (1949), 'The Virginia system of mixed enterprise', *Political Science Quarterly*, **64**: 355–87.

Goodrich, Carter (1960), *Government Promotion of American Canals and Railroads 1800–1890*, New York: Columbia University Press.

Goodrich, Carter (1968), 'State in, state out: a pattern of development policy', *Journal of Economic Issues*, **30**: 365–83.

Gordon, Scott (1954), 'The economic theory of a common property resource: the fishery', *Journal of Political Economy*, **62** (April): 124–42.

Gort, Michael (1969), 'An economic disturbance theory of mergers', *Quarterly Journal of Economics*, **83**: 624–42.

Grandy, Christopher (1993), *New Jersey and the Fiscal Origins of Modern American Corporation Law*, New York and London: Garland.

Granqvist, Gunnar (1971), *Ny trafikpolitik – en ostkustbana*, Lund.

Gravelle, Jane (1992), 'Equity effects of the Tax Reform Act of 1986', *Journal of Economic Perspectives*, **6**: 27–44.

Groenewegen, J. and J. Vromen (1997), 'Theory of the firm revisited: new and neo-institutional perspectives', in Magnusson and Ottosson (eds).

Group of 30 (1997), *Global Institutions, National Supervision and Systemic Risk: A Study Group Report*, Washington, DC: Group of 30.

Haas, George (1937), 'Tax revision studies: general statement, revenue estimates, summaries, and recommendations', College Park, MD: Tax Reform Programs and Studies; Records of the Office of Tax Analysis/Division of Tax Research; General Records of the Department of the Treasury, Record Group 56; National Archives, College Park, MD.

Hadley, Arthur T. (1886), 'Private monopolies and public rights', *Quarterly Journal of Economics*, **1** (October): 28–44.

Hadley, Arthur Twining (1903), *Railroad Transportation*, 10th edn, New York: G.P. Putnam's & Sons.

Hahn, Robert W. (1996), *Risks, Costs, and Lives Saved*, New York: Oxford University Press.

Hall, Peter A. (1986), *Governing the Economy*, New York: Oxford University Press.

Hall, Peter, A. (1989), 'Introduction', in Hall (ed.), *The Political Power of Economic Ideas: Keynesianism Across Nations*, Princeton, NJ: Princeton University Press.

Hallberg, M.C. (1992), *Policy for American Agriculture: Choices and Consequences*, Ames, IA: Iowa State University Press.

Hamilton, Gary G. and Nicole Woolsey Biggart (1988), 'Market, culture, and authority', *American Journal of Sociology*, **94**.

Handlin, Oscar and Mary F. Handlin (1947), *Commonwealth: A Study of the Role of Government in the American Economy: Massachusetts, 1774–1861*, Cambridge, MA: Harvard University Press.

Hannan, Michael T. and Glenn R. Carroll (1992), *Dynamics of Organizational Populations*, New York: Oxford University Press.

Hannan, Michael T. and John Freeman (1987), 'The ecology of organizational founding rates', *American Journal of Sociology*, **92**: 910–43.

Hannan, Michael T. and John Freeman (1989), *Organizational Ecology*, Cambridge, MA: Harvard University Press.

Hansen, Bent (1969), *Fiscal Policies in Seven Countries*, Paris: OECD.

Hansen, Robert G. and John R. Lott Jr. (1996), 'Externalities and corporate objectives in a world with diversified owner/shareholders', *Journal of Financial and Quantitative Analysis*, **31** (March): 43–68.

Harriss, John et al. (eds) (1995), *The New Institutional Economics and Third World Development*, London: Routledge.

Hartz, Louis (1948), *Economic Policy and Democratic Thought*, Cambridge, MA: Harvard University Press.

Headrick, D.R. (1981), *The Tools of Empire: Technology and European Imperialism in the Nineteenth Century*, Oxford, Oxford University Press.

Heckscher, Eli F. (1907), *Till belysning af järnvägarnas betydelse för Sveriges ekonomiska tillväxt*, Stockholm.

Heiner, Ronald A. (1983), 'The origin of predictable behavior', *American Economic Review*, **73** (4) (September): 560–95.

Helgesson, C.-F. (1995), 'Technological momentum and the "natural" monopoly', paper presented at the SHOT 1995 annual meeting, Stockholm: Stockholm School of Economics.

Helgesson, C.-F. (1999), *Making a Natural Monopoly: The Configuration of a Techno-Economic Order in Swedish Telecommunications*, Stockholm: EFI, Economic Research Institute, Stockholm School of Economics.

Henrekson, Magnus (1996), 'Sweden's relative economic performance: lagging behind or staying on top?', *Economic Journal*, **106**: 1747–59.

Henry, Robert S. (1945), 'The American land grant legend in American history texts', *Mississippi Valley Historical Review*, **32**: 171–94.

Heydinger, Earl L. (1954), 'The English influence on American railroads', *Railway and Locomotive History Bulletin*, **91**: 7–45.

Hicks, Alexander and Lane Kenworthy (1998), 'Cooperation and political economic performance in affluent democratic capitalism', *American Journal of Sociology*, **103**: 1631–72.

Hilton, George W. (1966), 'The consistency of the Interstate Commerce Act', *Journal of Law and Economics*, **19**: 87–113.

Hobsbawm, E.J. (1969), *Industry and Empire*, London: Penguin Books.

Hodgson, G.M. (1988), *Economics and Institutions*, Cambridge: Polity Press.

Hodgson, G.M. (1993), *Economics and Evolution*, Cambridge: Polity Press.

Hodne, Fritz (1988), *Statens grunnlagsinvesteringer. Stortingssalen som markedsplass 1849–1914*, Oslo: Universitetsforlaget.

Hoffman, Linwood, Mark Ash, William Lin and Stephanie Mercier (1990), 'U.S. feed grains: background for 1990 farm legislation', Agricultural Information Bulletin 604, UDSA Economic Research Service, Washington, DC: Government Printing Office.

Hoogenboom, Ari and Olive Hoogenboom (1976), *A History of the ICC: From Panacea to Palliative*, New York: W.W. Norton & Company.

House, Robert, Mark Peters, Harry Baumes and Terry W. Disney (1993), 'Ethanol and agriculture: effect of increased production on crop and livestock sectors', Agricultural Economic Report, No. 667, USDA Economic Research Service, Washington, DC: Government Printing Office.

Hughes, Thomas (1983), *Networks of power: Electrification in Western society, 1880–1930*, Baltimore: John Hopkins University Press.

Hultkrantz, L. (1996), 'Telepolitikens ekonomiska teori', CTS Working Paper 6, Centre for Research in Transport and Society, Borlänge: Högskolan Dalarna.

Ioannidis, D. (1998), *I nationens tjänst? Strategisk handling i politisk miljö*, Stockholm: EFI: Economic Research Institute, Stockholm School of Economics.

Isser, Steve (1996), *The Economics and Politics of the United States Oil Industry, 1920–1990: Profits, Populism, and Petroleum*, New York: Garland.

Jackson, P.M. and C.M. Price (1994), *Privatisation and Regulation: A Review of the Issues*, London: Longman.

Jeding, C. (1998), 'National politics and international agreements: British strategies in regulating European telephony, 1923–39', Working Papers in Transport and Communications History, Uppsala: Departments of Economic History, Umeå and Uppsala Universities.

Johansson, Anders L. and Lars Magnusson (1998), *LO andra halvseklet: fackföreningsrörelsen och samhället*, Stockholm: Atlas.

John, Richard R. (1997), 'Governmental institutions as agents of change: rethinking American political development in the early republic, 1787–1835', *Studies in American Political Development*, **11** (Fall): 347–80.

Johnson, Chalmers (1982), *MITI and the Japanese Miracle*, Stanford, CA: Stanford University Press.

Johnson, David R. and David Post (1996), 'Laws and borders: the rise of law in cyberspace', *Stanford Law Review*, **48** (May): 1367–1402.

Johnson, Ronald N. and Gary D. Libecap (1994), *The Federal Civil Service System and the Problem of Bureaucracy: The Economics and Politics of Institutional Change*, Chicago: University of Chicago Press.

Jonsson, Bo (1969), *Staten och malmfälten: en studie i svensk malmfältspolitik omkring sekelskiftet*, Dissertation, Stockholm: Almqvist & Wiksell.

Jonung, Lars (1999), *Med backspegeln som kompass: om stabiliseringspolitiken som läroprocess*, rapport till ESO – Expertgruppen för studier i offentlig ekonomi, Ds 1999:9 (with an English summary), Stockholm: Liber/Allmänna Förlaget.

Kaijser, A. (1994), *I fädrens spår: den svenska infrastrukturens historiska utveckling och framtida utmaningar*, Stockholm: Carlssons.

Kaijser, A. (1999), 'The helping hand. In search of a Swedish institutional regime for infrastructural systems', in Andersson-Skog and Krantz (eds).

Kanazawa, M.T. and R.G. Noll (1994), 'The origins of state railroad regulation: the Illinois Constitution of 1870', in Goldin and Libecap (eds), pp. 13–54.

Kane, Sally and Michael LeBlanc (1989), *Ethanol and U.S. Agriculture*, AIB-559, US Department of Agriculture, Economic Research Service, Washington, DC: Government Printing Office.

Kane, Sally M. and John M. Reilly (1989), 'Economics of ethanol production in the United States', USDA, Economic Research Service, Agricultural Economic Report 607, March, Washington, DC: Government Printing Office.

Karlsson, M. (1998), *The Liberalisation of Telecommunications in Sweden*, Linköping, Sweden: Department of Technology and Social Change, Linköping University.

Karpoff, Jonathan M. and John R. Lott, Jr. (1993), 'The reputational penalty firms bear from committing criminal fraud', *Journal of Law and Economics*, **36** (October): 757–802.

Katz, Joan M. (1970), 'The games bureaucrats play: hide and seek under the freedom of information act', *Texas Law Review*, **48**: 1261–84.

Katzenstein, Charles J. (1984), *Corporatism and Change*, Ithaca, NY: Cornell University Press.

Kennedy, Charles J. (1961), 'The influence of government regulation on the management decisions of forty-five New England railroads, 1830–1900', *Railway and Local Historical Society Bulletin*, **105**: 6–22.

Kennedy, Robert Dawson, Jr. (1991), 'The statist evolution of rail governance in the United States, 1830–1986', in John L. Campbell, J. Rogers Hollingsworth and Leon N. Lindberg (eds), *Governance of the American Economy*, New York: Cambridge University Press, pp. 138–81.

Kindleberger, C.P. (1983), 'Standards, as public, collective and private goods', *Kyklos*, **36**: 377ff.

Kirchstetter, Thomas W., Brett C. Singer, Robert A. Harley, Gary R. Kendall and Waymond Chan (1996), 'Impact of oxygenated gasoline use on California light-duty vehicle emissions', *Environmental Science and Technology*, **30** (2): 661–70.

Klein, Benjamin and Keith B. Leffler (1981), 'The role of market forces in assuring contractual performance', *Journal of Political Economy*, **89** (August): 615–41.

Knoke, D. et al. (eds) (1996), *Comparing Policy Networks. Labor Politics in the U.S, Germany, and Japan*, Cambridge: Cambridge University Press.

Koebel, P. (1990), 'Deregulation of the telecommunications sector: a movement in line with recent technological advances', in Majone (ed.), pp. 110–23.

Kolko, Gabriel (1965), *Railroads and Regulation, 1877–1916*, Princeton, NJ: Princeton University Press.

Korpi, Walter (1996), 'Eurosclerosis and the sclerosis of objectivity: on the role of values among economic experts', *Economic Journal*, **106**: 1727–46.

Korten, David (1995), *When Corporations Rule the World*, West Hartford, CT: Kamarian Press.

Krantz, Olle (2000), 'Swedish economic growth during the 20th century – a problematic history', *Economist Debate*, **1**: 7–15.

Krueger, A.O. (1974), 'The political economy of the rent seeking society', *American Economic Review*, **64**: 291–303.

Krueger, A.O. (1990), 'The political economy of control: American Sugar', in Maurice Scott and Deepak Lal (eds), *Public Policy and Development: Essays in Honour of Ian Little*, Oxford: Oxford University Press.

Krueger, A.O. (1996), 'The political economy of control: American Sugar', in Lee J. Alston, Thráinn Eggertsson and Douglass North (eds), *Empirical Studies in Institutional Change*, Cambridge: Cambridge University Press, pp. 169–218.

Langlois, Richard (ed.) (1989), *The Market as a Process*, Cambridge, MA: Cambridge University Press.

Lardner, Dionysius (1850), *Railway Economy: A Treatise on the New Art of Transport, Its Management, Prospects, and Relations, Commercial, Financial, and Social*, London: Taylor, Walton & Maberly.

LeBlanc, Michael and John Reilly (1988), *Ethanol: Economic and Policy Tradeoffs*, AER-585, US Department of Agriculture, Resources and Technology Division.

Lee, Dwight R. and Richard B. McKenzie (1989), 'The international political economy of declining tax rates', *National Tax Journal*, **42**: 79–83.

Leibowitz, S.J. and S.E. Margolis (1995), 'Path dependence, lock-in, and history', *Journal of Law, Economics, and Organization*, **7** (1): 206ff.

Levi, Margaret (1988), *Of Rule and Revenue*, Berkeley, CA: University of California Press.

Levitt, Steven D. and James M. Snyder (1997), 'The impact of federal spending on house election outcomes', *Journal of Political Economy*, **105** (February): 30–53.

Levy, P.T. and B. Spiller (1994), 'The institutional foundations of regulatory commitment: a comparative analysis of telecommunications regulation', *Journal of Law, Economics and Organization*, **10** (2): 201–46.

Lewin, Leif (1970), *Planhushållningsdebatten* (The debate on planning), Stockholm: Almquist & Wicksell.

Lin, William, Peter Riley and Sam Evans (1995), 'Feed grains: background for 1995 farm legislation', USDA, Economic Research Service, Agricultural Economics Report, 714, April.

Lindberg, Leon and John L. Campbell (1991), 'The state and the organization of economic activity', in John L. Campbell, J. Rogers Hollingsworth and Leon N. Lindberg (eds), *Governance of the American Economy*, New York: Cambridge University Press, pp. 356–95.

Lindbeck, Assar (1997), *The Swedish Experiment*, Stockholm: SNS Förlag.

Lindgren, Håkan (1994), *Aktivt ägande. Investor under växande konjunkturer* (Active ownership: investors and the Wallenberg group), Stockholm: Norstedts.

Lipset, Seymour Martin (1963), *The First New Nation*, New York: Norton.

Lipton, Kathryn L. (1989), 'Changes in U.S. agriculture and emerging issues for legislation in the 1990s', USDA, Economic Research Service, Agriculture Information Bulletin 584, December.

Lissitzyn, Oliver J. (1942), *International Air Transport and National Policy*, New York: Council on Foreign Relations.

Locklin, David (1954), *Economics of Transportation*, 4th edn, Homewood, IL: Irwin.

Locklin, David (1965), *The Economic Effects of Regulation*, Cambridge, MA: MIT Press.

Lufttrafikkommittén (1921), *Betänkande och förslag angående reguljär lufttrafik och åtgärder från statens sida för dess främjande*. Avgivet av den av Kungl. Maj:t den 2 maj 1919 för ändamålet tillsatta kommitté: Stockholm.

Lundberg, Stellan (1992), 'Botniabanan och det regionala samspelet', in Gidlund and Sörlin (eds).

Lupia, Arthur W. and Mathew D. McCubbins (1997), *The Democratic Dilemma: Can Citizens Learn What they Need to Know?*, Cambridge: Cambridge University Press.

Lyth, Peter J. (1993), 'The history of commercial air transport: a progress report, 1953–93', *Journal of Transport History*, 3rd ser., **14** (2): 166–80.

Lyth, Peter J. (1997a), 'Institutional change and European air transport, 1910–1985', in Magnusson and Ottosson (eds).

Lyth, Peter J. (1997b), 'Experiencing turbulence: regulation and Deregulation in the international air transport industry, 1930–1990', in James McConville (ed.), *Transport Regulation Matters*, London and Washington: Pinter.

MacAvoy, Paul W. (1965), *The economic effects of regulation : the trunk-line railroad cartels and the interstate commerce commission before 1900*, Cambridge, MA: MIT Press.

Magnusson, L. (1996), *Sveriges ekonomiska historia*, Stockholm: Tiden, Rabén och Sjögren.

Magnusson, Lars (2000), *An Economic History of Sweden*, London: Routledge.

Magnusson, L. and J. Ottosson (1996), 'Transaction Costs and Institutional Change', in John Groenewegen (ed.), *Transaction Cost Economics and Beyond*, Boston, MA, Dordrecht and London: Kluwer Academic, pp. 351–64.

Magnusson, L. and J. Ottosson (eds) (1997), *Evolutionary Economics and Path Dependence*, Cheltenham: Edward Elgar.

Majone, G. (1990a), 'Introduction', in Majone (ed.), pp. 1–6.

Majone, G. (ed.) (1990b), *Deregulation or Regulation? Regulatory Reform in Europe and the United States*, London: Pinter.

Mannino, David M. and Ruth A. Etzel (1996), 'Are oxygenated fuels effective? an evaluation of ambient carbon monoxide concentrations in 11 western states, 1986 to 1992', *Journal of the Air and Waste Management Association*, **46** (January): 20–24.

Mark, Gregory A. (1995), 'Some observations on writing the legal history of the corporation in an age of theory', in Lawrence E. Mitchell (ed.), *Progressive Corporate Law*, Boulder, CO: Westview, pp. 67–92.

Marris, Robin (1964), *Economic Theory of 'Managerial' Capitalism*, New York: Free Press.

Massachusetts, Board of Railroad Commissioners (1869–1922), *Annual Report of the Railroad Commissioners*, Boston: Commonwealth of Massachusetts.

Massachusetts, Committee on Railways and Canals (1838–1856), *Annual Report of the Railroad Corporations of Massachusetts*, Boston: Commonwealth of Massachusetts.

Massachusetts, General Court of (1825–1922), *Acts and Resolves of the General Court of Massachusetts*, Boston: State Printers.

Massachusetts, Secretary of the Commonwealth (1857–1869), *Returns of the Railroad Corporations of Massachusetts*, Boston: Commonwealth of Massachusetts.

Mayhew, David R. (1974), *Congress: The Electoral Connection*, New Haven, CT: Yale University Press.

Mayotte, Stephen C., Christian E. Lindhjem, Venkatesh Rao and Michael S. Sklar (1994a), 'Reformulated gasoline effects on exhaust emissions. Phase I: Initial investigation of oxygenate, volatility, distillation and sulfur effects', SAE Technical Paper Series, 941973.

Mayotte, Stephen C., Venkatesh Rao, Christian E. Lindhjem and Michael S. Sklar (1994b), 'Reformulated gasoline effects on exhaust emissions. Phase II: Continued investigation of oxygenate type, volatility, sulfur, olefins, and distillation parameters', SAE Technical Paper Series, 941974.

McCraw, Thomas K. (1984), *Prophets of Regulation*, Cambridge, MA: Harvard University Press.

McCraw, Thomas K. (1997), *Creating Modern Capitalism*, Cambridge, MA: Harvard University Press.

McDaniel, Paul and Stanley Surrey (1985), *International Aspects of Tax Expenditures: A Comparative Study*, Deventer, The Netherlands: Kluwer.

Meekhof, Ronald L., Wallace E. Tyner and Forrest D. Holland (1980), 'U.S. agricultural policy and gasohol: a policy simulation', *American Journal of Agricultural Economics*, **62** (3): 408–15.

Meyer, John W. and Brian Rowan (1977), 'Institutionalized organizations', *American Journal of Sociology*, **83**: 340–63.

Miles, Kristi A. (1989), 'The Freedom of Information Act: shielding agency deliberations from FOIA disclosure', *George Washington Law Review*, **57** (5): 1326–1341.

Miller, George H. (1971), *Railroads and the Granger Laws*, Madison, WI: University of Wisconsin Press.

Miller, Paul J., Environmental Defense Fund (1994), 'Regulation of fuels and fuel additives: renewable oxygenate required for reformulated gasoline', Comments to the Environmental Protection Agency Notice of Proposed Rulemaking, Public Docket A-93–49, February 14.

Millward, R. and J. Singleton (eds) (1995), *The Political Economy of Nationalisation in Britain 1920–1950*, Cambridge: Cambridge University Press.

Mitchell, Brian R. (1998a), *International Historical Statistics: Europe, 1750–1993*, Basingstoke: Macmillan.

Mitchell, Brian R. (1998b), *International Historical Statistics: The Americas 1750–1993*, Basingstoke: Macmillan.

Mokyr, J. (1990), *The Lever of Riches: Technological Creativity and Economic Progress*, Oxford: Oxford University Press.

Morgenson, Gretchen (1999), 'Market watch: a company worth more than Spain?', *New York Times*, December 26, sec. 3, p. 1.

Murhem, Sofia and Jan Ottosson (2000), 'The changing foundations of Swedish model labour market policies', in Rolf Prigge, Reiner Buchegger and Lars Magnusson (eds), *Strategien Regionaler Beschäftigungsförderung. Schweden, Österreich und Deutschland im Vergleich*, Frankfurt/New York: Campus Verlag.

National Advisory Panel on Cost-Effectiveness of Fuel Ethanol Production (1987), *Fuel Ethanol Cost-effectiveness Study*, Washington, DC: Government Printing Office, November.

National Research Council Committee on Tropospheric Ozone Formation and Measurement (1991), *Rethinking the Ozone Problem in Urban and Regional Air Pollution*, Washington, DC: National Academy Press.

National Research Council, Committee on Toxicological and Performance Aspects of Oxygenated Motor Vehicle Fuels (1996), *Toxicological and Performance Aspects of Oxygenated Motor Vehicle Fuels*, Board on Environmental Studies and Toxicology, Commission on Life Sciences, Washington, DC: National Academy Press.

National Science and Technology Council Committee on Environment and Natural Resources (1997), *Interagency Assessment of Oxygenated Fuels*, Executive Office of the President, Washington, DC: Government Printing Office.

Nelson, R.R. (1994), 'Economic growth via the co-evolution of technology and institutions', in L. Leydesdorff and P. van den Besselaar (eds), *Evolutionary Economics and Chaos Theory*, London and New York: Pinter.

Nelson, R.R. and S.G. Winter (1982), *An Evolutionary Theory of Economic Change*, Cambridge, MA: Harvard University Press.

Nimmo, Joseph Jr. (1881), *The Railroad Problem: Cost of Transportation, Railroad Confederations or Pooling Arrangements, and the Governmental Regulation of Railroads; Being a Part of the Annual Report on the Internal*

Commerce of the United States, Washington, DC: Government Printing Office.

Niskanen, W.A. (1993), 'Reduce Federal regulation', in D. Boaz and E.H. Crane (eds), *Market Liberalism: A Paradigm for the 21st Century*, Washington, DC: Cato Institute, pp. 103–14.

Noam, E. (1992), *Telecommunications in Europe*, New York: Oxford University Press.

Noll, R.G. (1989), 'Economic perspectives on the politics of regulation', in Richard Schmalensee and Robert D. Willig (eds), *Handbook of Industrial Organization*, vol. II, Amsterdam, New York, Oxford, Tokyo: North-Holland, pp. 1254–87.

Nordlund, Sven (1989), *Upptäckten av Sverige. Utländska direktinvesteringar i Sverige 1895–1945*, Umeå Studies in Economic History 12, Umeå: University of Umeå, Department of Economic History.

Norrländsk uppslagsbok. Ett uppslagsverk på vetenskaplig grund om den norrländska regionen (1993), vols I–IV, Höganäs, Umeå 1994–1996.

North, Douglass C. (1981), *Structure and Change in Economic History*, New York: Norton.

North, D.C. (1990), *Institutions, Institutional Change and Economic Performance,* Cambridge: Cambridge University Press.

North, Douglass C. (1995), 'The New Institutional Economics and Third World development', in John Harriss (ed.), *The New Institutional Economics and Third World Development*, London & New York: Routledge.

Novak, William J. (1996), *The People's Welfare: Law and Regulation in Nineteenth-Century America*, Chapel Hill, NC and London: University of North Carolina Press.

O'Reilly, James T. (1994), 'Applying Federal open government laws to congress: an explorative analysis and proposal', *Harvard Journal on Legislation*, **31**: 415–68.

OECD (1988), *Why Economic Policies Change Course*, Paris: Organization for Economic Cooperation and Development.

OECD (1989), *International Direct Investment and the New Economic Environment*, Paris: Organization for Economic Cooperation and Development.

OECD (1991), *Taxing Profits in a Global Economy: Domestic and International Issues*, Paris: Organization for Economic Cooperation and Development.

OECD (1997), *Taxing International Business: Emerging Trends in APE and OECD Countries*, Paris: Organization for Economic Cooperation and Development.

OECD (1999), *Financial Market Trends*, No. 73, June.

Olson, Mancur (1965), *The Logic of Collective Action*, Cambridge, MA: Harvard University Press.

Olson, Mancur (1982), *The Rise and Decline of Nations. Economic Growth, Stagflation, and Social Rigidities*, New Haven, CT and London: Yale University Press.

Olson, Mancur (1990), *How Bright are the Northern Lights? Some Questions about Sweden*, Crafoord lectures, Lund: Lund University Press.

Oredsson, Sverker (1969), *Järnvägarna och det allmänna. Svensk järn-vägspolitik till 1890*, Lund: Rahms Boktryckeri.

Ostkustbanekommitténs, betänkande (1922), Stockholm.

Ousaager, Sveen (1988), *Politikk på skinner. Lokalbanesporsmålet og Nordfyns privatbaner i dansk trafikpolitik ca 1920–1970*, Odense: Odense universitetsforlag.

Paarlberg, Robert L. (1988), *Fixing Farm Trade: Policy Options for the United States*, Cambridge, MA: Ballinger.

Palme, Mårten (1993), *Five Empirical Studies on Income Distribution in Sweden*, Stockholm.

Peacock, Alan and Weisman, Jack (1961), *The Growth of Public Expenditure in the United Kingdom*, Princeton, NJ: National Bureau of Economic Research.

Pechman, Joseph A. (ed.) (1987), *Comparative Tax Systems: Europe, Canada and Japan*.

Pechman, Joseph A. (ed.) (1988), *World Tax Reform: A Progress Report*, Washington, DC: Brookings Institution.

Peltzman, S. (1976), 'Toward a more general theory of regulation', *Journal of Law and Economics*, **19**: 211–40.

Peltzman, S. (1989), 'The economic theory of regulation after a decade of deregulation', *Brookings Papers on Economic Activity: Microeconomics*, pp. 1–59, reprinted in Bailey and Rothenberg Pack (eds) (1995), pp. 168–208.

Petrulis, Mindy, Judith Sommer and Fred Hines (1993), 'Ethanol production and employment', Agricultural Information Bulletin, No. 678, USDA Economic Research Service, Washington, DC: Government Printing Office.

Pettersson, Thomas (1999a), *Att kompensera för avstånd? Transportstödet 1970–1995. Ideologi, ekonomi och stigberoende* (Compensating for distance? Transport aid, 1970–1995. Ideology, economy and path dependence), dissertation, Umeå: Department of Economic History, Umeå University.

Pettersson, Thomas (1999b), 'Institutional rigidity and economic change. A comparison between Swedish transport subsidies', in Andersson-Skog and Krantz (eds).

Polyani, Karl (1994), *The Great Transformation: The Political and Economic Origins of our Time*, New York: Rhinehart.

Pontusson, Jonas, and Peter Swenson (1996), 'Labor markets, production strategies, and wage bargaining institutions: the Swedish employer offensive in comparative perspective', *Comparative Political Studies*, **29**: 223–50.

Poor, Henry V. (1860), *History of the Railroads and Canals of the United States of America, Exhibiting Their Progress, Cost, Revenues, Expenditures and Present Condition*, New York: John H. Schultz.

Porter, Michael E. (1990), *The Competitive Advantage of Nations*, New York: Free Press.

Preissl, B. (1998), 'The regulation of telecommunication in Europe', in *Vierteljahrshefte zur Wirtschaftsforschung*, Berlin: Deutsches Institut für Wirtschaftsforschung, pp. 40–49.

Pressman, S. (1999), 'Theories of the state', in Phillip Anthony O'Hara (ed.), *Encyclopedia of Political Economy*, London: Routledge.

Putnam, Robert D. (1993), *Making Democracy Work. Civic Traditions in Modern Italy*, Princeton, NJ: Princeton University Press.

Radaelli, Claudio (1997), *The Politics of Corporate Taxation in the European Union: Knowledge and International Policy Agendas*, London and New York: Routledge.

Ramstad, Y. (1994), 'On the nature of economic evolution: John R. Commons and the metaphor of artificial selection', in L. Magnusson (ed.), *Evolutionary and neo-Schumpeterian Approaches to Economics*, Boston, MA: Kluwer Academic Press.

Reese, Thomas (1980), *The Politics of Taxation*, Westport, CT: Quorum Books.

Renewable Fuels Association (1998), *Ethanol Report*, May 7.

Renewable Fuels Association (1999), *Ethanol Industry Vows to Continue Fight to Open California Gasoline Market to Ethanol*, RFA Ethanol Report, No. 87, January 7.

Report of the Directors of the Boston & Worcester Rail Road, to the Stockholders, at Their Ninth Annual Meeting, June 1, 1840 (1840), Boston: Samuel N. Dickinson.

Riksdagens revisorers förslag angående Inlandsbanan (1995), Riksdagens Revisorer, Stockholm: Swedish Parliament.

Ripley, William Z. (1912), *Railroads, Rates, and Regulation*, New York: Longmans, Green.

Ripley, William Z. (1915), *Railroads, Finance and Organization*, New York: Longmans, Green.

Rodriguez, Enrique (1980), *Offentlig inkomstexpansion: En analys av drivkrafterna bakom de offentliga inkomsternas utveckling i Sverige under 1900-talet*, Uppsala: CWK Gleerup.

Rodriguez, Enrique (1981), *Den Svenska skattehistorien* (Swedish tax history), Lund: Liber Läromedel.

Rodrik, Dani (1997), *Has Globalization Gone too Far?* Washington, DC: Institute for International Economics.

Romano, Roberta (1998), 'Empowering investors: a market approach to securities regulation', in Klaus J. Hopt, Hideki Kanda, Mark J. Roe, Eddy

Wymeersch and Stefan Prigge (eds), *Comparative Corporate Governance: The State of the Art and Emerging Research*, Oxford: Clarendon, pp. 143–217.

Rosenberg, N. (1994), *Exploring the Black Box. Technology, Economics and History*, Cambridge: Cambridge University Press.

Rosin, John and Peter Helmberger (1974), 'A neoclassical analysis of the U.S. farm sector, 1948–1970', *American Journal of Agricultural Economics*, **56** (November): 717–29.

Roy, William G. (1997), *Socializing Capital*, Princeton, NJ: Princeton University Press.

Russo, Thomas A. (1997), 'Finding common ground for global markets', *New York Times*, March 16, sec. 3, p. 14.

Rutherford, M. (1994), *Institutions in Economics. The Old and the New Institutionalism*, Cambridge: Cambridge University Press.

Sabine, B.E.V. (1966), *A History of Income Tax*, London: George Allen & Unwin.

Sabine, B.E.V. (1980), *A Short History of Taxation,* London: Butterworths.

Samuels, W.J. (1992), 'Some fundamentals of the economic role of government', in Samuels, *Essays on the Economic Role of Government*, Vol. 1, Houndmills, Basingstoke: Macmillan, pp. 156–61.

Sanders, M. Elizabeth (1981), *The Regulation of Natural Gas*, Philadelphia: Temple University Press.

Sandford, Cedric (1993), *Successful Tax Reform: Lessons from an Analysis of Tax Reform in Six Countries*, Bath, UK: Fiscal Publications.

Sannerstedt, Anders (1979), *Fri konkurrens eller politisk styrning? 1963 års trafikpolitiska beslut – debatten om innehåll, tillämpning och effekter*, Dissertation, Lund: Department of Political Science, Lund University.

Sansonetti, Patrick (1989), 'International venture capital: reaching new markets', *Small Business Reports*, **14**: 40–42.

Scheiber, Harry N. (1975), 'Federalism and the American economic order, 1789–1910', *Law and Society Review*, Fall: 57–118.

Scheiber, Harry N. (1981), 'Regulation, property rights, and definition of "the market"', *Journal of Economic History*, **41**: 103–9.

Schlesinger, Jacob M. (1997), 'G-7 summit to unveil policies that aim to stave off global financial crisis', *Wall Street Journal*, June, 17, sec. A, p. 2.

Schnittker Associates and US National Alcohol Fuels Commission (1980), *Ethanol: Farm and Fuel Issues*, Washington, DC: Government Printing Office, August.

Sciulli, David (1999), *Corporations vs. the Court*, London: Lynne Rienner.

Scott, W. Richard (1995), *Institutions and Organizations*, Thousand Oaks, CA: Sage.

Setterfield, M. (1993), 'A model of institutional hysteresis, *Journal of Economic Issues*, **27** (3) (September).

Shepherd, William G. (1979), *The Economics of Industrial Organization*, Englewood Cliffs, NJ: Prentice-Hall.

Shonfield, Alfred (1965), *Modern Capitalism*, London: Oxford University Press.

Skårfors, R. (1997), 'Telegrafverkets inköp av enskilda telefonnät: omstruktureringen av det svenska telefonsystemet 1883–1918', Working Papers in Transport and Communications History, Uppsala: Departments of Economic History, Umeå and Uppsala Universities.

Skocpol, T. (1979), *States and Social Revolutions. A Comparative Analysis of France, Russia, and China*, Cambridge: Cambridge University Press.

Skoglund, G. and K. Mähler (1944), Motion AK 1944:126, Stockholm: Swedish Parliament.

Skowronek, Stephen (1982), *Building a New American State: The Expansion of National Administrative Capacities, 1877–1920*, Cambridge: Cambridge University Press.

Sobczak, Deanne M. (1989), 'A survey of recent developments under the freedom of information act', *Administrative Law Journal*, **3**: 181–213.

Söderberg, Nils (1990), 'KABA när flyget var ungt', *Flyghistorisk Revy 34*, Stockholm: Svensk Flyghistorisk Förening.

Sörlin, Sverker (1988), *Framtidslandet: debatten om Norrland och naturresurserna under det industriella genombrottet*, Dissertation, Stockholm: Carlssons.

Stackelberg, Heinrich (1952), *The Theory of the Market Economy*, New York: Oxford University Press.

Stagliano, Vito (1994), 'The impact of a proposed EPA rule mandating renewable oxygenates for reformulated gasoline: questionable energy security, environmental and economic benefits', Washington, DC: Resources for the Future, Discussion Paper 9417.

Statens Järnvägar 50 år. 1856–1906 (1906), Vol. I, Stockholm.

Statens Järnvägar 75 år. 1906–1931 (1931), Vol. I, Stockholm.

Statens Offentliga Utredningar (1924), SOU 1924:30, *SJ som allmänt affärsverk*, Stockholm.

Statens Offentliga Utredningar (1929), SOU 1929:21, *Betänkande och förslag rörande understöd åt den civila luftfarten,* Avgivet den 30 september av sakkunniga, tillkallade inom kommunikationsdepartementet, Luftfartssakkunniga, Stockholm.

Statens Offentliga Utredningar (1933), SOU 1933:13, *Betänkande angående statsinlösen av Ostkustbanan och Uppsala – Gävle järnvägar*, Stockholm.

Statens Offentliga Utredningar (1946), SOU 1946:84, *Vissa åtgärder till förbättrade transportförhållandena i Norrland*, Stockholm.

Statens Offentliga Utredningar (1992), SOU 1992:70, *Telelag. Betänkande av Telelagsutredningen* (Report of the government's commission on a new telecommunications act), Stockholm.

Statens Offentliga Utredningar (1996), SOU 1996:95, *Botniabanan*, Stockholm.

Stein, Herbert (1969), *The Fiscal Revolution in America,* Chicago: University of Chicago Press.

Steinmo, Sven (1986), 'So what's wrong with tax expenditures: a re-evaluation based on Swedish experience', *Journal of Public Budgeting and Finance.*

Steinmo, Sven (1993), *Taxation and Democracy: Swedish, British and American Approaches to Financing the Modern State,* New Haven, CT: Yale University Press.

Steinmo, Sven, Kathleen Thelen and Frank Longstreth (1992), *Structuring Politics. Historical Institutionalism in Comparative Analysis*, Cambridge: Cambridge University Press.

Stigler, George (1968), *The Organization of Industry,* Homewood, IL: Irwin.

Stigler, George (1971), 'The theory of economic regulation', *Bell Journal of Economics*, **2**: 3–21.

Stigler, George (1992), 'Law or economics?', *Journal of Law and Economics*, **35** (October): 455–68.

Storer, John F. (1970), *The Life and Death of the American Railroad*, New York: Oxford University Press.

Surrey, Stanley and William Hellmuth (1969), 'The tax expenditure budget – response to Professor Bittker', *National Tax Journal*, **22**.

Svenska Män och Krinnor (1949), vol. 5, Stockholm: Albert Bonniers Förlag.

Svenskt flyg och dess män. Ett samlingsverk utgivet till förmån för Kungl. Svenska Aeroklubbens verksamhet till det svenska flygets främjande (1940), 2nd edn, Stockholm: Kungliga Svenska Aeroklubben.

Swank, Duane (1996), 'Funding the Welfare State. Part I: Global capital and the taxation of business in advanced market economies', in *Annual American Political Science Association Meeting,* San Francisco, CA.

Tanzi, Vito (1995), *Taxation in an Integrating World*, Washington, DC: The Brookings Institution.

Taylor, B.B. (1874), 'Commercial corporations', *Overland Monthly and Out West Magazine*, **13** (6): 498–503.

Taylor, George Rogers (1968 [1951]), *The Transportation Revolution, 1815–1860*, New York: Harper & Row.

Tennessee Valley Authority (1985), Office of Natural Resources and Economic Development, *Effect of the Use of Gasohol on Ozone Formation for Cities in the Tennessee Valley Region*, Muscle Shoals, Alabama.

Thelen, K. and S. Steinmo (1992), 'Historical institutionalism in comparative politics', in Steinmo et al. (eds), pp. 1–32.

Thorp, Willard Long (1926), *Business Annals*, New York: National Bureau of Economic Research.

Thue, L. (1995), 'Electricity rules – the formation and development of Nordic electricity regimes', in A. Kaijser and M. Hedin (eds), *Nordic Energy Systems: Historical Perspectives and Current Issues*, Canton, MA: Science History Publications, pp. 11–29.

Tipton, Frank B. (1976), *Regional Variations in the Economic Development of Germany During the Nineteenth Century*, Middleton, CT: Wesleyan University Press.

Tipton, Frank B. (1999), 'Bureaucracy and the railways in Germany and Japan', in Andersson-Skog and Krantz (eds), pp. 14ff.

Tirole, Jean (1988), *The Theory of Industrial Organization*, Cambridge, MA: MIT Press.

Tocqueville, Alexis de (1945), *Democracy in America*, reprint ed. Henry Reeve and Phillips Bradley, trans., New York: Vintage.

Tucker, David J., Jitendra V. Singh and Agnes G. Meinhard (1990), 'Organizational form, population dynamics, and institutional change', *Academy of Management Journal*, **33**: 151–78.

Tullock, Gordon (1967), 'The welfare cost of tariffs, monopolies, and theft', *Western Economic Journal*, **5**: 224–32.

Tullock, Gordon (1989), *The Economics of Special Privilege and Rent Seeking*, Boston, MA: Kluwer Academic.

Twenty-fifth Annual Report of the President and Directors to the Stockholders of the Baltimore and Ohio Rail Road (1851), Baltimore, MD: John Murphy & Co.

Tyner, Wallace E. and Carroll J. Bottum (1979), 'Agricultural energy production: economic and policy issues', *Purdue University Agr. Exp. Sta. Bull.*, No. 240.

US Bureau of the Census (1960), *Historical Statistics of the United States, Colonial Times to 1957*, Washington, DC.

US Department of Energy (1980), *Gasohol*, Washington, DC: Energy Research Advisory Board, April 29.

US Department of Energy (1996), *Alternatives to Traditional Transportation Fuels 1995*, Vol 1, DOE/EIA-0585, Washington, DC: p. 20.

US Environmental Protection Agency (1993), 'Assessment of Potential Health Risks of Gasoline Oxygenated with Methyl Tertiary Butyl Ether (MTBE)', Office of Research and Development, EPA/600/R93/206, November.

US Environmental Protection Agency (1995), 'Origin of the Reformulated Gasoline Program', Office of Mobile Sources, EPA 420-F-95–001.

US General Accounting Office (1984), *Importance and Impact of Federal Alcohol Fuel Tax Incentives*, GAO/RCED-84–1, Washington, DC: Government Printing Office.

US General Accounting Office (1990), *Alcohol Fuels, Impacts from Increased Use of Ethanol Blended Fuels*, RCED-90–156, Washington, DC: Government Printing Office, July.

US General Accounting Office (1996), *Motor Fuels – Issues Related to Reformulated Gasoline, Oxygenated Fuels and Biofuels*, GAO/RCED-96–121, Washington, DC: Government Printing Office.

US General Accounting Office (1997a), 'Ethanol, clean air, and farm economy', Hearing before the Committee on Agriculture, Nutrition, and Forestry, Washington, DC.

US General Accounting Office (1997b), *Tax Policy: Effects of the Alcohol Fuels Tax Incentives*, GGD-97–41, Washington, DC: Government Printing Office.

US National Alcohol Fuels Commission (1980), 'Public Hearing', Washington, DC, June 18 and 19, Washington, DC: Government Printing Office.

US National Alcohol Fuels Commission (1981), *Fuel Alcohol: An Energy Alternative for the 1980s, Final Report*, Washington, DC: Government Printing Office.

Usher, J.A. (1994), 'Utilities, deregulation and competition policy', RUSEL Working Paper, No. 19, Exeter: Department of Politics, University of Exeter.

Vallinder, T. (1962), *I kamp för demokrati*, Stockholm: Natur och Kultur.

Vanberg, V.J. (1988), 'Rules and choice in economics and sociology', *Jahrbuch für Neue Politische Oeconomie*, 7: 2f.

Vanberg, V.J. (1994), *Rules and Choices in Economics*, London: Routledge.

Vietor, Richard (2000), 'Government regulation of business', in Stanley L. Engerman and Robert E. Gallman (eds), *The Cambridge Economic History of the United States, Volume III: The Twentieth Century*, Cambridge: Cambridge University Press.

Vogel, David (1995), *Trading Up: Consumer and Environmental Regulation in a Global Economy*, Cambridge, MA: Harvard University Press.

Vogel, S.K. (1996), *Freer Markets, More Rules*, Ithaca, NY: Cornell University Press.

Waara, Lennart (1980), *Den statliga företagssektorns expansion. Orsaker till förstatliganden i ett historiskt och internationellt perspektiv*, Stockholm: Liber Förlag.

Wade, Robert (1990), *Governing the Market*, Princeton, NJ: Princeton University Press.

Wallace, Cynthia (1990), 'Foreign direct investment in the Third World: U.S. corporations and government policy', in C.D. Wallace (ed.), *A New Climate in the Third World*, Dordrecht, Netherlands: Martinus Nijhoff.

Waltman, Jerold (1985), *Political Origins of the U.S. Income Tax*, Jackson, MS: University of Mississippi Press.

Waters, Richard (1999), 'US Regulators Stand in Way of Global Rules', *Financial Times* (US Edition), 25 March 1999, p. 5.

Weber, Caroline and Aaron Wildavsky (1986), *A History of Taxation and Expenditure in the Western World*, New York: Simon & Schuster.

Weber, Max (1946), 'Religious rejections of the world and their directions', in H.H. Gerth and C. Wright Mills (eds), *From Max Weber*, New York: Oxford University Press, pp. 323–59.

Weber, Max (1978), *Economy and Society*, Berkeley, CA: University of California Press.

Weingast, Barry R., Kenneth A. Shepsle and Christopher Johnsen (1981), 'The political economy of benefits and costs: a neoclassical approach to distributive politics', *Journal of Political Economy*, **89** (August): 642–64.

Weir, Charlie (1997), 'Corporate governance, performance, and take-overs', *Applied Economics*, **29**: 1465–75.

Weir, M. and T. Skocpol (1985), 'State structures and the possibilities for "Keynesian" responses to the Great Depression in Sweden, Britain, and the United States', in P. Evans, D. Rueschemeyer and T. Skocpol (eds), *Bringing the State Back In*, New York: Cambridge University Press.

Westin, L. and A. Östhol (1992), 'City networks and the search for regional potential', Umeå: CERUM Working Paper No. 13.

Westlund, Hans (1993), *Regionala utvecklingsmöjligheter från Atlanten till Bottenhavet*, Östersund, Sweden: Länsstyrelsens tryckeri.

Wikstrand, Rolf (1987), *Herremakt och folkstyre. En studie kring de svenska landstingen 1863–1889*, Stockholm: Landstingsförbundet tnr. 849/1987–02, pp. 27ff.

Wilcox, Clair (1960), *Public Policies Toward Business*, rev. edn, Homewood, IL: Irwin.

Wilkins, Mira (1970), *The Emergence of Multinational Enterprise: American Business Abroad from the Colonial Era to 1914*, Cambridge, MA: Harvard University Press.

Wilkins, Mira (1974), *The Maturing of Multinational Enterprise: American Business Abroad from 1914 to 1970*, Cambridge, MA: Harvard University Press.

Williams, David (1991a), *Trends in International Taxation*, London: International Fiscal Association, British Branch.

Williams, David (1991b), *Trends in International Taxation*, London: International Fiscal Association.

Williamson, Oliver E. (1996), *The Mechanisms of Governance*, New York: Oxford University Press.

Williamson, Oliver E. (1998), 'Public and private bureaucracies: a transactions cost economics perspective', Working paper, Haas School of Business, Berkeley, CA: University of California.

Wilson, J.Q. (ed.), (1980), *The Politics of Regulation*, New York: Basic Books.

Wilson, J.Q. (1989), *Bureacracy. What Government Agencies Do and Why They Do It*, New York: Basic Books.

Winiecki, Jan (1996), 'Impediments to institutional change in the former Soviet system. Why economic reform fails in the Soviet system: a property rights-based approach', in Lee J. Alston, Thráinn Eggertsson and Douglass North (eds), *Empirical Studies in Institutional Change*, Cambridge: Cambridge University Press.

Winston, C. (1993), 'Economic deregulation: days of reckoning for micro-economists', *Journal of Economic Literature*, **31** (3) (September): 1263–89, reprinted in Bailey and Rothenberg Pack (eds) (1995), pp. 587–613.

Witte, John (1985), *The Politics and Development of the Federal Income Tax*, Madison, WI: University of Wisconsin Press.

Wittman, Donald (1995), *The Myth of Democratic Failure: Why Political Institutions Are Efficient*, Chicago: University of Chicago Press.

Yonay, Yuval P. (1998), *The Struggle over the Soul of Economics*, Princeton, NJ: Princeton University Press.

Zelizer, Viviana A. (1988), 'Beyond the polemics on the market', *Sociological Forum*, **4**: 614–34.

Zukin, Sharon and Paul DiMaggio (1990), 'Introduction', in Zukin and DiMaggio (eds), *Structures of Capital*, Cambridge: Cambridge University Press, pp. 1–36.

Zysman, John (1983), *Governments, Markets, and Growth*, Ithaca, NY: Cornell University Press.

Index